The Art of Tsukamaki

Second Edition

THOMAS BUCK

Lloyd & Tutle Publishing, Limited

ISBN: 0-9843779-5-6
ISBN-13: 978-0-9843779-5-4

DEDICATION

This work is dedicated to the intangible fellowship of sword lore masters who have guided me on this quest. Specifically, thanks go to my Sensei(s) Mr. Carl Braafadt, Dr. W. Y. Takahashi, Mr. Takahiro Ichinose, Mr. John Grimmitt, and Sir Gary Montgomery.

CONTENTS

ACKNOWLEDGMENTS

I would like to thank all those without whom this work would not have been finished. In particular, my appreciation goes to Dr. W. M. Takahasi and Tsukamaki-shi Takao Ichinose for their time and energy, and many years of allowing me to tap their vast stores of knowledge; Mr. Robert Benson and Dr. R. M. Lewert for the beautiful photos of Master Ichinose's work; Mark Hinton at Christie's; Tsukamaki-shi Yasuo Toyama and Saya-shi Kazuki Takayama; the conservancy and staff members of the Asian Arts section at the Denver Art Museum; and, Mr. Nobuo Ogasawara for classic images of the Japanese Imperial Collection. My thanks especially goes out to my friend, and personal Managing Editor, Andrea Novel Buck, who has patiently and repeatedly read my text and made supportive contributions and suggestions.

1 A Brief Chronology

1.1 Koto: Early Sword Era

Ancient Period (before 794)

In Ancient Japan, all aspects of Japanese life, from politics to science, were strongly influenced by the continental cultures and technologies. The manufacture of swords was no exception and the domestic product was considered low-grade to the swords made in China and Korea, which led to a large import of arms from the continent. At its peak, the Empress Suiko (554-628) imported the bulk of the imperial house swords from the ancient Chinese province of Go. The earliest swords in Japan were of the Straight Sword (*Chokuto)* variety.

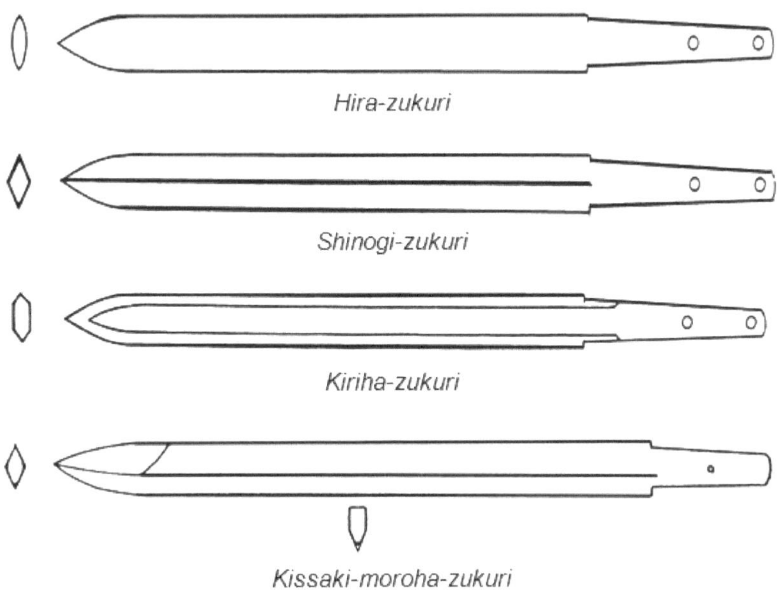

Figure 1.1 Varieties of Chokuto

Chokuto can be divided into four classifications: (1) *Hira-zukuri,* flat blades without a ridge line, or *Shinogi*, (2) *Shinogi-zukuri,* double-edged blades with a ridge line down the center, (3) *Kiriha-zukuri,* double-edged blades with a ridge line near the cutting edge, and (4) *Kissaki-moroha-zukuri,* blades with a double edge only at the tip. *Hira-zukuri* and *Kiriha-zukuri* blades are the oldest, followed by *Kissaki-moroha-zukuri* blades, with the double-edged *Shinogi-zukuri* being the newest of the ancient styles.

These Ancient period swords primarily were thrusting weapons, and were hung from the waist edge-down.

Along with the import of these swords, came many Chinese and Korean craftsmen who began teaching their art of sword making to the indigenous smiths. This was a significant milestone in the evolution of the Japanese sword.

Toward the end of the Ancient Sword Period a transition from straight double-edged swords to single-edged curved blades began to occur. In fact, by the beginning of the Heian Period, although straight swords where still in wide use, the Japanese warrior class showed a marked preference for this new style of sword.

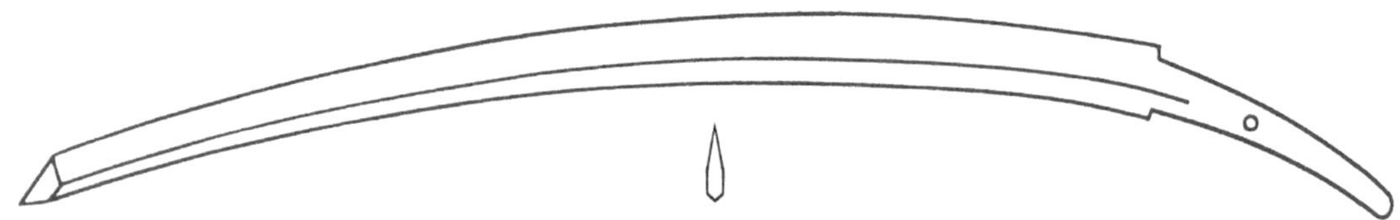

Figure 1.2 Single-edged curved blade of the *Shinogi-zukuri* style.

Heian Period (794 – 1184)

During the Heian Period, the warrior class in Japan began to gain power. The aristocrats, led by the Fujiwara family, had come into power by destroying the old clan system and flourished in conjunction with the development of the manor system of government in which land estates were leased to lords and the peasants were made dependent on the land and their lords. Along with the powerful families in the outlying areas, the urban lords found it necessary to form and maintain large military forces within their own clans. In addition, separate warrior families grew up among the military groups attached to these manors. Among these the Genji and Heike clans made the most rapid rise to power.

In 1156, the Heike clan, under the leadership of Taira Kiyomori, succeeded in putting down a rebellion and took over the reins of the government in Kyoto. This is the first time in Japanese history that the government had been in the hands of a warrior family. As a result, a significant shift occurred in the fighting methods: the old group warfare foot soldier method was being replaced in importance by the mounted warrior, and increased focus was placed more on individual hand-to-hand combat with swords, bows and arrows.

Around the mid-Heian Period, the curved single-edged Japanese Sword (*Nippon-to*) was perfected and came into general use. The adoption of the curved sword was not only due to the shift to horseback fighting techniques in which a striking sword rather than a stabbing sword became necessary, but was also due to the quality of the steel available and the great advance in forging techniques.

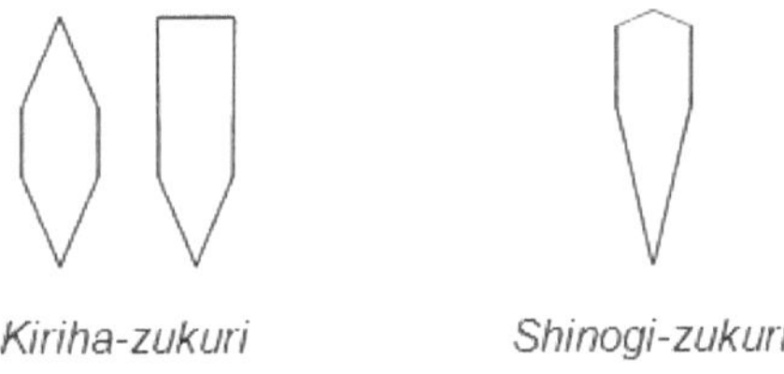

Figure 1.3 Blade cross sections.

As illustrated in Figure 1.3, the change from *Kiriha-zukuri* to *Shinogi-zukuri* was merely a moving of the ridge line (*Shinogi*) closer to the top ridge of the blade. This produced a much broader cutting surface and a more acute angle to the cutting edge, and added a dynamic keenness to the cutting edge.

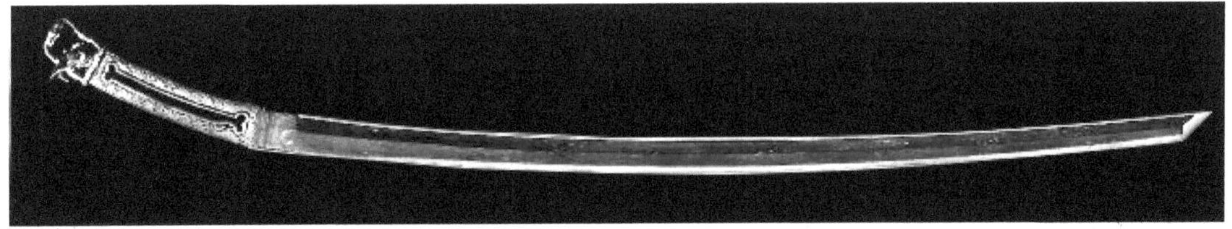

Figure 1.4 Kenuki-gata style tachi.

The evolution of the straight to the curved blade and from *Kiriha-zukuri* to *Shinogi-zukuri* was not a direct process. Intermediate stages in this process can be seen in the *Kenuki-gata* style *tachi* (Fig. 1.4) that is said to have been owned by Fujiwara Hidesato in

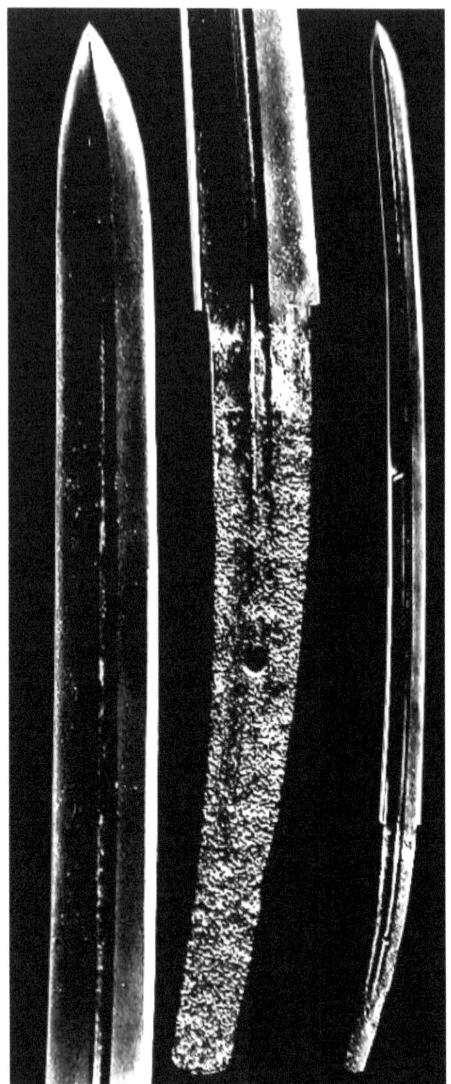

Figure 1.6 The Kogarasu Maru tachi, Circa 800

the 10th century, and the famous *Kogarasu Maru tachi* (Fig. 1.5), a prized possession of the Heike family.

Over time, the classic curved Japanese Sword (*Nihonto)* came to replace the older straight sword because of both its greater practical applications, as well as progress in sword-making techniques and improvements in materials. Initially, the sword-making process of curving a blade would seem relatively easy, but the actual procedure involved in bending the folded steel back in the direction of the thick *mune* (back edge) from the thinner *ha* (cutting edge) are exceptionally complex and difficult. The birth of the curved sword was not only an improvement for battle tactics, but a significant accomplishment in engineering and metallurgy. By the end of the Heian Period, the evolution was complete, and the traditional curved single-edge of the *Shinogi-zukuri* style *Nihonto* was perfected.

Early Kamakura Period (1184 – 1231)

The 150 years of the Kamakura Period were divided into roughly three parts: under the leadership of Minamoto Yoritomo's new warrior government in Kamakura, the first 50 years redefined the warrior class; the next 50 years redefined the economy; and, the last 50 were redefined by stagnation. Although in many ways, the evolution of the Japanese sword mirrored these changes in society, Early Kamakura Period swords paralleled those of the previous period in design and function, such as the *Kitsune-ga-*

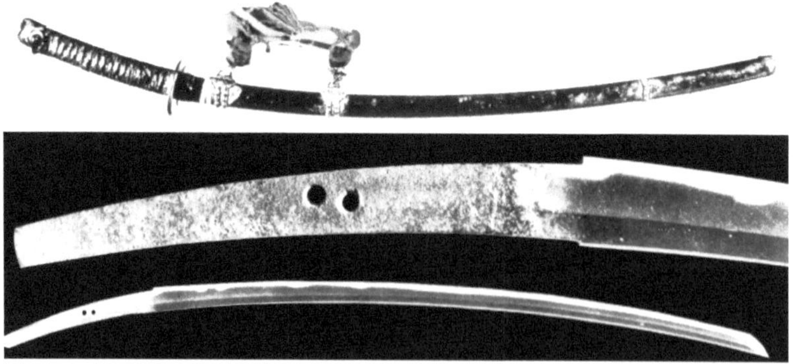

Figure 1.5 The Kitsune-ga-saki blade by Tametsugu

saki blade (Fig. 1.6) made by Tametsugu from Bitchu. This was also exemplified by the large number of Bizen swordsmiths that still flourished under the imperial court as it had been during the last part of the Heian Period. The greatest change during this period occurred to the sword mountings and fittings, or *koshirae*.

During the Early to Middle Kamakura Period, three general types of *tachi koshirae* (sword mounts worn edge down) were

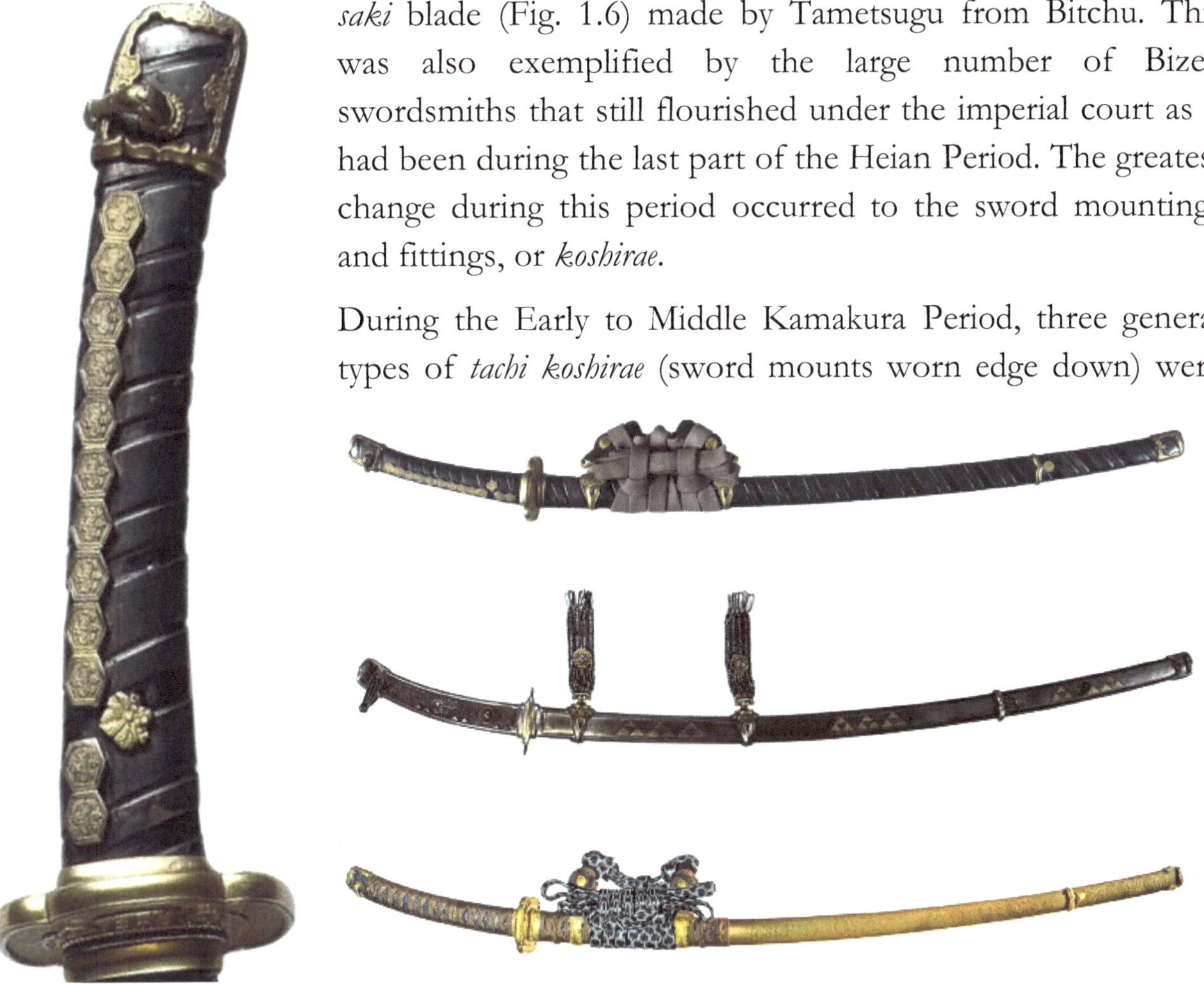

Figure 1.7 Three types of Early to Middle Kamakura Period sword mountings: from top to bottom, Hiru-maki-no-tachi Koshirae, Hyogo-gusari Koshirae, and Ito-maki-no-tachi Koshirae.

used (Fig. 1.7): the *hiru-maki-no-tachi koshirae* is comprised broad metal bands wrapped in a spiral fashion around both the *tsuka* (handle) and *saya* (scabbard); the *hyogo-gusari koshirae* is covered with a combination of metal plates and bands; and the *ito-maki-no-tachi koshirae* has the saya wrapped, at least in part, in silk braid.

Middle Kamakura Period (1232 – 1287)

During the Kamakura Period, the samurai felt it necessary to be as austere and warrior-like as possible. To further this mindset, in 1232 an official code of ethics was established which focused on thrift and strength of character, as well as extensive martial training in archery, horsemanship and swords.

The Middle Kamakura Period was also a time of great advancement in the art of sword making. In general, the blades became stronger, broader and thicker. In particular, the Yamashiro school of Bizen became preeminent with its distinct curve and its variations of the *choji midare* temperline.

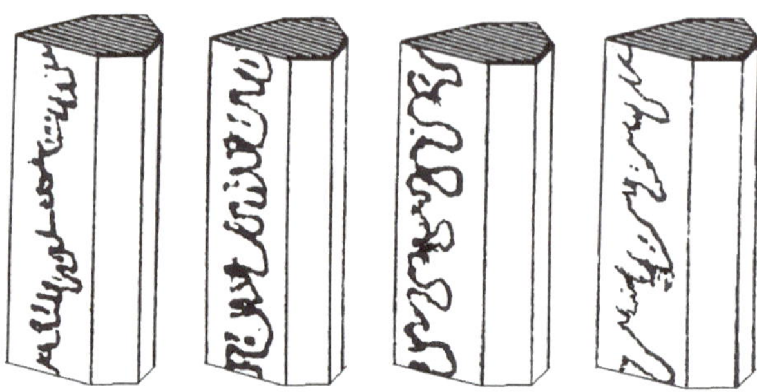

Figure 1.8 Variations of the Bizen Choji Midare Temperline

This part of the Kamakura Period was a time of refinement for the sword, and set the standards for all future Japanese swords. In addition to the long swords, *tanto* (daggers) *wakizashi* (short swords) and *naginata* (halberds) were all in large supply, and their production did not decline during this middle period. It was also during this time that five separate and distinct schools of sword making became formally established. Famous swordsmiths of this period include Kunitsuna of the Awataguchi school, Saburo Kunimune from Bizen, and Sukezane of the Ichimonji.

Late Kamakura Period (1288 - 1335)

The two Mongol invasions in 1274 and 1281 gave birth to drastic changes in Japanese war tactics and weapons. The Japanese discovered through this experience that group warfare was much more effective than the mounted individual combat style that they had been using up to that time.

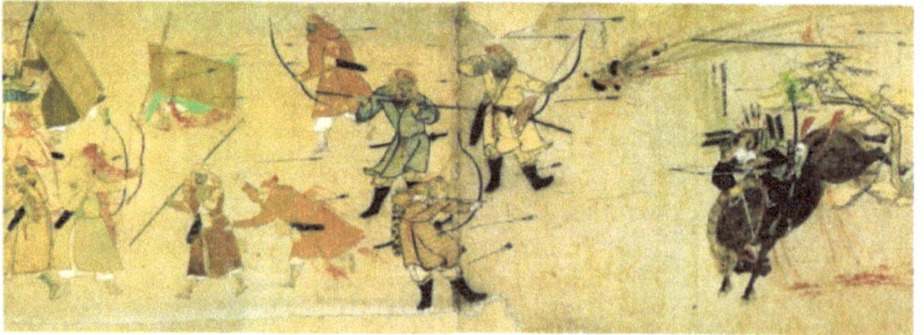

Figure 1.9 Scroll depicting the battle at Hakata in 1274.

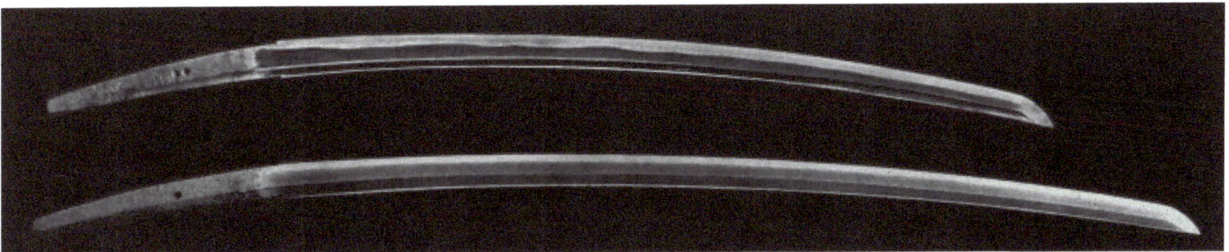

Figure 1.10 From top to bottom, shapes of Middle and Late Kamakura blades.

The blades became longer and more even in width throughout their entire length and the sword mountings of this period became more refined, focusing on detail and

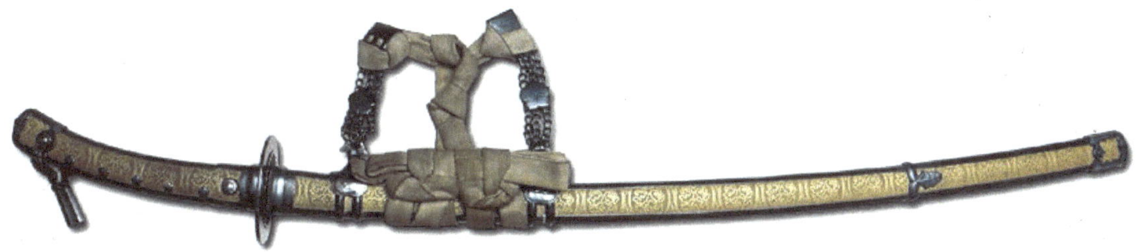

Figure 1.11 Hyogo-gusari style tachi of with brocade silk panels.

quality. *Tanto* became straighter, thicker and slightly longer than those of the previous period, and *naginata* blades became curved (see Fig. 1.13).

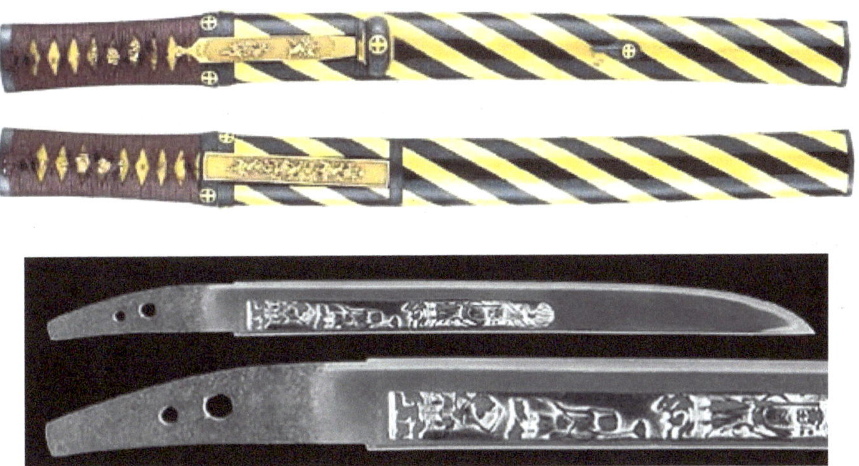

Figure 1.12 A period hira-zukuri (no ridge) style tanto.

The most significant effect the Mongol invasions brought was the awareness of the need for a strong national defense. This resulted in swordsmiths springing up in all parts of the country. The most famous swordsmith to appear during this period was a

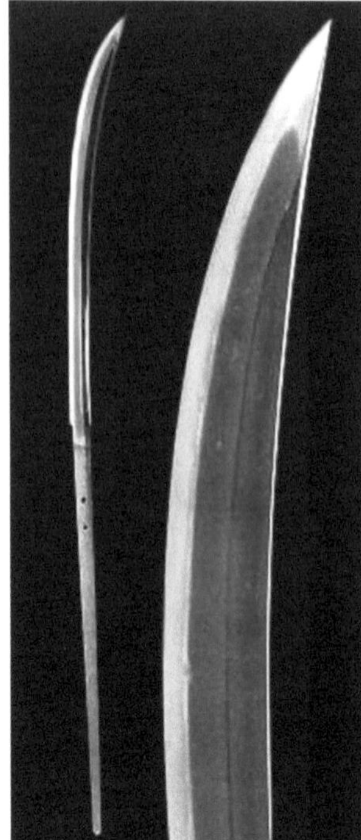

Figure 1.13 (Above) Late Kamakura *naginata* blade.

student of Shintogo Kunimitsu named Masamune. He inherited the traditions of his teacher's style and developed that style to produce stronger, more resilient, more beautiful swords.

Masamune's influence spread throughout the country and everyone began to imitate his style, even to the extent that during the Edo Period there were ten famous swordsmiths known as the Masamune Jittetsu, who made blades in his style but none of who seem to have had any direct relationship to the master himself.

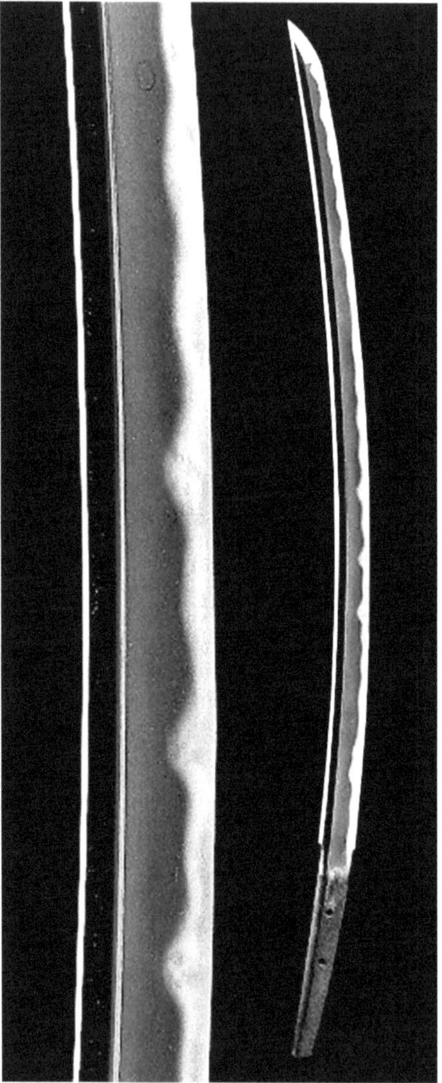

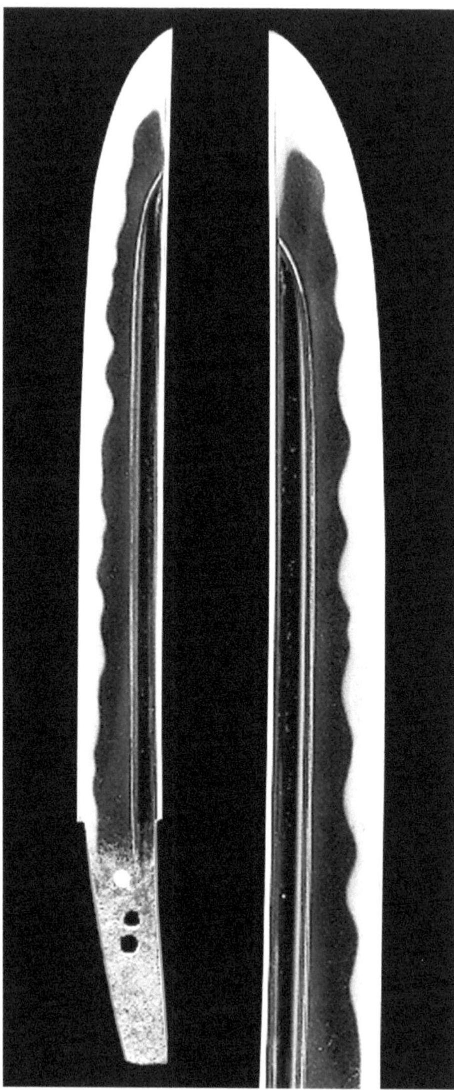

Figure 1.14 (Right) Two works attributed to Masamune; left to right, 66.2cm tachi and 29.3cm tanto.

The actual student of Masamune who is said to have succeeded the best in learning the master's style was Sadamune. He was active throughout the Late Kamakura and well into the Nanbokucho Period.

Nanbokucho Period (1336 – 1393)

During the Nanbokucho Period, also known as the Northern and Southern Courts period, the Japanese government was divided into two groups, with the Emperor Godaigo at Yoshino in the south (*Nan*), and the shogun Ashikaga Takauji and Emperor Komyo in the north (*Hoku*). Warring between these two factions didn't end until nearly sixty years later, when Emperor Gokomatsu took the throne in 1392.

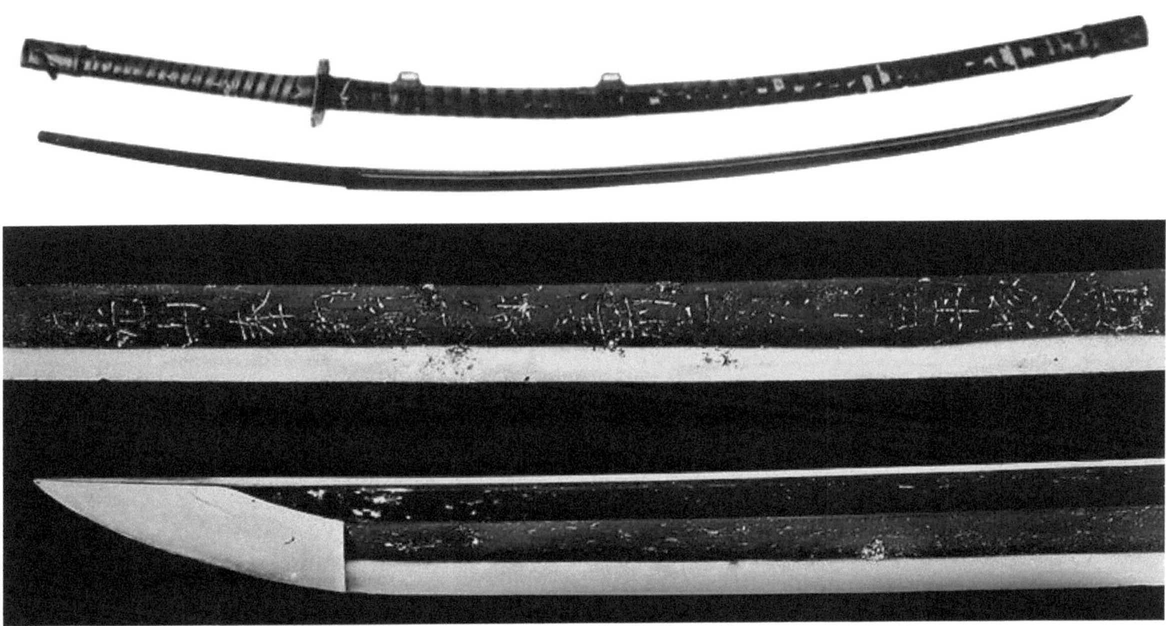

Figure 1.15 The Kashiwa Tachi.

During this time, swords and pole arms became greatly exaggerated. Examples of this can be seen in the Nambokucho swords named *Kashiwa Tachi*, or the Oak Sword (Fig. 1.15), and the *Tomomitsu Odachi* (Fig. 1.16).

The blade of the Oak Sword has a *nagasa* (cutting edge) of 136.6 cm, with a *nakago* (tang) of 54.4 cm, and is *mumei* (unsigned); its *tsuka* and *saya* are black lacquered and wrapped in opposite directions with a thin strip of leather.

The Tomomitsu Odachi has a *nagasa* of 126.0 cm and a *sori* (curve) of 5.8 cm, and a *kissaki* of 6.7 cm in length; and it is signed by Tomomitsu and dated 1366.

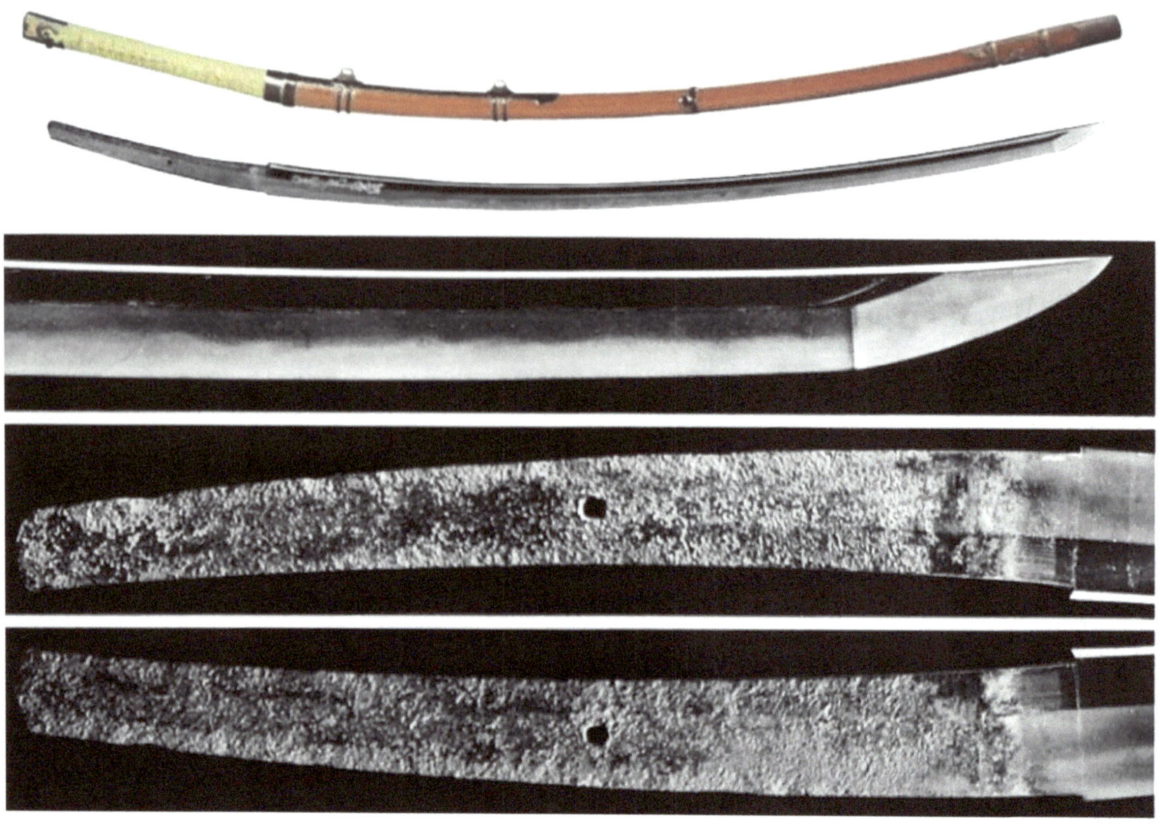

Figure 1.16 The Tomomitsu Odachi.

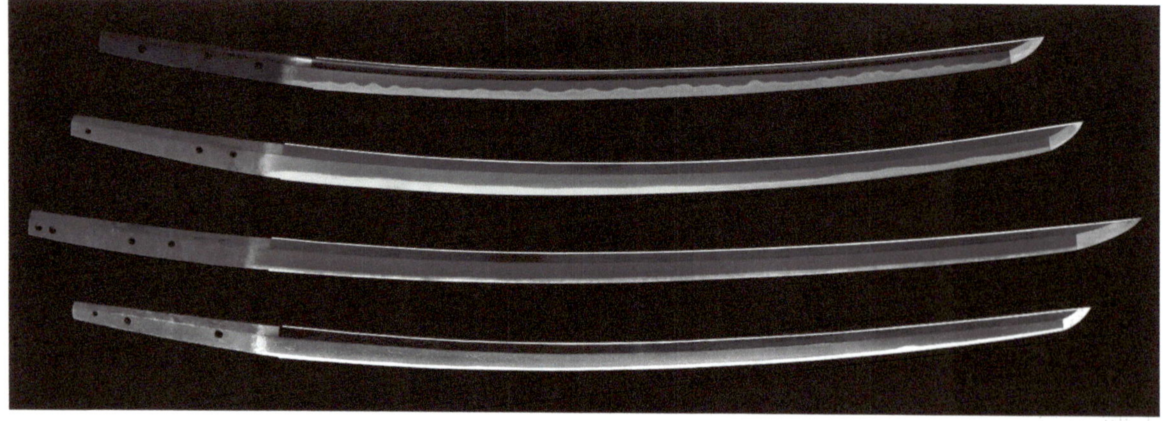

Figure 1.17 Shortened Nanbokucho Period swords.

Ironically, the primary significance of these oversized arms came during the following period when it became common practice to cut down the blades to make them a more useful length, as seen in Figures 1.17 and 1.18.

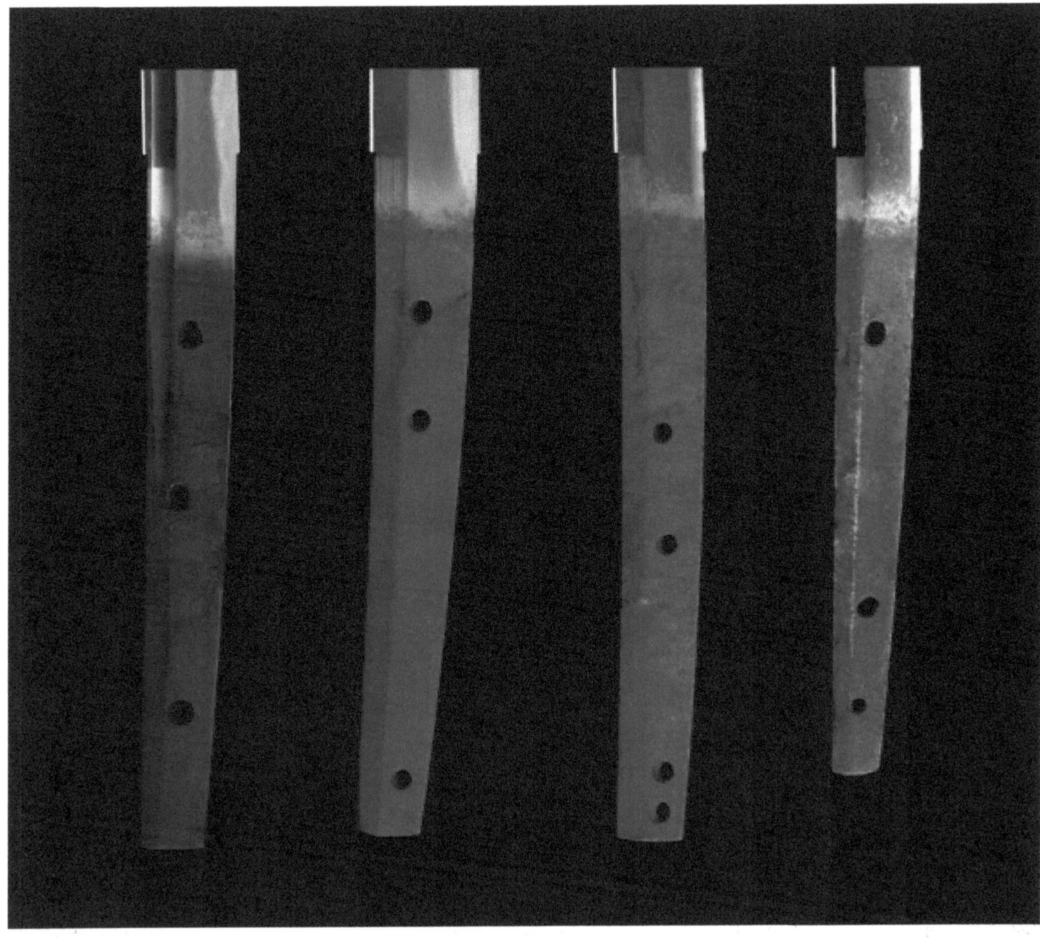

Figure 1.18 Nakago of shortened Nanbokucho Period swords.

From top to bottom (Fig. 1.17), and left to right (Fig. 1.18), *mumei* (unsigned) Omiya school sword with a blade length of 63.6 cm; *mumei* sword with a blade length of 69.7 cm; *mumei* Hoju school sword with a blade length of 82.0 cm; and, *mumei* Chikushi Ryokai sword with a blade length of 71.0 cm.

As a sign of things to come, there were also blades of only about 70 cm made that were worn unlike the *tachi*, thrust through the belt (*obi*) with the edge pointing up. This style became known as the *uchigatana.*

Muromachi Period (1392 – 1573)

In 1393 the north and south warring factions were united by emperor Ouchi Yoshihiro, allowing Ashikaga Yoshimitsu to become shogun, creating a general state of peace and ushering in the new age known as the Muromachi Period.

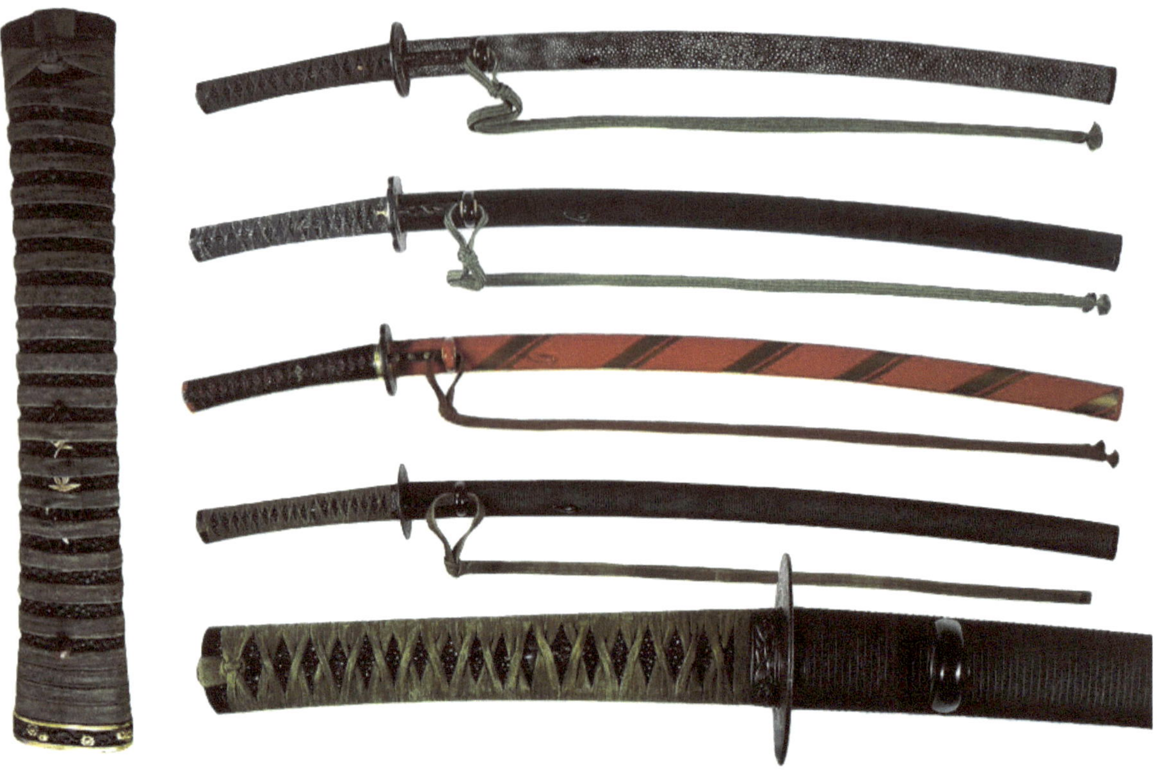

Figure 1.19 Modern reproductions of Muromachi Period akechi tsuka & uchigatana koshirae by Kazuki Takayama and Yasuo Toyama

It was during this period that the *tachi* began to disappear and the *uchigatana* took its place. Similar to the *koshirae* in Figure 1.19, common features of *uchigatana koshirae* of this period include a *tsuka* wrapped with leather over black lacquered *same'*, and a black horn *kashira* (pommel) with the wrap crossing over its top. This shift in *koshirae* occurred primarily because of the change in battle tactics from mounted individual fighting back to the group combat on foot, and can be traced back to the two Mongol invasions (1274 and 1281).

The Muromachi period was marked by repeated rebellions and civil war, including the Eikyo Rebellion in 1439 and the Onin Rebellion in 1467. After Yoshimitsu, the successor shoguns were relatively short-lived and changed rapidly, until the 15th Shogun was driven out of the capital by Oda Nobunaga in 1568.

In general, government was broken up among various regional feudal lords who established their own castle towns, which in turn became commercial centers where merchants and craftsmen could gather and supply the ever-increasing demand for

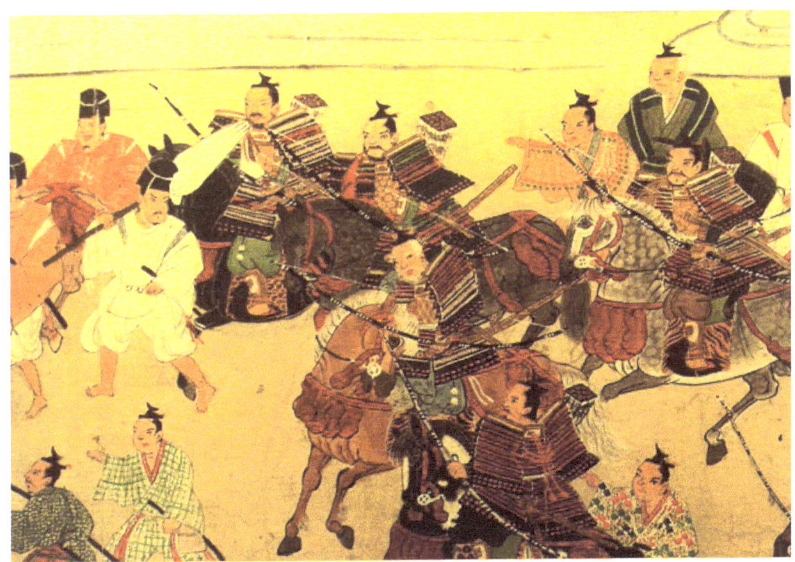

Figure 1.20 Muromachi Period warriors preparing for battle.

weapons. Because of the constant stream of battles in all parts of the country, weapon production was at an all-time high, and, consequently, the quality of workmanship fell to an all-time low.

Sword mountings of this period covered the spectrum from inexpensive functional *akechi koshirae* (see Fig. 1.19), to elaborate high quality works for the nobility that in ways mirrored pieces from the Kamakura period.

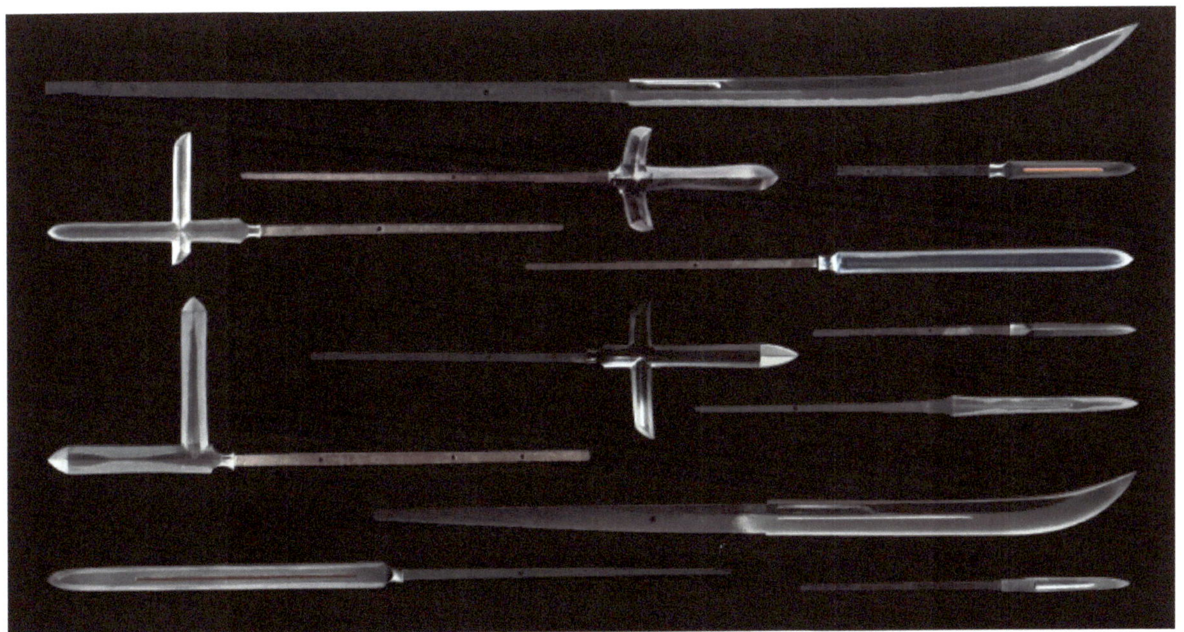

Figure 1.21 Examples of period naginata and yari blades.

Because of their usefulness in the new foot soldier battle tactics, a great variety of styles, shapes and sizes of pole arms were developed and produced (Fig. 1.21). In addition to *naginata*, the most common pole arms of the Muromachi period were *yari*, or lances, of which there are two major types, the *su yari* (those with straight blades) and *kama yari* (those with crossbars on the blade). Oversized *su yari* are referred to as *omi no yari. Jumonji yari* are *kama yari* with crossbars of equal length, and *katakama yari* have either a single sided crossbar or crossbars of unequal length.

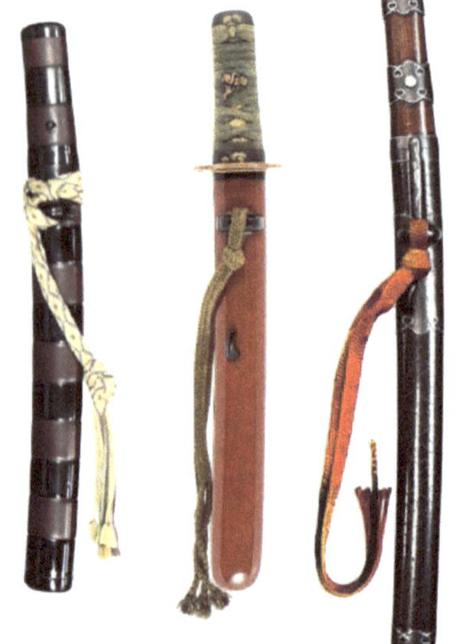

Figure 1.22 Muromachi Period tanto.

In addition to long swords and lances, a wide variety of *koshirae* for *tanto* (daggers) and *wakizashi* (short swords) were also introduced during this period, as shown in Figure 1.22 and 1.23.

During the 181 years of the Muromachi period, arguably the most dramatic change occurred in its last 30 years the introduction of the gun to Japan in 1543. Its impact was felt across the Japanese social strata, and directly influenced sword production and battle tactics. The gun gave Oda Nobunaga the political and military edge he needed to end the period of civil wars and unify Japan.

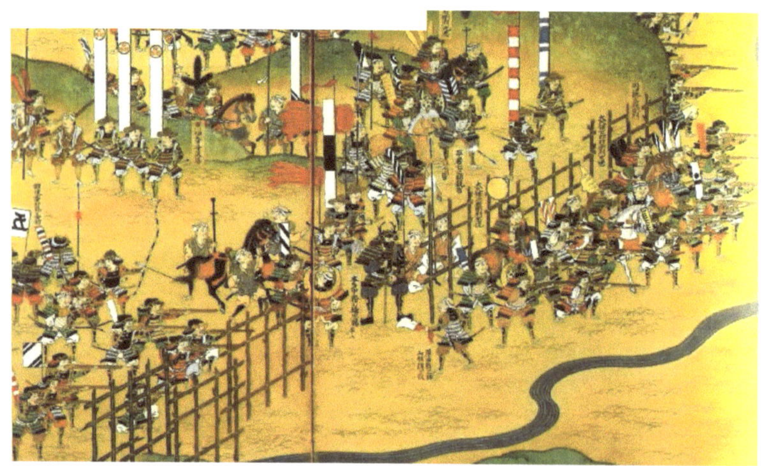

Figure 1.24 (Above) The Battle of Nagashino in 1575 (left) was a major turning point in the use of guns in Japanese battle tactics.

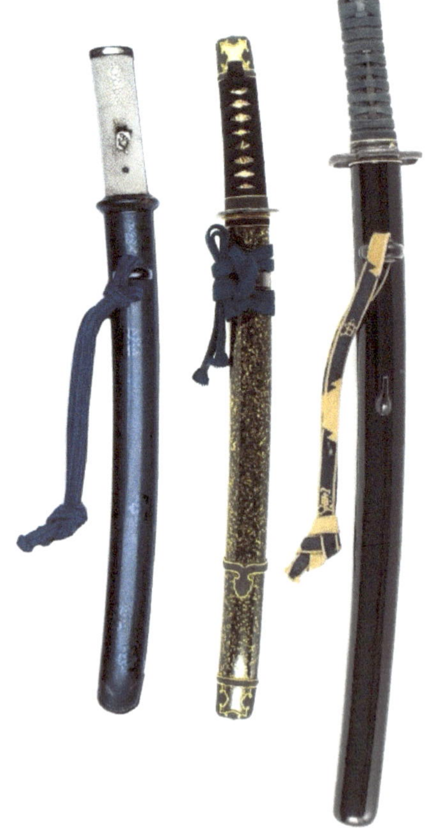

Figure 1.23 (Right) Muromachi Period wakizashi.

1.2 SHINTO & SHIN-SHINTO: NEW SWORD ERAS

In the context of sword production, the Shinto Period traditionally is broken up into three distinct eras: the *Keicho Shinto* era (1596 – 1660); the *Kanbun Shinto* era (1661 – 1780); and the *Shin-shinto* (New New Sword) era, which began in 1781 and lasted until the end of the Tokugawa Period. In a historical context, the Shinto period arguably spans the Momoyama period, beginning in 1573, all the way through the end of the Meiji Restoration in 1868.

The period name *Shinto* (New Sword) wasn't derived simply from the production of new blades, but came about because of a change in styles and methods of production, as well as a societal shift in government and culture, characterized by a new prosperity and a revitalization of traditional social values and ideals.

Momoyama Period (1573 – 1615)

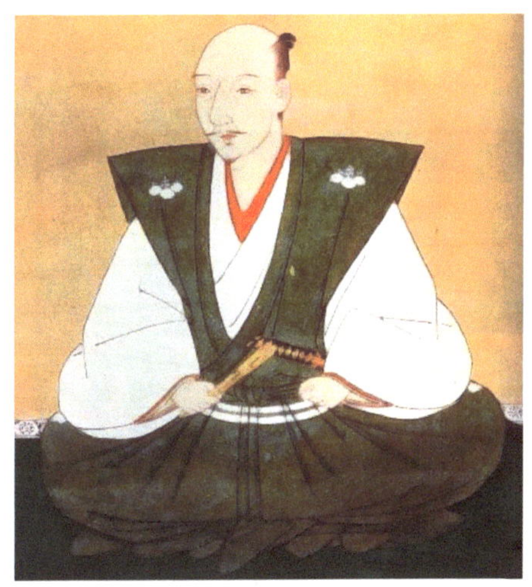

Figure 1.25 Portrait of Oda Nobunaga.

Although the Momoyama Period began in 1573, its foundations were laid in 1568 with the end of Ashikaga Shogunate. From that point on until his death in 1582, Oda Nobunaga's string of conquests and alliances brought the country under a more unified rule with a strong central government. By 1590, Hideyoshi, one of Nobunaga's former allies, had completed the unification of Japan, formalized his rule and issued an order banning the ownership of swords by farmers and peasants. It was during Hideyoshi's reign of peace that castle towns became less the fortresses of war and more the peaceful centers of politics, economies, transportation and culture, filled with craftsmen and merchants. The most direct influence this had on sword production was a shift from a focus on quantity to a greater interest in quality.

One of the more noticeable differences in sword design directly attributed to the peaceful urbanization of the Momoyama Period was the shifting of the *sori* (curve) from being off centered and closer to the *nakago* (often referred to as a "*Bizen-sori*") as seen on *tachi*, to a more central point (*saki-sori*) that made the sword easier to draw when worn edge up, as with a *katana*.

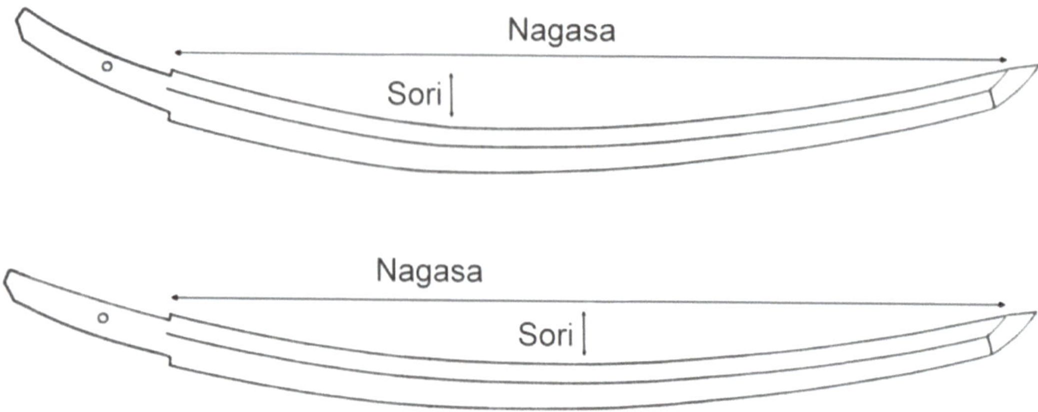

Figure 1.26 Shift from "Bizen-sori" (top) to "Saki-sori" (bottom).

Early Edo Period

During the Edo Period the Tokugawa Shogunate government remained strong until the first half of the 18th century, and was still in control of the economies as well as the government. Thus the whole society was built upon warrior-like ideals and the demand for swords was great. Sword makers moved from the old capital Kyoto and gathered in the new capital Edo and in the thriving commercial center in Osaka.

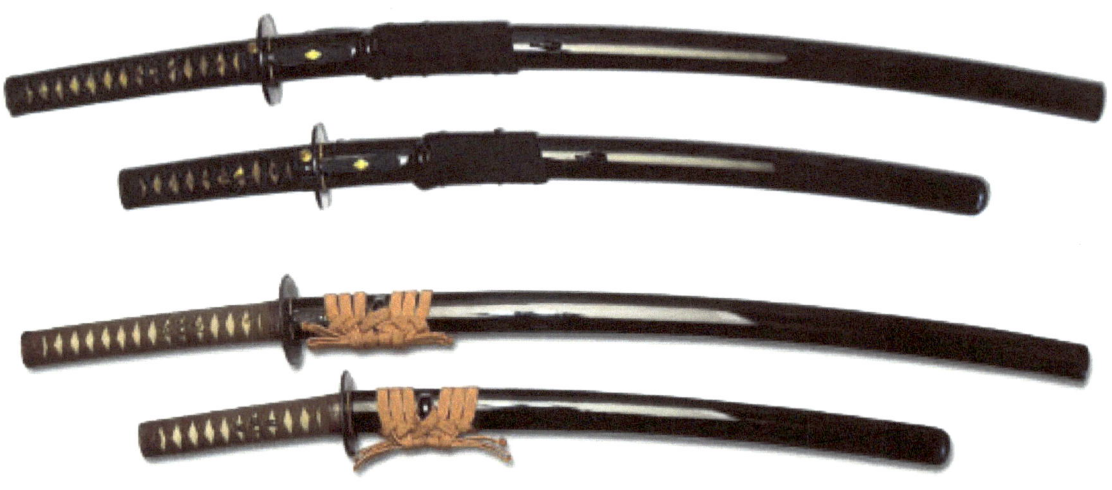

Figure 1.27 Two examples of Daisho Koshirae.

Swords of this period were characterized by a great deal of show with gold inlay and other decorative ornaments. Kotetsu was the most influential swordsmith, and Ishido the most famous school, from this period.

Late Edo Period

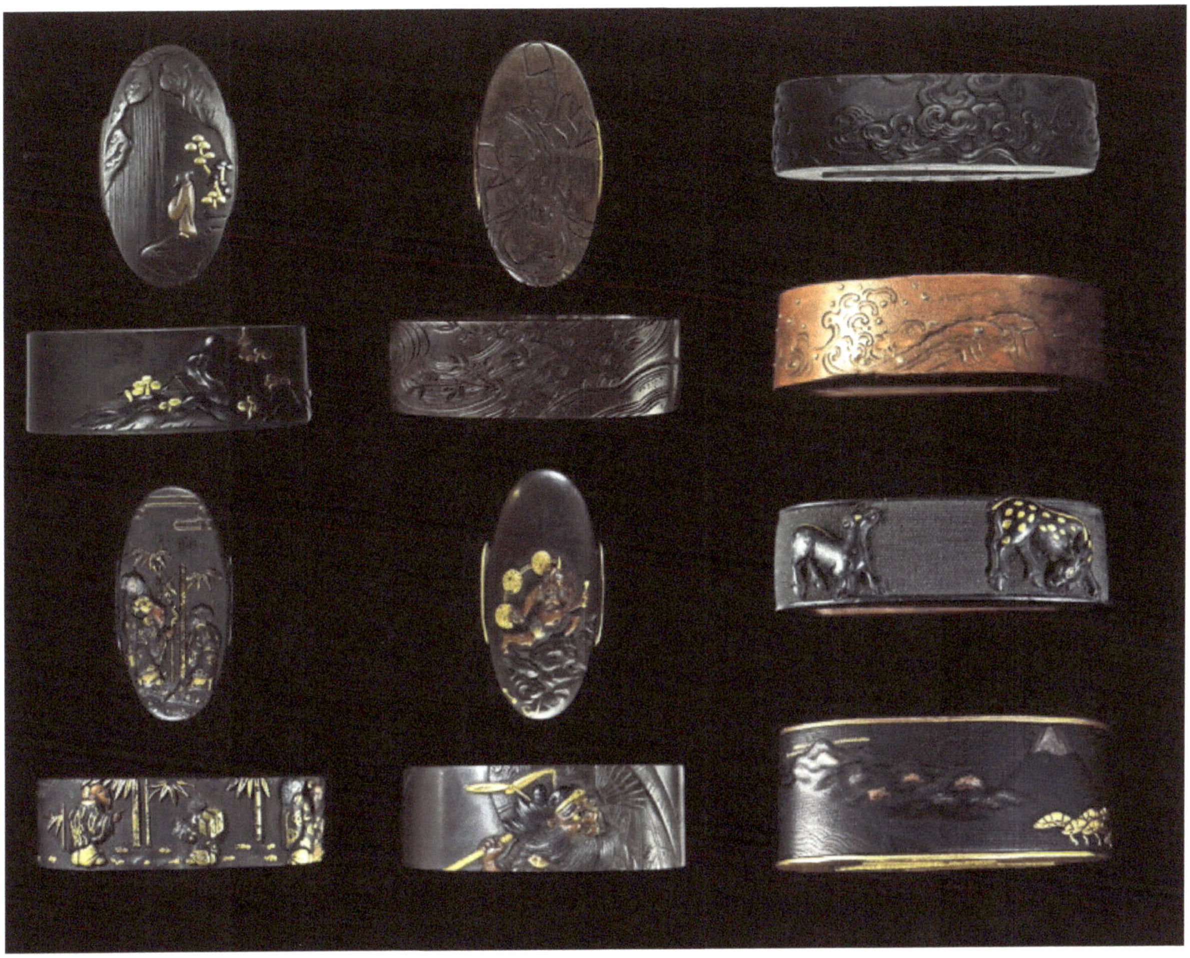

Figure 1.28 Late Edo Period fuchi and kashira.

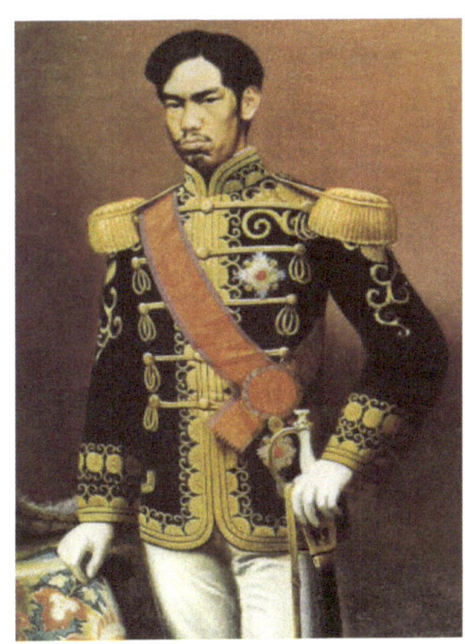

During the same 130 years after the Genroku Period until the end of the Shogunate, the creation of mountings and fittings was the most significant development in the evolution of the Japanese sword. All kinds and colors of metals, lacquers, woods and fabrics were used to produce extremely decorative swords which, in many respects, had become more a matter of social status and part of the samurai's costume than an actual combat weapon.

Figure 1.29 (Left) Mutsuhito, Emperor Meiji of Japan 1867-1912

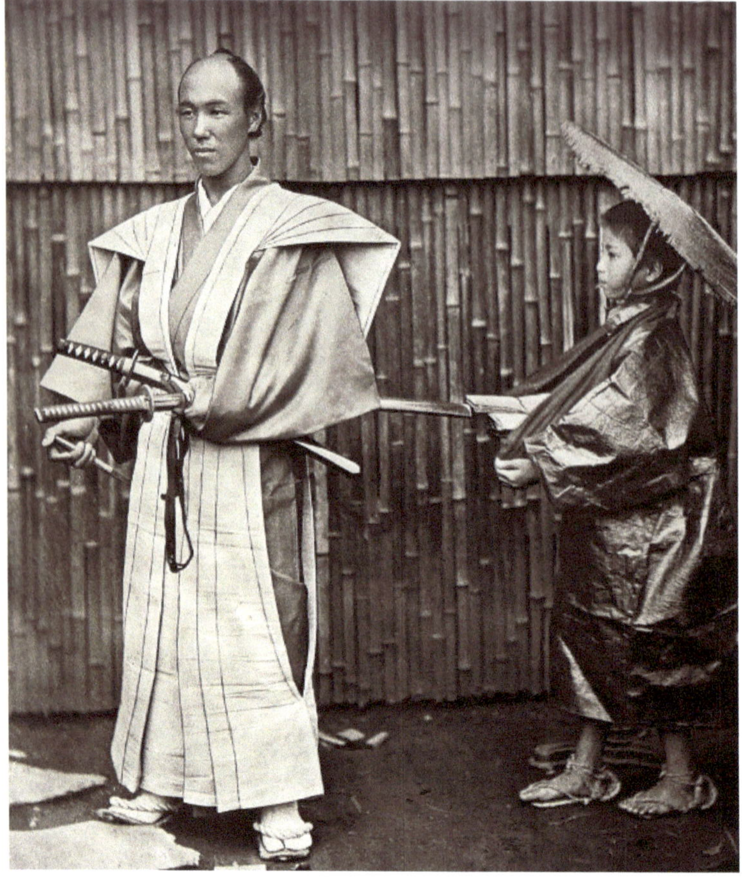

Figure 1.30 Late Edo Period (circa 1860) photo of a samurai in formal wear with his daisho, followed by an attendant.

The coming of Commodore Perry to Japan with his 'black ships' in 1853 marked a period of unrest and internal strife that lasted until the Meiji Restoration in 1868. In the fourth year after the Meiji Restoration, 1871, the Emperor issued the Dampatsurei Edict, forcing the samurai to cut their top knots. This was followed in 1876 by the Heitorei Edict, a strict order for all citizens to stop the carrying of swords. Consequently, the sword lost its last use, causing the swordsmiths to literally go out of business. Swordsmiths went into such jobs as producing cookware and cutlery, and the fittings artists turned their hands to such things as jewelry, vases and sculpture.

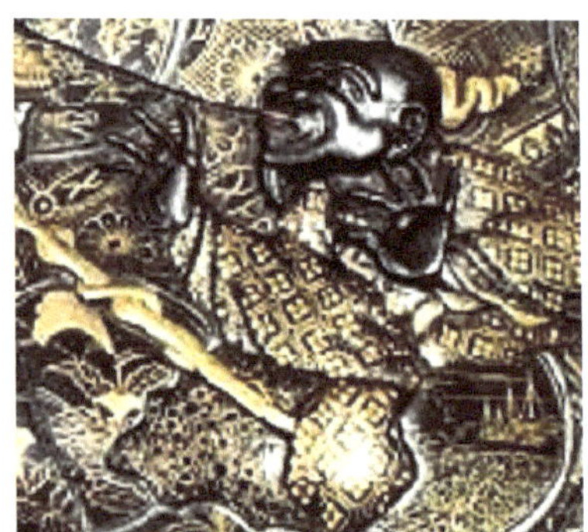

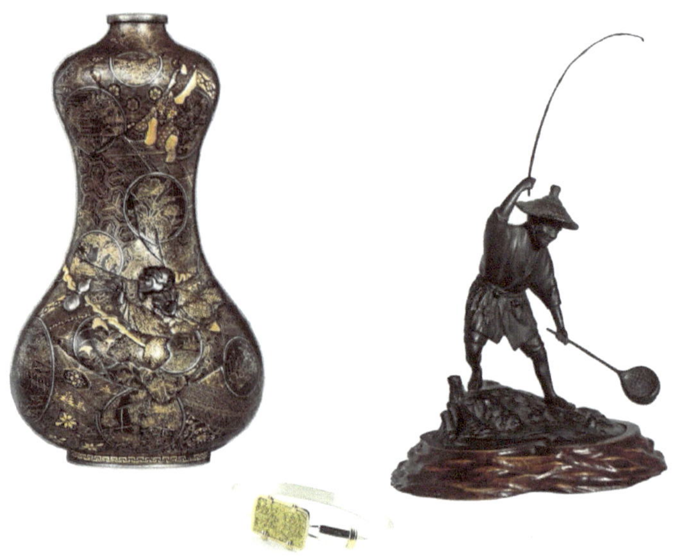

Figure 1.31 Meiji era works by former sword artist; (from left to right) iron vase with gold & silver inlay, a gold & silver bracelet, a bronze statue, and (above) a close up of vase.

2 ANATOMY OF TSUKAMAKI

2.1 A VISUAL GUIDE TO TSUKA PARTS, SHAPES & LENGTHS

A Definition of Terms

In this chapter I shall bring together descriptions of common materials, methods of construction, as well as a general overview of the different types, shapes and sizes of Japanese sword mounts. But first, a number of the common terms used in Japanese swords in general, and *tsukamaki* in particular, need to be defined.

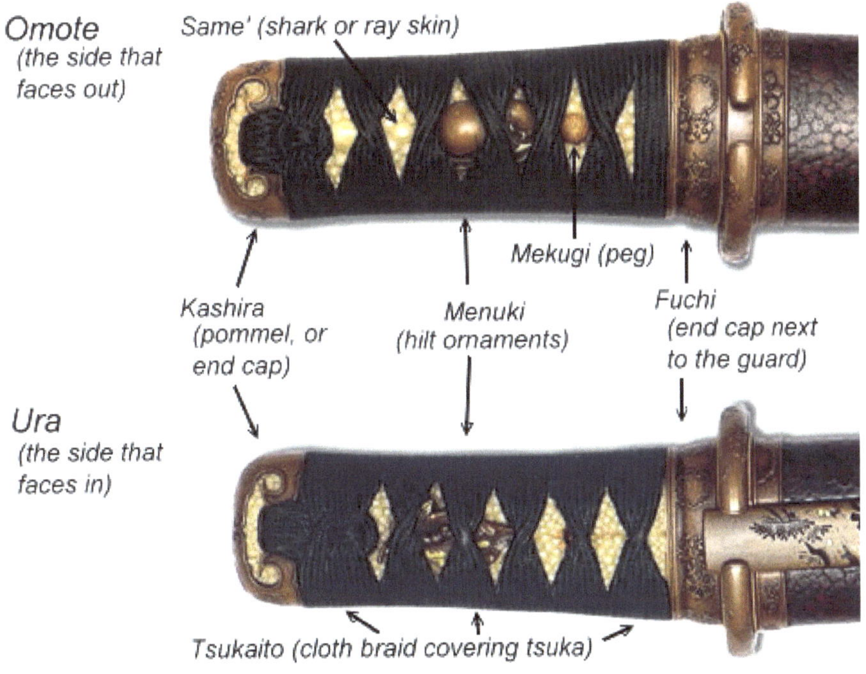

Figure 2.1 Common terms used in tsukamaki.

In general terms, the *tsuka* (hilt) was always made of wood, and was covered by a single piece of *same'* (ray skin) with its seam placed down the center of the *ura* (back) side, and the row of three large nodes placed on the *omote* (front) side near the *kashira* (end cap). Occasionally, the *tsuka* or the wood core had two wide strips of *same'* placed on either side.

All of this was covered by the *tsukaito* (hilt wrapping) created by a single piece of *ito* (flat silk braid). The center of the *ito* is placed flush with the *omote* side of the *fuchi* (hilt collar). It is then wrapped around the *tsuka* and tied in two knots, the first on the *ura* side to secure the *ito*, and the second on the *omote* side to secure the *kashira.*

The Tsuka – General Shapes and Lengths

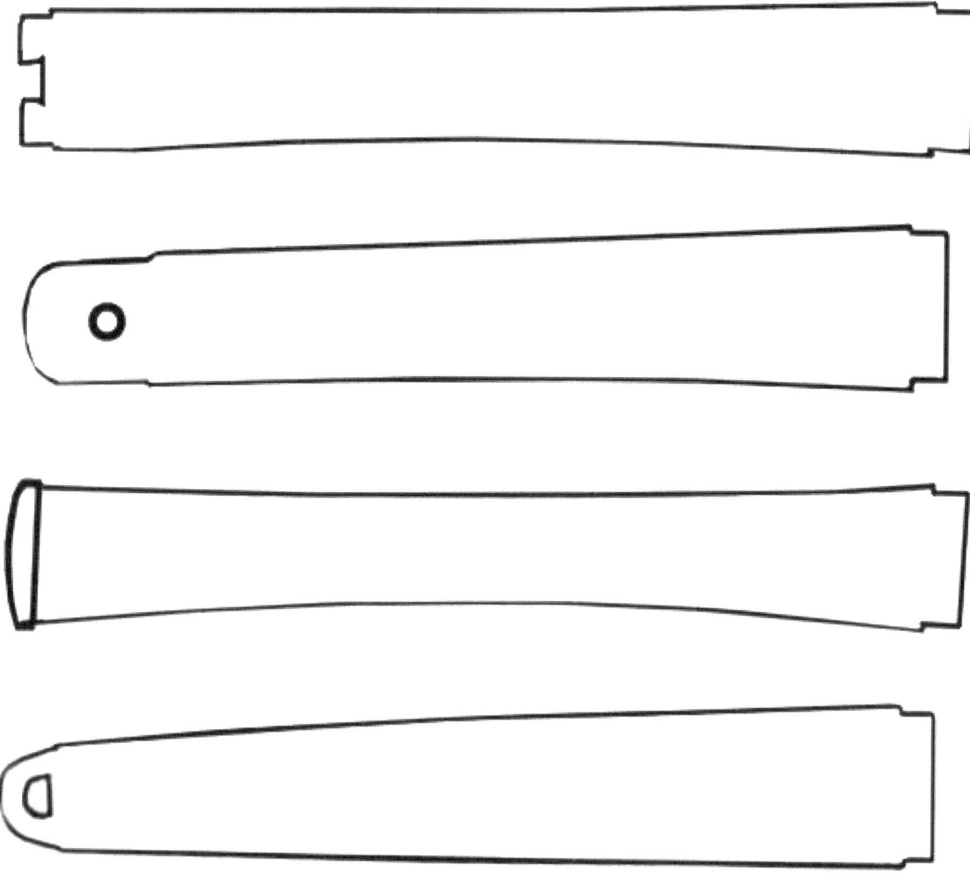

Figure 2.2 Four general tsuka shapes, from top to bottom: Haichi (concave bottom), Morozori (even curve and taper), Rikko (hourglass) and Imogata (potato).

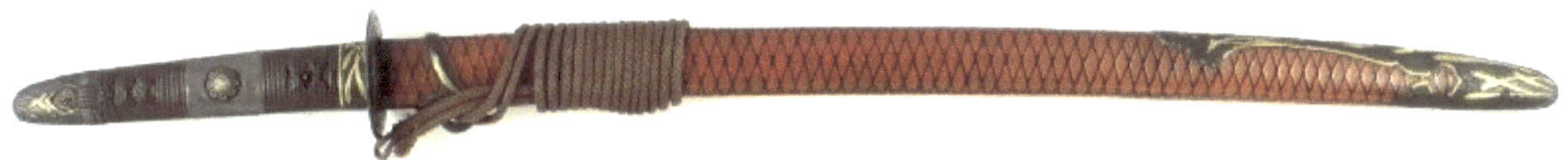

Figure 2.3 An example of a sword with the Imogata shaped tsuka.

In general there are four basic shapes of *tsuka* (see Fig. 2.2 & Fig. 2.3). The *Haichi* is the most common, with the *ha* side almost straight and the *mune* side slightly following the lines of the sword. Next is the *Morozori* which closely follows the shape of the *saya*, and is mostly found on *tachi* and *handachi koshirae*. Then there is the *Rikko* style which has a distinct hourglass shape. And, finally, the *Imogata* (potato) shape with both sides straight, or even slightly convex.

The traditional formula for *tsuka* length was based on a combination of the blade length and the individual owner's hand width. The blade length categorized the general parameters (*katana, wakizashi, tanto*), within which the owner's hand width was used as the specific unit of measurement. With this in mind, the pre-described *tsuka* lengths are as follows: *katana* equals 2 hand widths plus 2 finger widths (or .5 hand widths); the *wakizashi* equals 1.5 hand widths; and the *tanto* equals one hand width. To put this in more conventional terms, if an individual's hand width is 10 cm (nearly 4 inches), and a finger width of 2 cm (about 3/4 inches), the correct *tsuka* length would be 24 cm. And, in fact, the average length of a *katana tsuka* during the Edo period was 24 cm (or 9.5 inches).

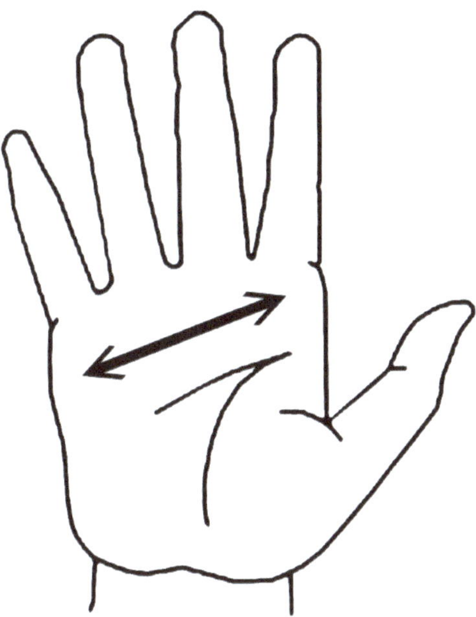

Figure 2.4 Width of a hand.(1W).

2.2 TSUKAMAKI: THE BASIC TOOLS, MATERIALS & TECHNIQUES

The Tools

For holding the *tsuka*: a stand (see Fig. 2.5b & Fig. 2.5c) that will hold the *tsuka* firmly in place for both wrapping and tightening, and will allow work to be done easily on both the *omote* and *ura* sides.

For inserting the paper wedges, and adjusting the *ito*: tweezers, a pick (any small pointed tool) and any small hand held tool with a blunt wedge shaped tip. For holding the *ito* in place: a special clamp that can be worked around freely, will not allow the *ito* to shift, and goes on and comes off readily.

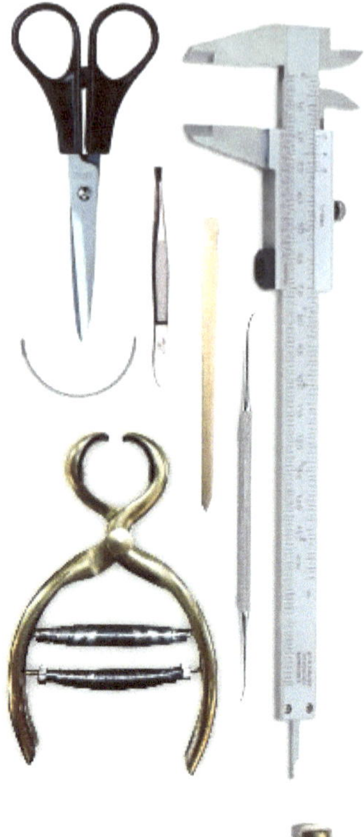

Figure 2.5a Various tools.

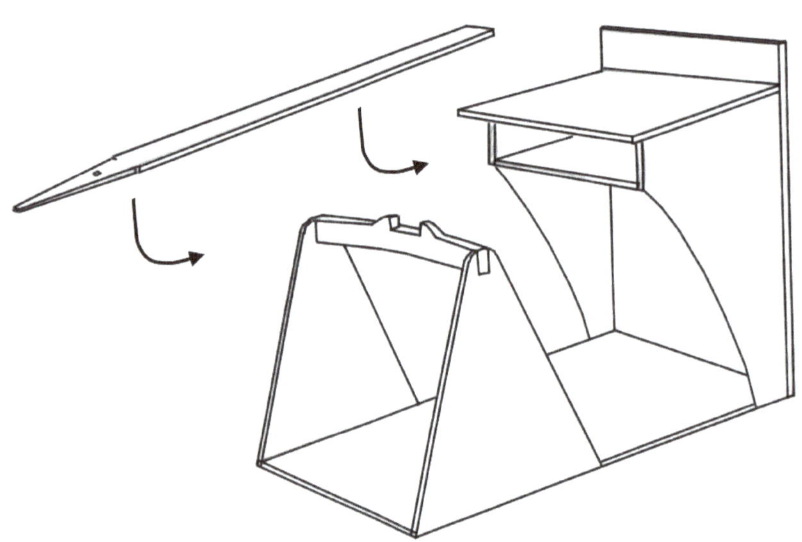

Figure 2.5b Diagram of a wooden wrapping stand.

The Materials

Aside from the *tsuka* itself, the basic materials in *tsukamaki* are the *ito*, paper and glue. The glue can either be purchased (such as Elmer's) or produced by boiling rice, working it into a paste while still warm, and adding a small amount of water.

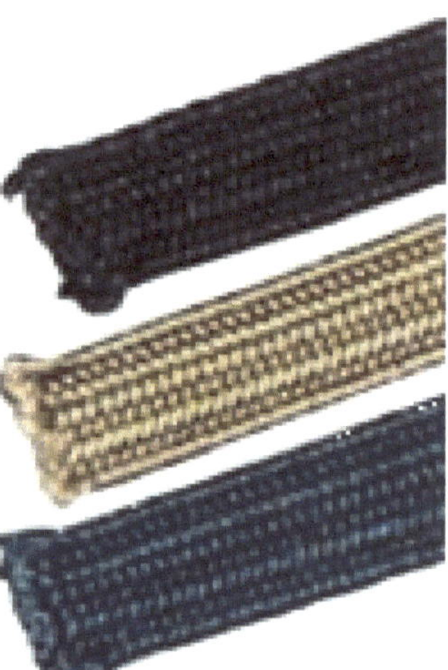

Figure 2.6 Ito examples.

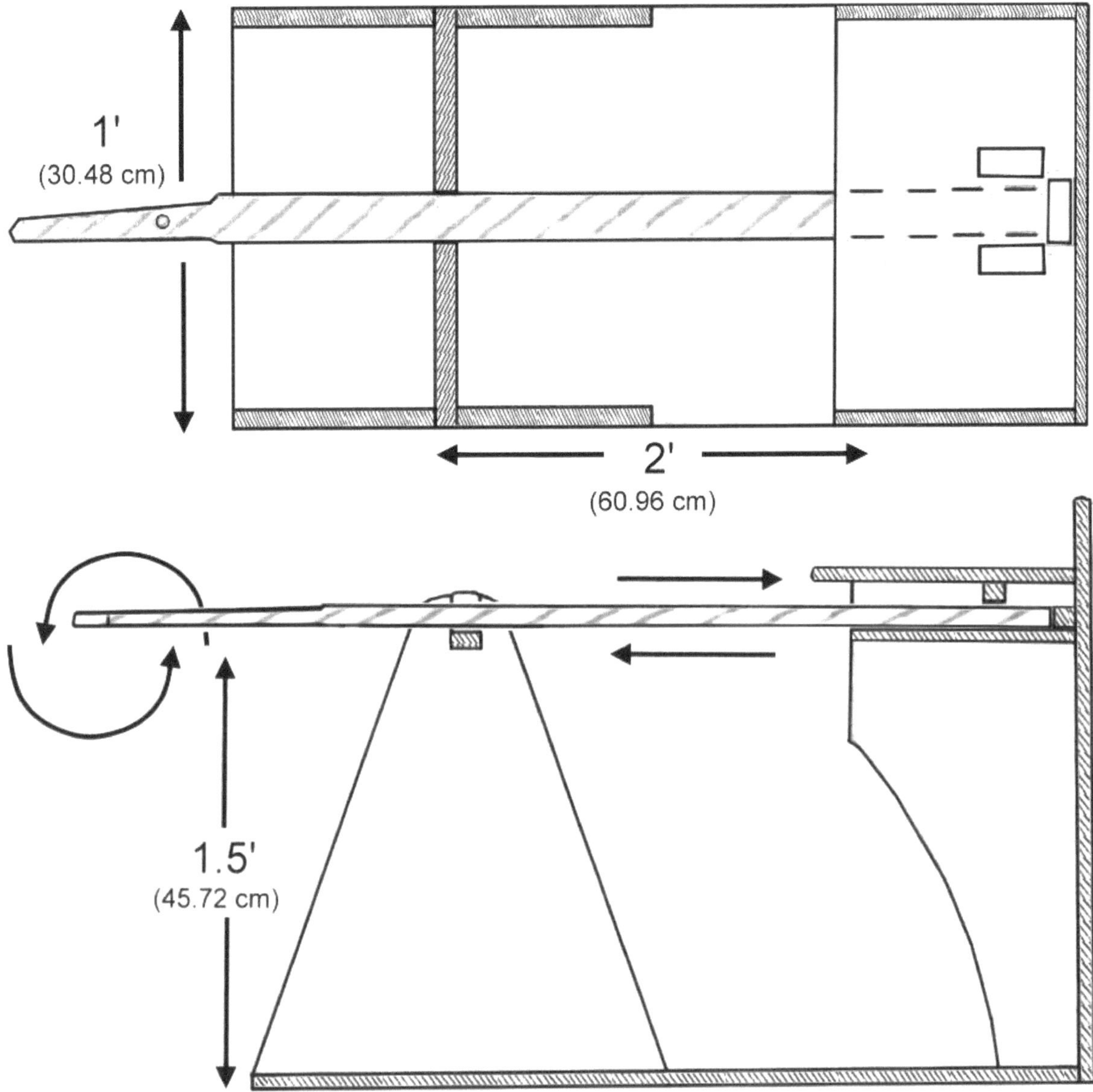

Figure 2.5c Schematics of a wooden wrapping stand.

The paper can be of nearly any weight, but ideally it should be relatively close to newsprint in weight and consistency.

During the wrapping, be sure to moisten the paper wedges before inserting them under the *ito*. This will allow the wedges to conform more readily to both the *ito* and the *same'*.

Although the *ito* is available in a wide range of colors, it is only manufactured using two different types of fibers (natural and synthetic). When trying to identify an unknown *ito*, a burn test is often helpful. The following chart (Fig. 2.7) gives tests for the principle natural fibers and synthetics.

Fiber	Flame	Odor	Residue
COTTON	*Luminous, rapid*	*Burning paper*	*Fine, gray*
SILK	*Slow orange/yellow*	*Burning hair*	*Brittle bead*
RAYON	*Sparks, orange*	*Burnt paper*	*Black ash*
NYLON	*Melts, no flame*	*Like celery*	*Hard bead*

Figure 2.7 Burn test to identify types of ito.

Suggested Ito Lengths

Although there are several different ways to derive the required length of *ito*, ranging from special formulas and ratios to wrapping the tsuka from end to end and half-way back, I tend to follow the simple guidelines given me by Takahashi-sensei.

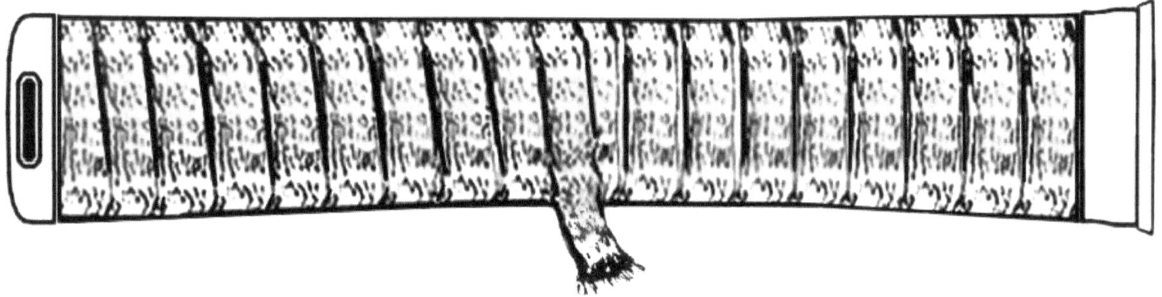

Figure 2.8 Ito length determined by wrapping the tsuka 1½ times.

TANTO tsuka (10cm | 4in)	2m or 6ft of ito
WAKIZASHI tsuka (15cm | 6in)	2.5m or 8ft of ito
KATANA tsuka (25cm | 10in)	3.5m or12ft of ito

Figure 2.9 Takahashi's suggested ito lengths.

Preparing the Tsuka

In preparing the *tsuka*, start by stretching a sample of the desired *ito* tight and measuring its width (1W).

Using a small amount of rice paste glue, place thin paper strips along both the *ha* and the *mune* sides of the *tsuka*. By layering the paper you will define the finished shape of the *tsuka*, and also guard the *ito* from snagging on surface of the *same'*. Continue the layering until the *fuchi/kashira* will be flush with the edges of the *tsuka* after the *ito* is in place.

the

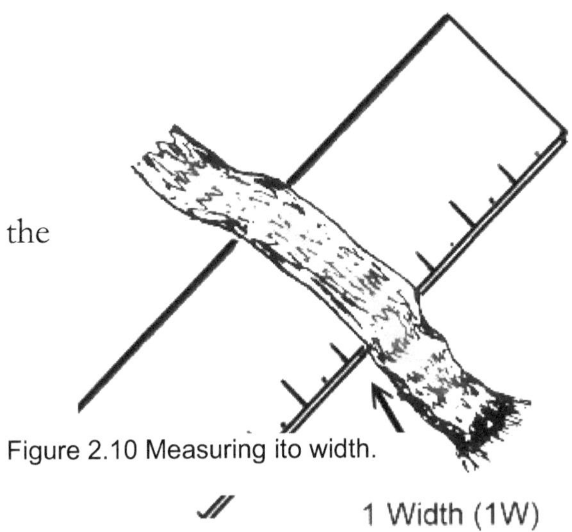

Figure 2.10 Measuring ito width.

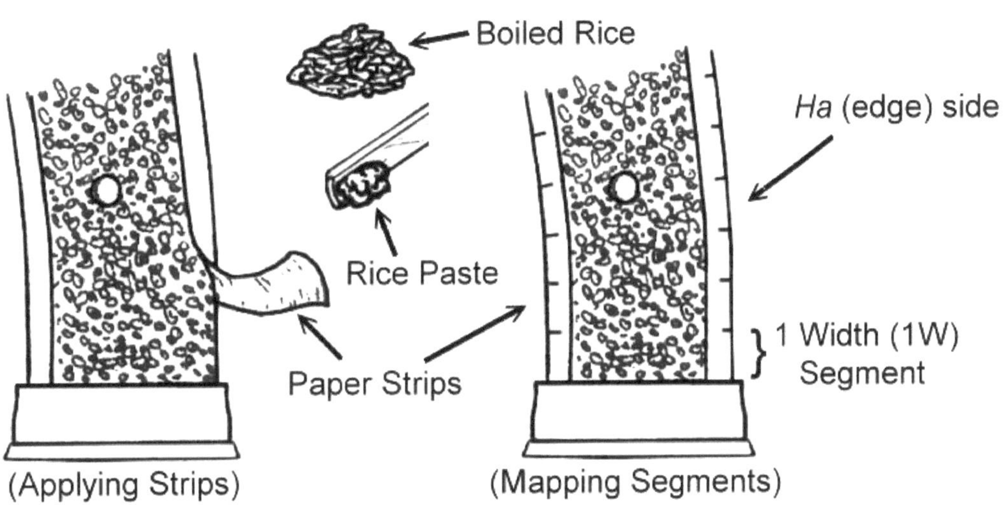

Figure 2.11 Applying paper strips and mapping the width (1W) segments.

Measure and mark the *ha* and *mune* sides in *tsukaito* width segments (1W). The distance between the *fuchi* and *kashira* should measure an odd number of width units along both the *ha* and *mune*. If not, either the *tsuka* may have to be altered, or a different weight *ito* may have to be selected in order to fit within an odd number of spaces.

Hishi-Gami (The Paper Wedges)

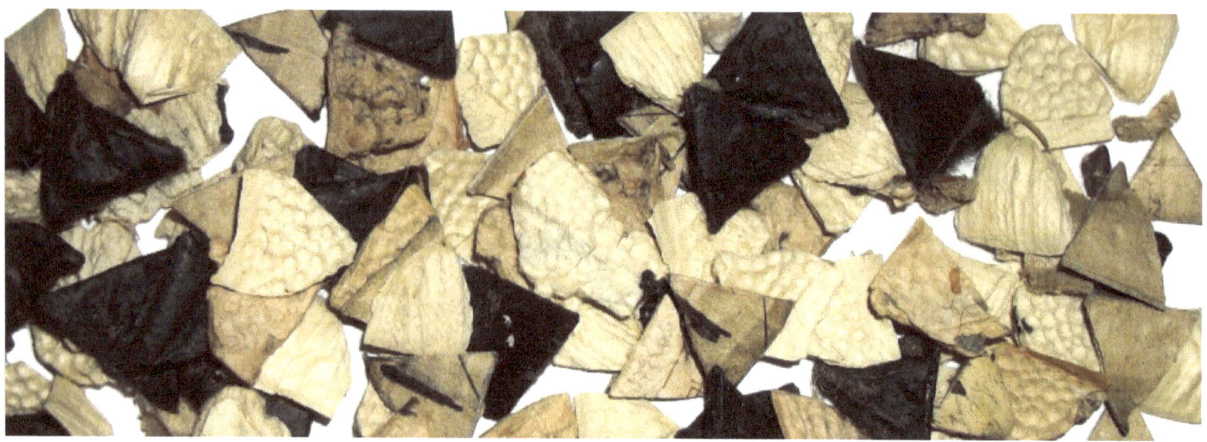

Figure 2.12 Hishi-gami from 18th and 19th century swords.

To give the *maki* a proper shape, the *tsukaito* is folded over various styles of *hishi-gami*, or small paper wedges. Here are a few of the many different styles used.

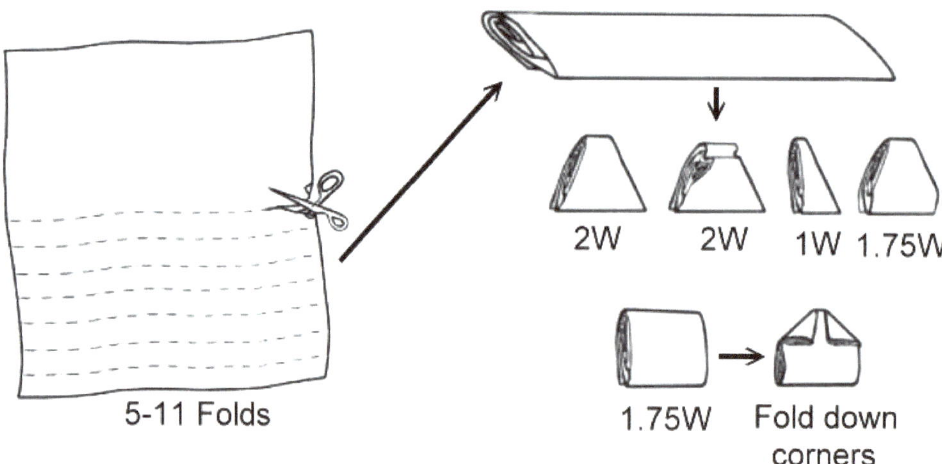

Figure 2.12b Various examples of hishi-gami.

In making the wedges, begin by folding a sheet of newsprint or standard weight paper five to eleven times. Cut off the excess paper, then cut the folded paper into two width (2W) segments. Use these to make any of the wedge styles illustrated in Figure 2.12.

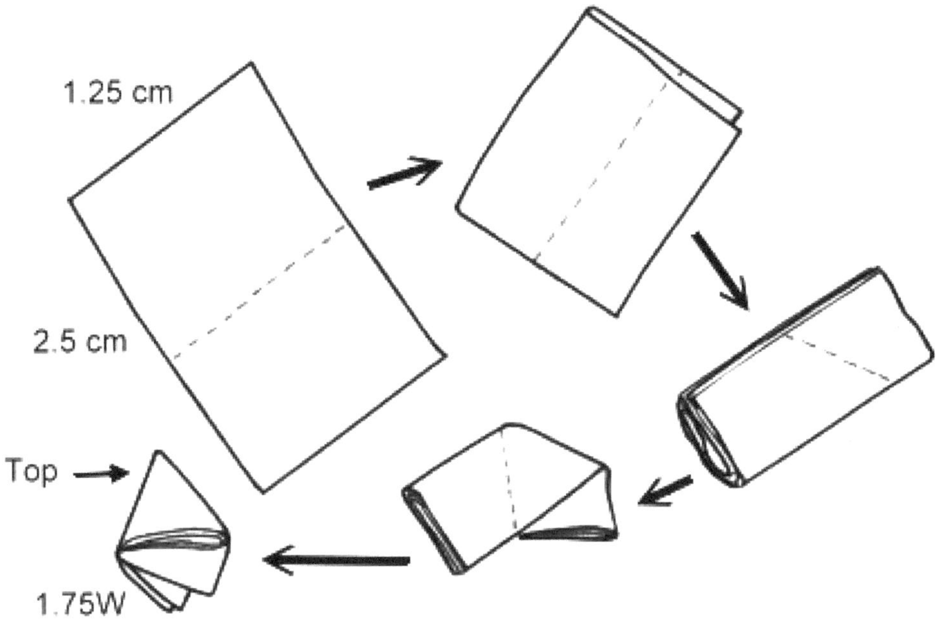

Figure 2.13 Alternate hishi-gami using a 2.5 x 1.25cm piece of paper

A flatter and more ridged *hishi-gami* can be made from a 2.5 x 1.25 cm (1" x 1/2") piece of paper folded (Fig. 2.13).

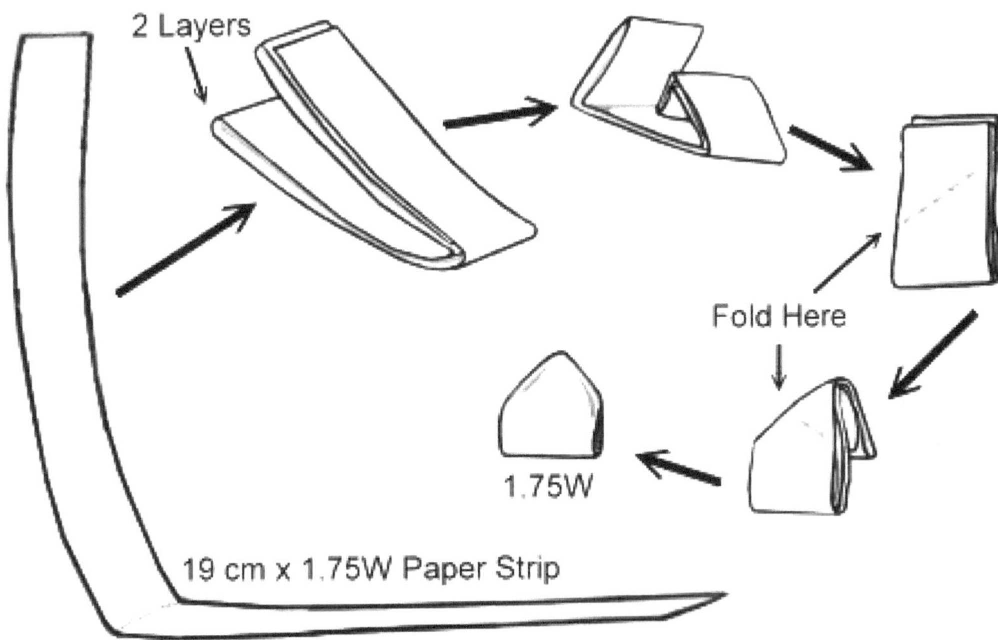

Figure 2.14 Alternate hishi-gami using 19cm x 1.75W strip of paper.

Another, thicker and more rounded wedge can be made from a piece of paper 19 cm (7 1/2") x 1.75W folded (Fig. 2.14).

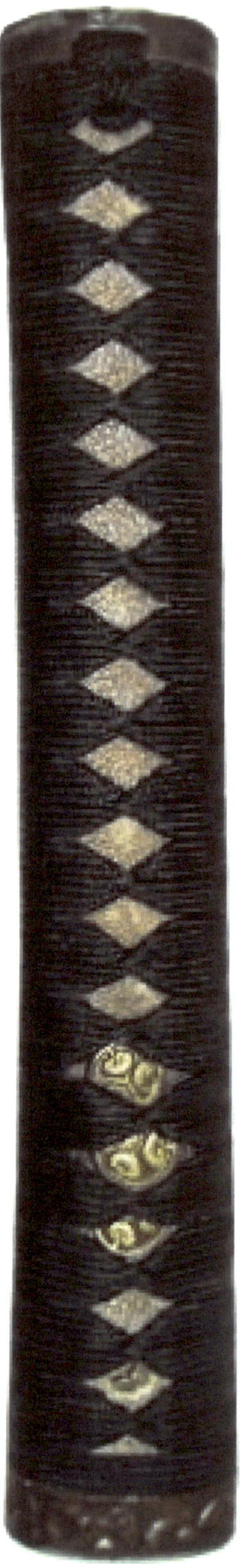

Figure 2.15 Tsuka in the menpumaki moyo iri wrapping style.

The Wrapping of the Handle

To begin with, it should be stated that Japanese tradition dictates that *tsukamaki* be started and completed on the *omote*, or side of the *tsuka* that faces outward when being worn. This is almost always true regardless of the style of wrap. The actual wrapping process begins in much the same way for many of the *maki* styles, using the following steps:

- Measure half the length of the *tsukaito.*
- Place the first two paper wedges on the *ura* (side opposite the *omote*), and align them with the marks on the paper strips. (Fig. 2.16).
- Make the first two *tsukaito* folds overlap the paper wedges.
- Bring the other half of the braid around and make the next two folds.
- Repeat with other length of *ito.*
- Continue this procedure on the other side, alternating the direction of the folds.

During the wrapping, tightness should be a primary concern. Each fold should be drawn or stretched so that there is no slackness or looseness.

Throughout the process, continually monitor and adjust the symmetry of the folds and open areas, and try to maintain a smooth surface appearance along the *ha* and *mune* edges of the *tsuka*. A quality *tsukamaki* is consistently symmetric, smooth and tight.

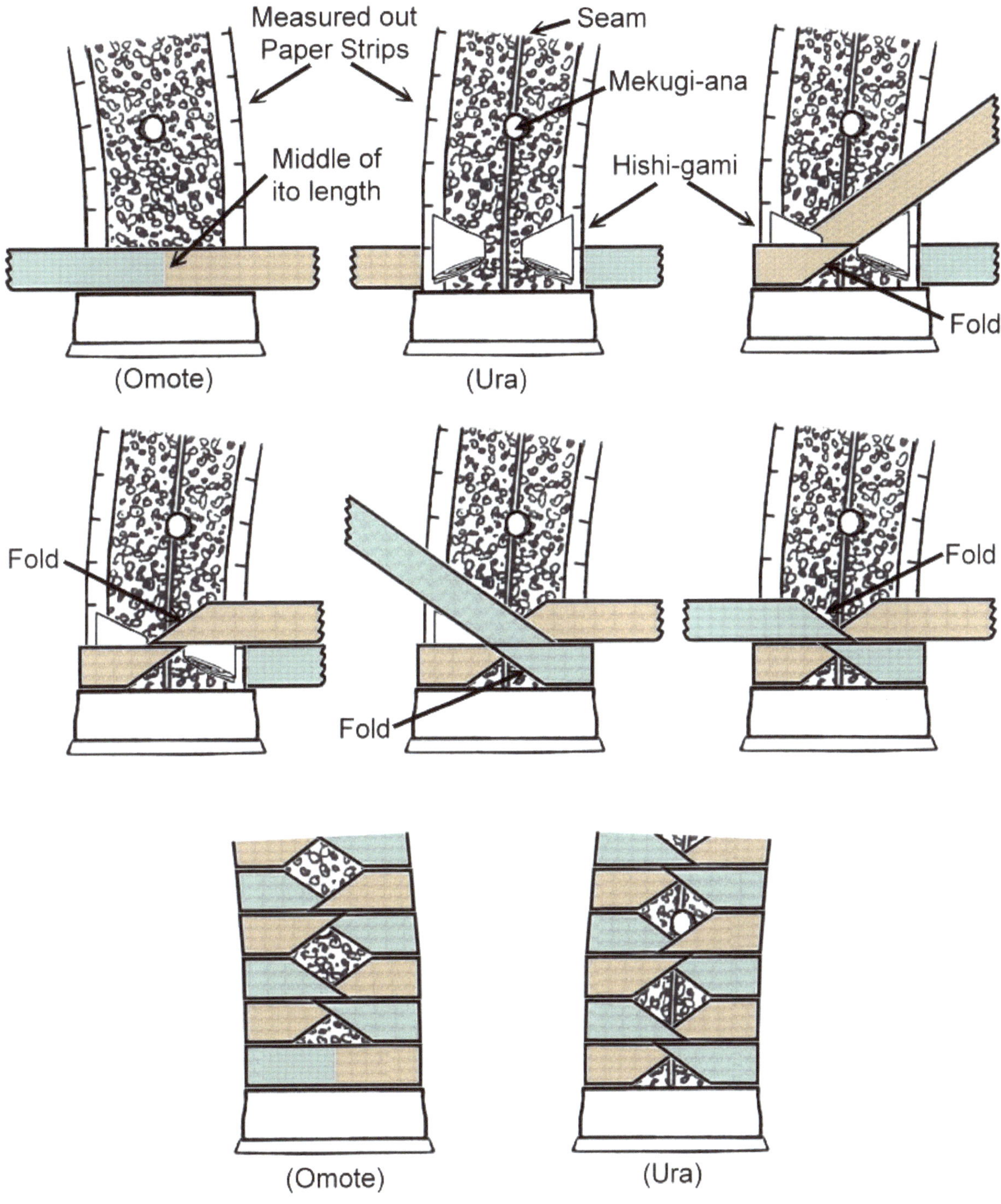

Figure 2.16 Tsukamaki in the menpumaki moyo iri wrapping style

Placing the Menuki

On the *katana*, as well as the *tachi*, the *menuki* usually are placed after the third set of folds from the *fuchi* on the *omote* side and three sets of folds from the knot on the *ura* side (Fig. 2.17). On the *wakizashi* and *tanto*, the *menuki* commonly are placed after the second or third set of folds. In any event, the positioning may vary because of *tsuka* size, *menuki* size, *ito* width, or placement of the *mekugiana* (peg hole). Also, when placing *menuki,* multiple layers of *hishi-gami* are used.

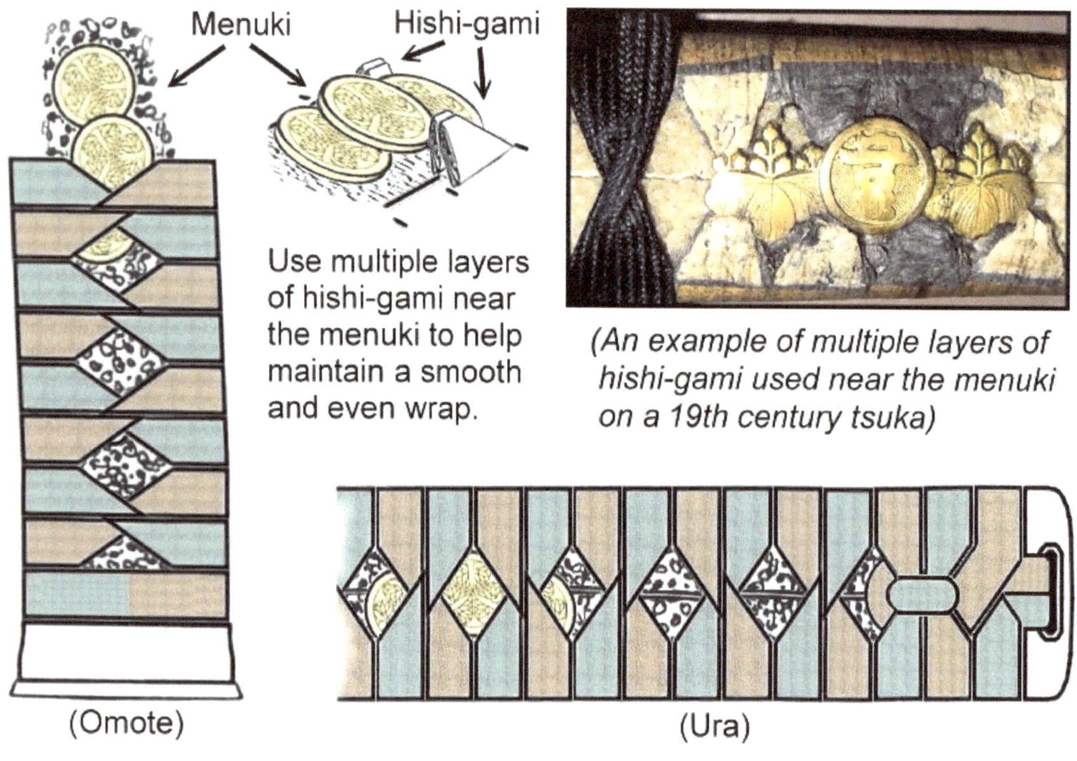

Figure 2.17 Menuki placement and use of hishi-gami.

Tying the Knots

One of the more difficult aspects of *tsukamaki* is tying the *ura* and *omote* side knots. To begin, at the end of the *tsuka* on the *ura* side, pass the end of the *tsukaito* over and then under the preceding fold. Then, pass the second end over the other end, and under the previous fold, making a loop. Bring it back again under the fold. Thread both ends through the *shitadome*, if present, and the *kashira* side-by-side. (Fig. 2.18).

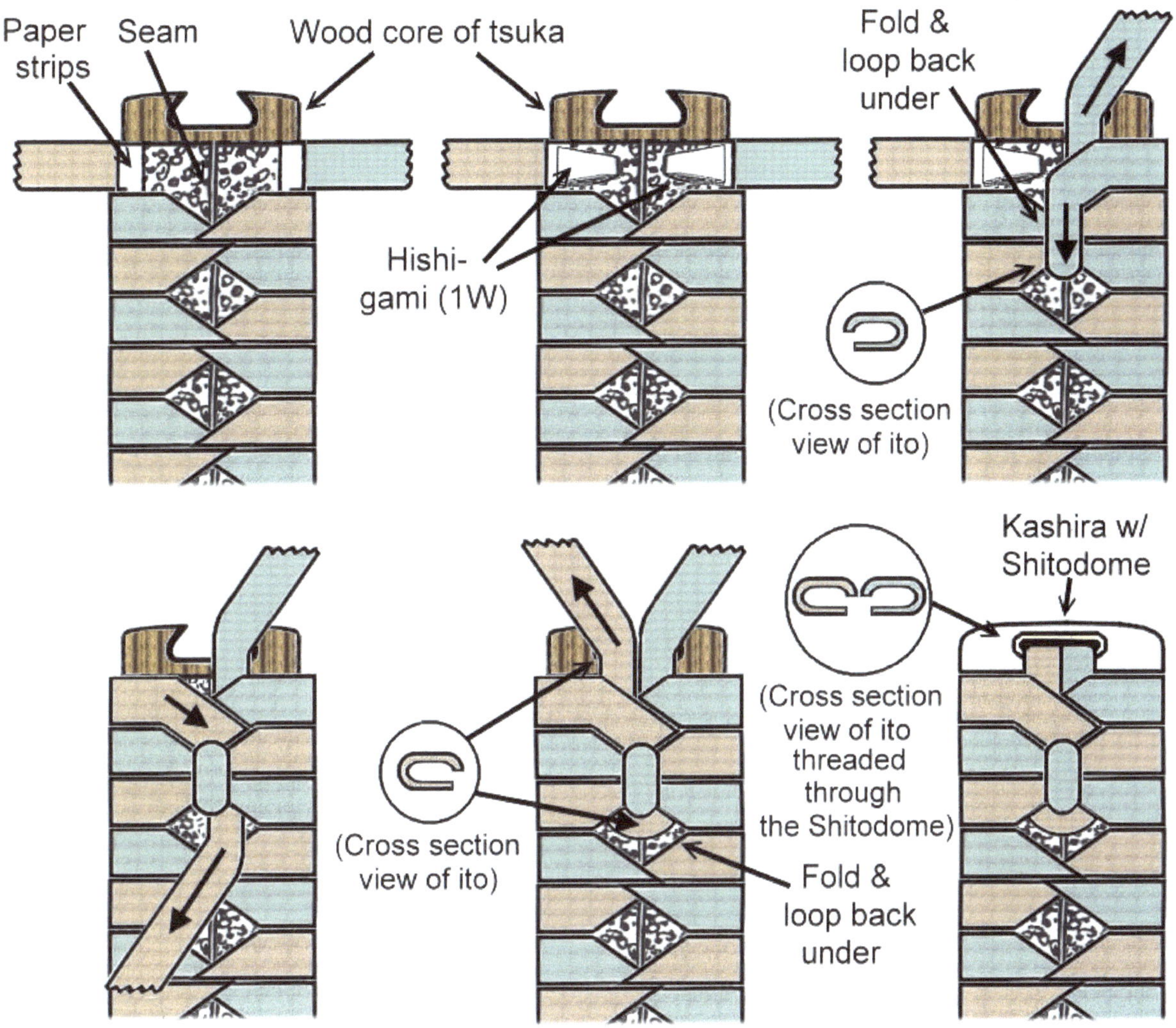

Figure 2.18 The tying of the ura side knot.

To start the *omote* knot, pass the bottom end of the *tsukaito* under the top set of folds, pull the braid over the fold, cut off, apply rice paste glue, and tuck under. (Fig. 2.21). Take the top end of the *tsukaito* under the top set of folds, repeating the first part of the previous step. Then, make a loop by bringing it back again under the folds. At this point, insert a small wad of paper and fold the *tsukaito* over and tighten. Bring the top length around to the left and down again, cut off, apply and paste glue and tuck under. (Fig. 2.21b).

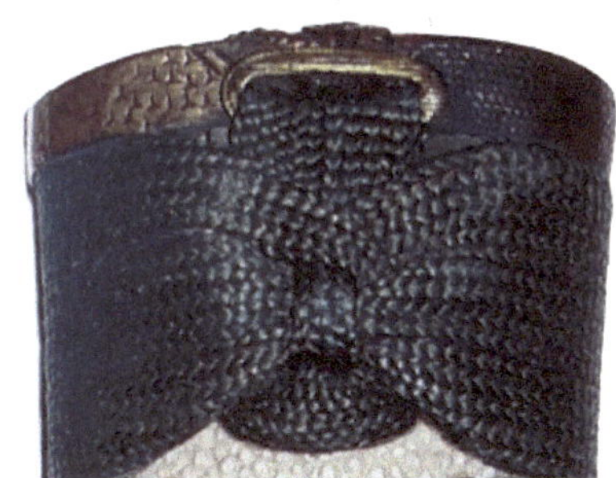

Figure 2.19 A ura side knot. Note the side-by-side folded ito passing through the shitodome.

Figure 2.20 (Right) An omote side knot. Note the positioning of the large same' node next to the knot.

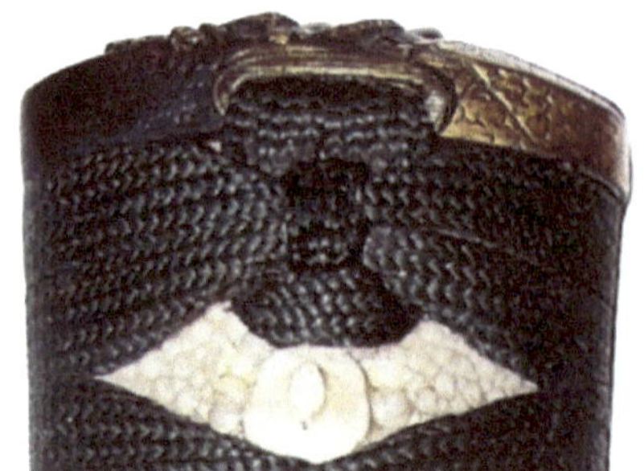

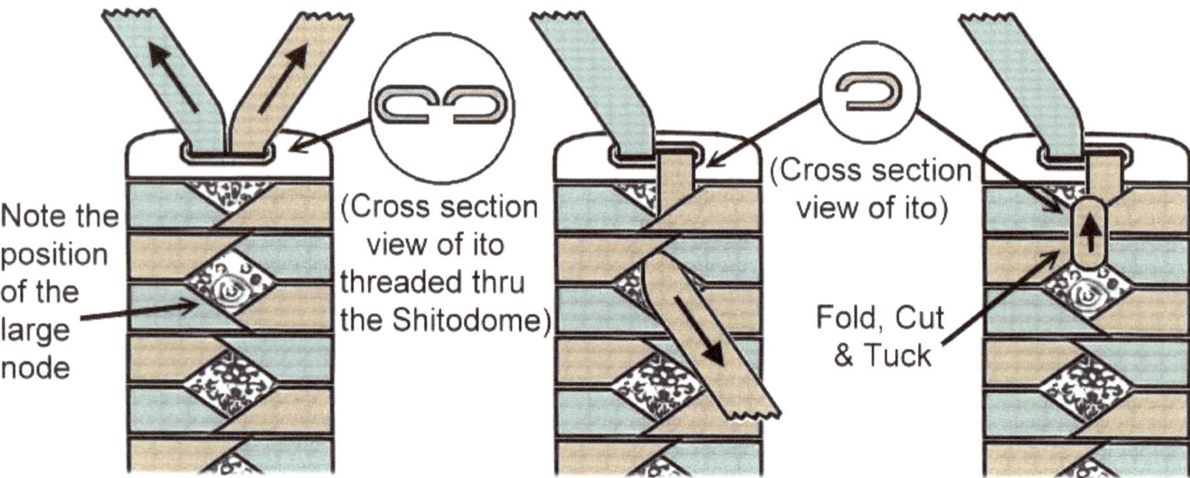

Figure 2.21a The tying of the omote side knot.

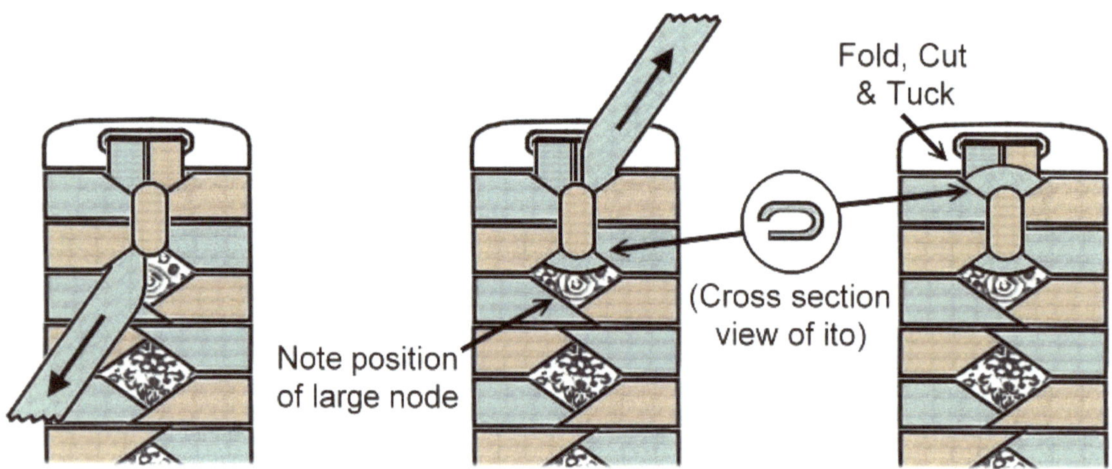

Figure 2.21b The tying of the omote side knot.

Threading the Ito

One of the more challenging aspects of tying the *tsuka* knots is threading the *ito* under tight *tsukamaki* folds. There are several innovative methods, but one of the simplest involves a curved needle and thread or string. First, you will need to acquire a needle with a relatively large eye (Fig. 2.22), and some string. Most any fabrics store should have both. Next, thread the needle with the string, looping it through several times, then put the end of the *ito* that you want to pull into the loops (Fig. 2.23).

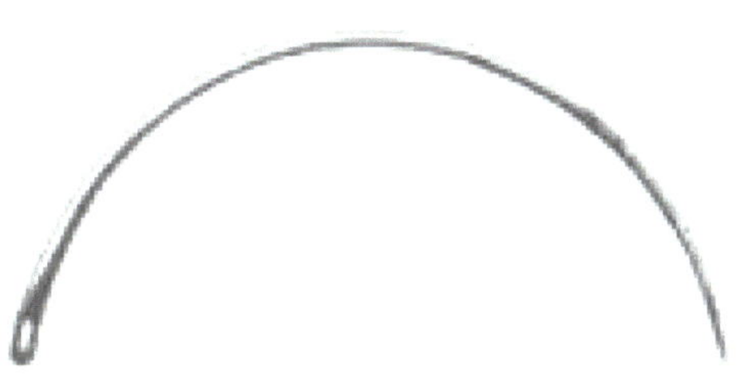

Figure 2.22 A curved needle

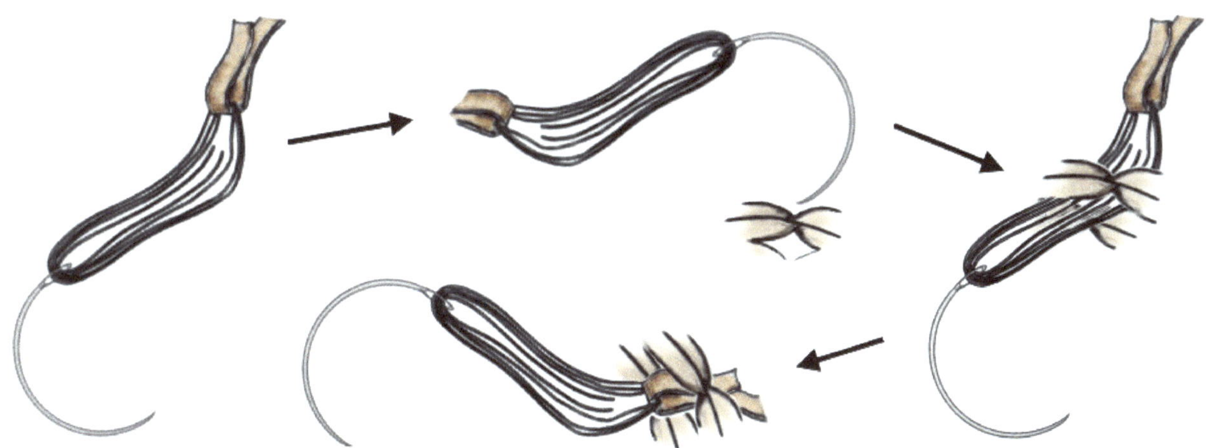

Figure 2.23 Using a curved needle to thread ito under tsukamaki folds.

Finally, after sliding the tip of the needle under the twists, you should be able to pull the needle, string and *ito* all the way under. You should be able to remove the needle and string by reversing the processes, except leaving the *ito* in place.

Variations on the Common Knots

Although countless *shingunto koshirae* (military sword mounts) use similar knots to the ones previously discussed, many use a variation where the *omote* side is finished first with a simple twisted knot, and without passing through the *kashira.* The *ura* side is completed by cutting and tucking both ends of the *ito.*

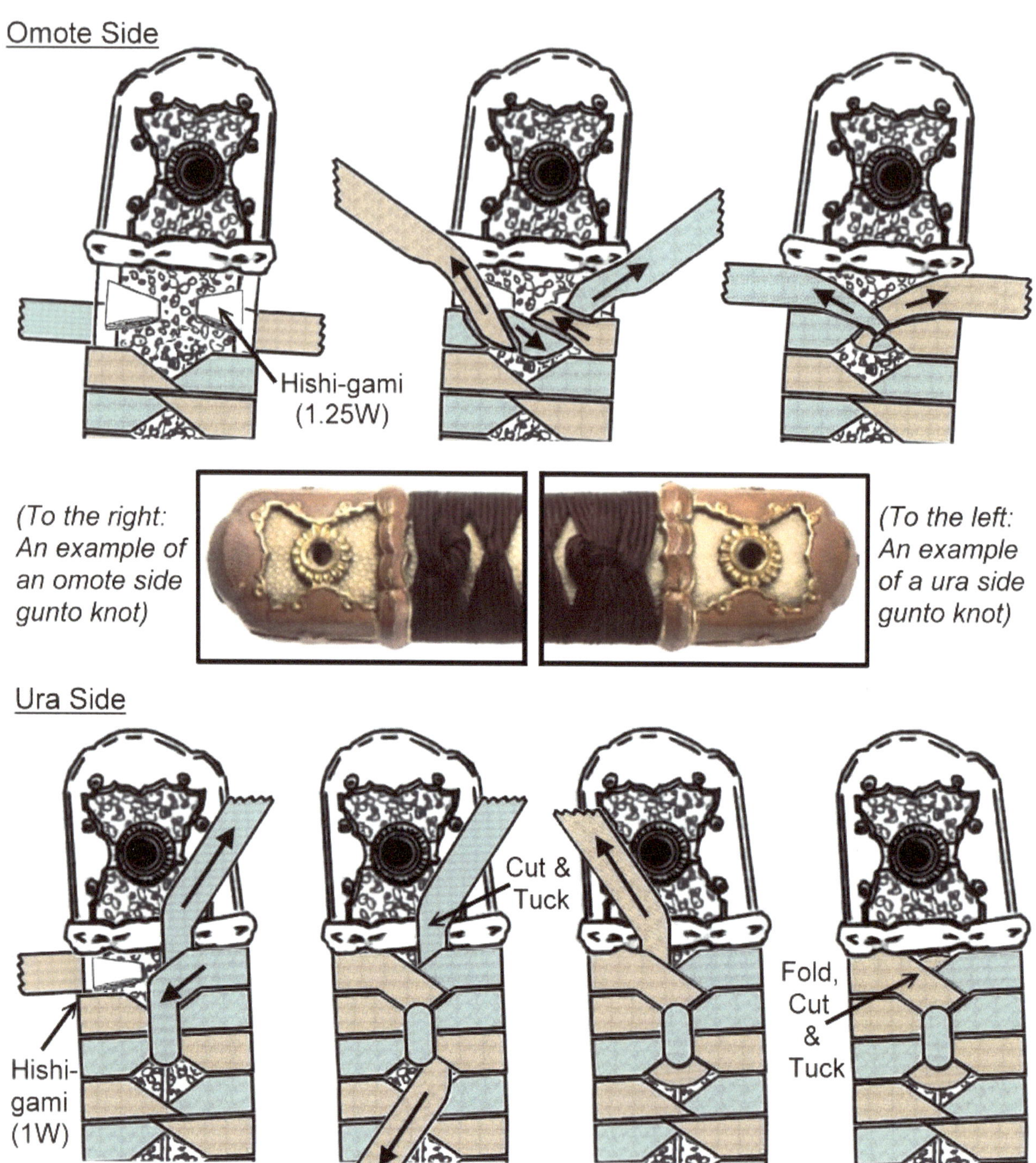

Figure 2.24 Common ura & omote side gunto knots.

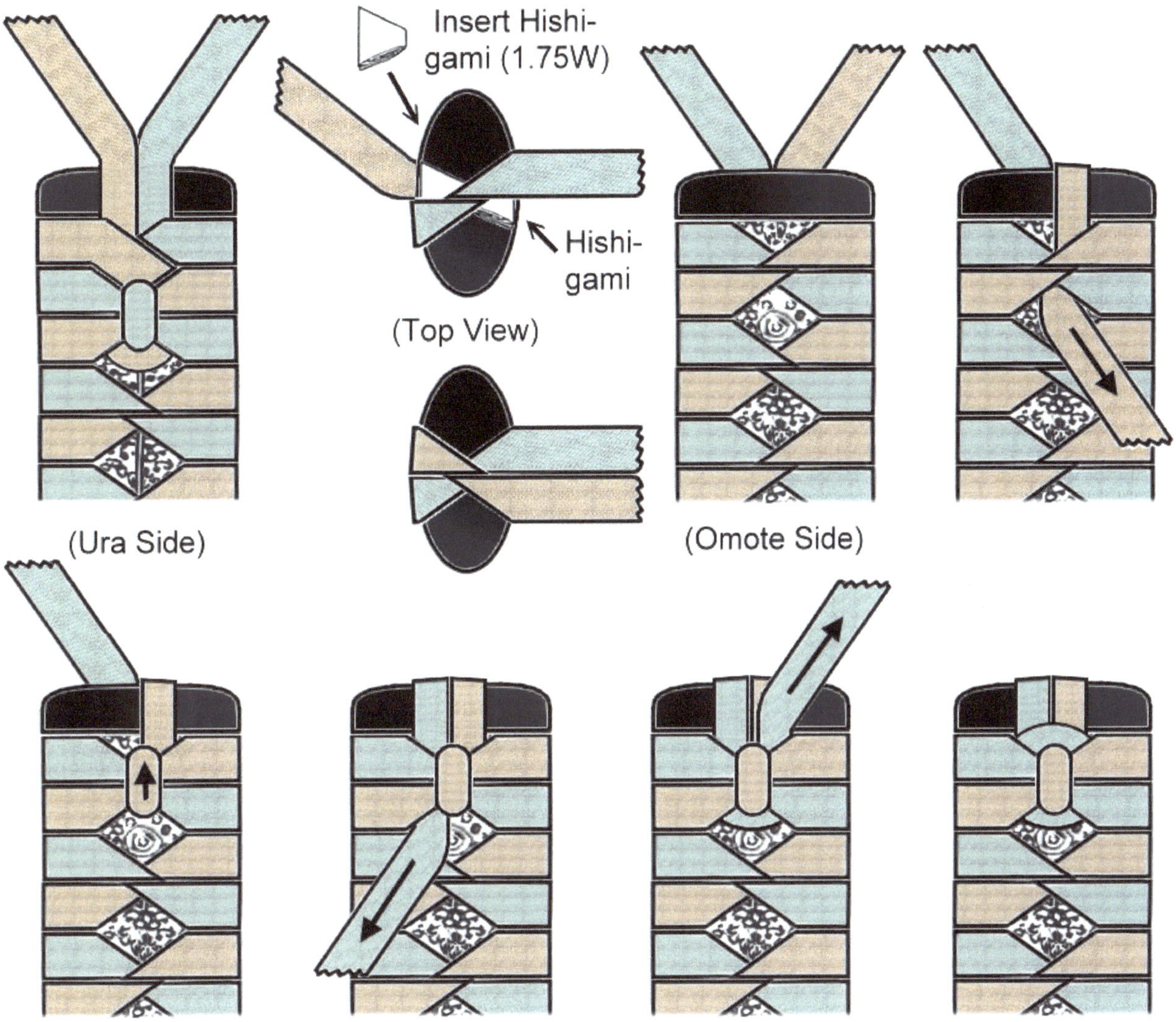

Insert Hishi-gami (1.75W)

Hishi-gami

(Top View)

(Ura Side)

(Omote Side)

Figure 2.25 Makikake no kashira.

Another knot variation (Fig. 2.25) is *makikake no kashira*, or the practice of crossing over a *kashira* of plain black water buffalo horn. During the Edo period, this style became a standard for formal wear, with the *fuchi* made of *shakudo* (a metal alloy with a deep bluish black patina) and the *menuki* of gold with a *nanako* (surface of small raised bumps) background most often displaying the owner's family crest.

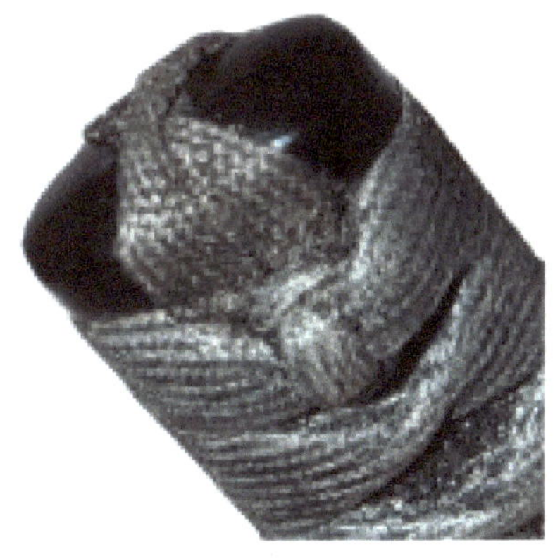

Figure 2.26 (Right) Ito wrapped over a water buffalo horn kashira.

2.3 TSUKAMAKI: THREE RESTORATION CASE STUDIES

Case 1: Restoration of a Shingunto Tsuka

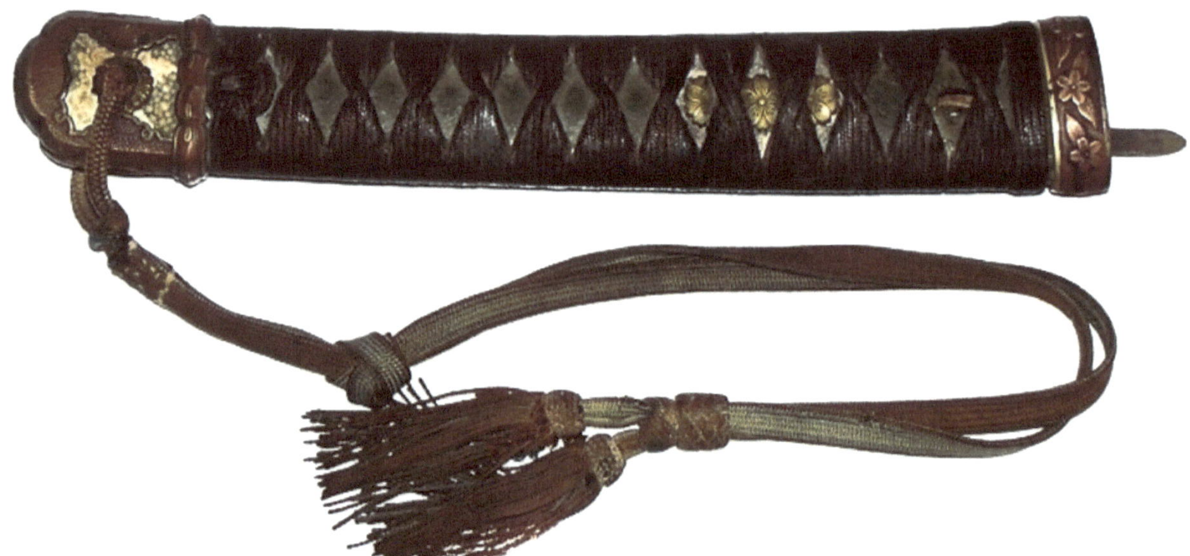

Figure 2.27 Shingunto tsuka from a koto blade in regulation mounts.

The *shingunto*, or neo-army sword, was introduced in 1933 to replace the *kyu-gunto*. Its *koshirae* are based on the traditional *tachi,* and is the most common of all Japanese military swords. It was carried throughout World War II, and it housed both newly made and ancestral blades.

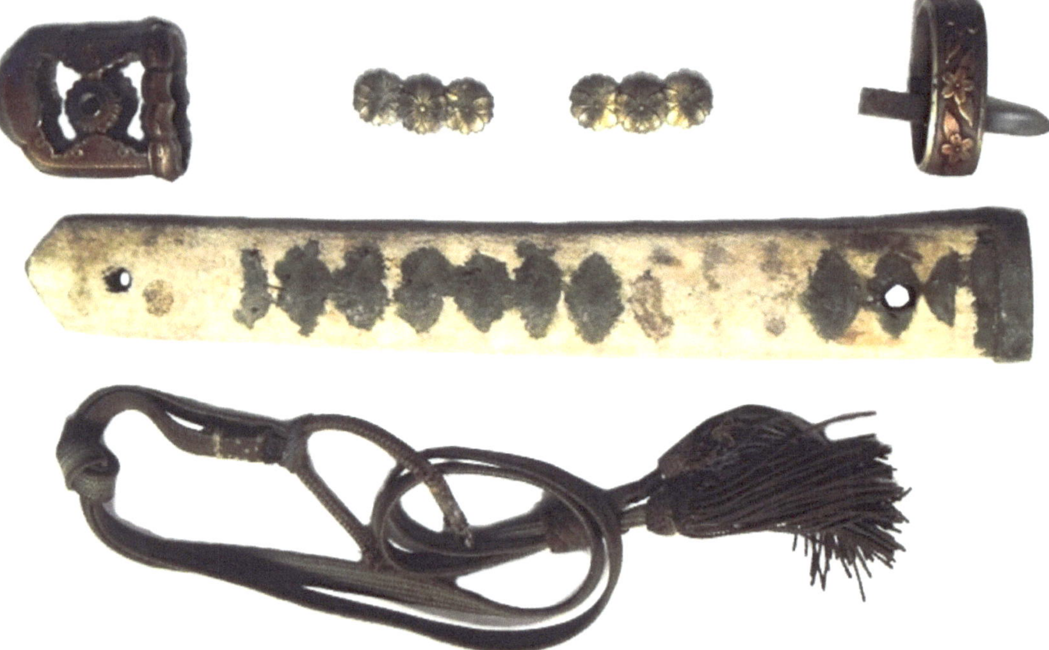

Figure 2.28 The tsuka and parts after the removal of the old same' and ito.

The Case 1 *tsuka* is from a sword in *shingunto* mounts. The *fuchi/kabuto-gane* and *menuki* are standard regulation mounts. The *ito* was applied in a slightly more complex fashion than normal, combining *tsumami* (see section 3.29) and *menpumaki* (Fig. 2.16) styles. Also, the *omote* knot is unusual for this style of mounts, and the tassel is attached to the *kabuto-gane* with a cord. At some point, the *tsuka* lost the majority of its *same'*, and the exposed wood was covered with a flat olive drab paint.

Figure 2.29 New same' applied (top) and prepared for wrapping (bottom).

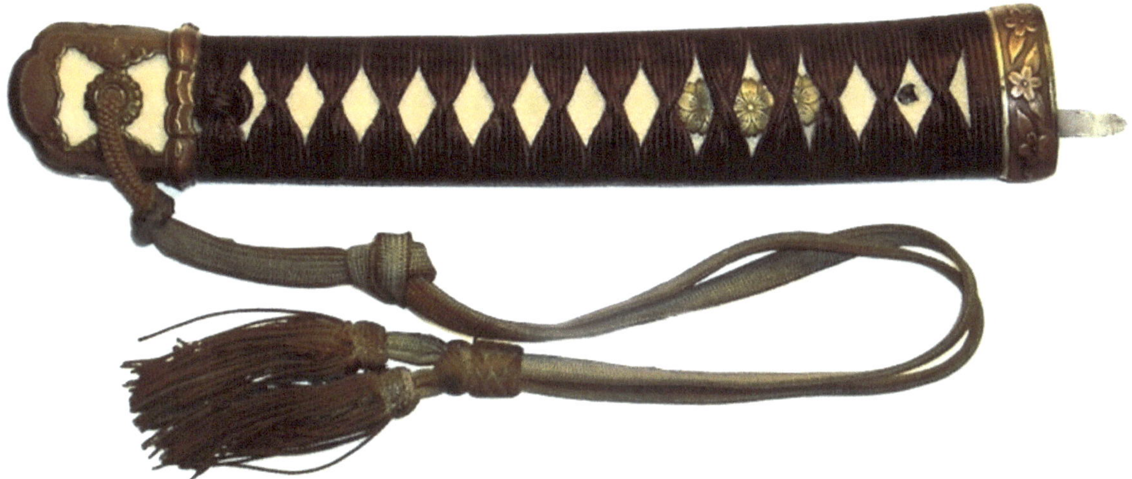

Figure 2.30 Following the original design, the tsuka was rewrapped with new brown silk ito, and the tassel was reattached.

Case 2: Restoration of an Edo Period Wakizashi Tsuka

Originally, the *tsuka* was wrapped in a wider, maybe 10 mm, gold silk *ito* which was faded, worn through and glued in place in spots. Notice the circular discolored patch of *same'* in the second opening from the fuchi (Fig. 2.31). This is evidence of either recycled *same'* or a *tsuka* from a different sword refitted to this one.

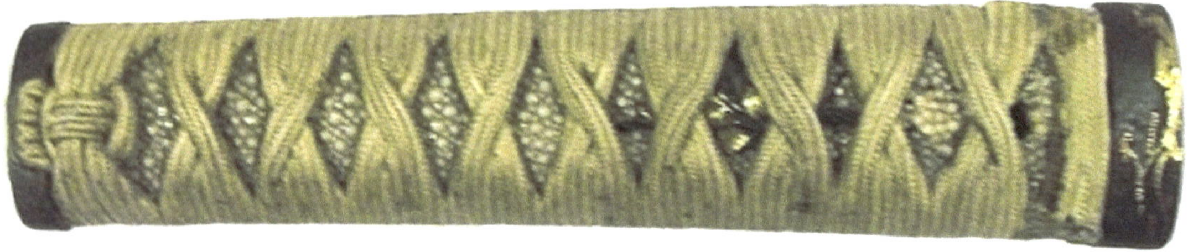

Figure 2.31 Edo period wakizashi tsuka before restoration.

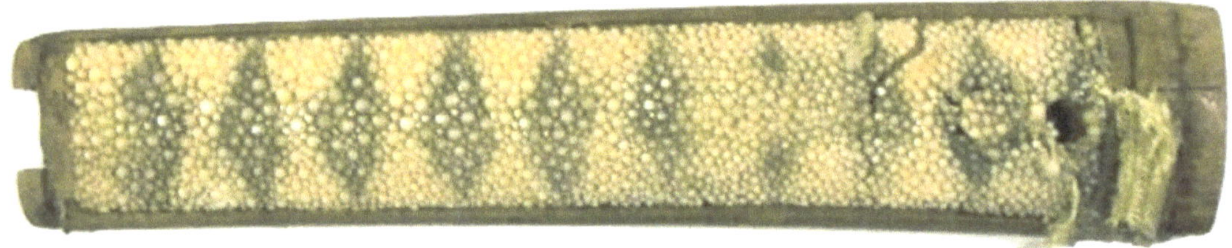

Figure 2.32 Tsuka with the ito removed.

After splitting open the *tsuka*, it became evident that this was a refitted *tsuka.* A shim and a plugged *mekugiana,* in combination with the carved out section being a different size and shape than the *nakago* of the blade it was currently on, attested to this (Fig. 2.33).

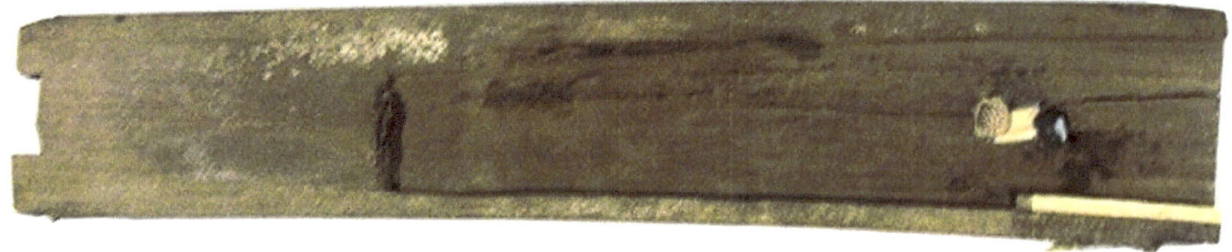

Figure 2.33 Inside of tsuka, notice shim and mekugiana plug.

Instead of restoring the *tsuka*, it was decided to replace it with one newly carved that matched the older one in shape and size. Japanese *honoki* was chosen as the wood for the new *tsuka*. *Honoki* wood is aged for several years to produce a very stable foundation that is salt free. It has a very low moisture content compared to other woods.

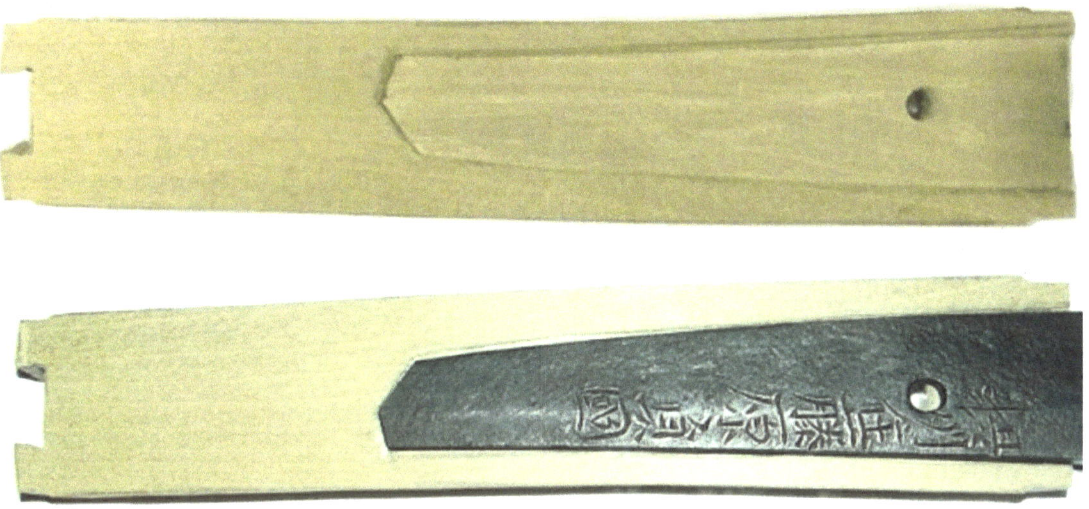

Figure 2.34 An interior view of the two newly carved halves of the tsuka.

In making a new *tsuka*, two separate pieces of wood are carved to fit the *nakago*, or tang, of the sword. Then the exterior is shaped using a small hand plane to match the original.

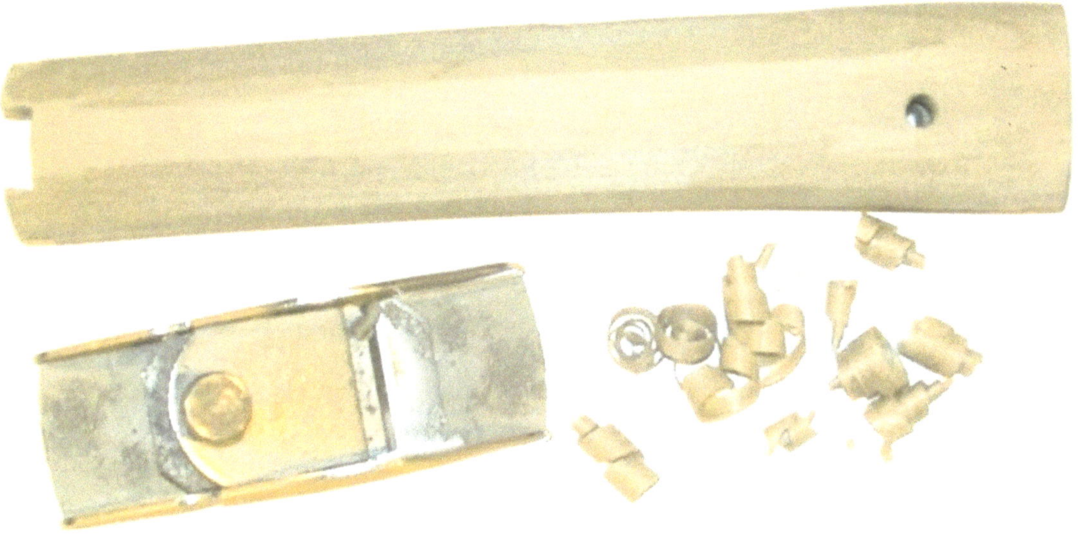

Figure 2.35 Above, shaping the exterior of the new tsuka.

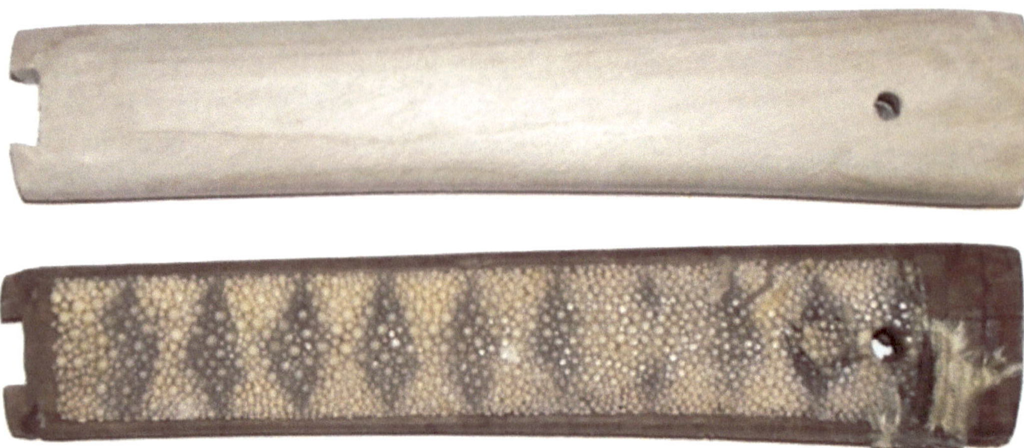

Figure 2.36 A side-by-side comparison of the original tsuka and the new.

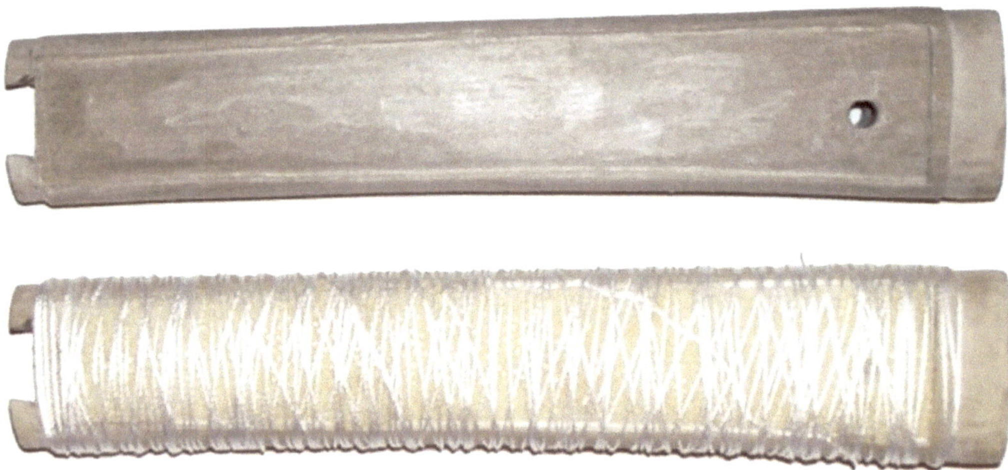

Figure 2.37 Above, carving completed and application of ray skin.

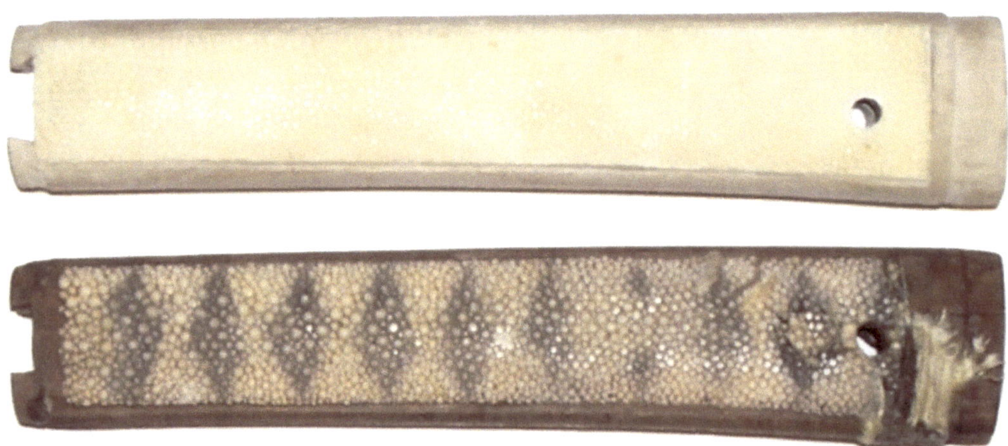

Figure 2.38 Above, a side-by-side comparison of the original and new tsuka.

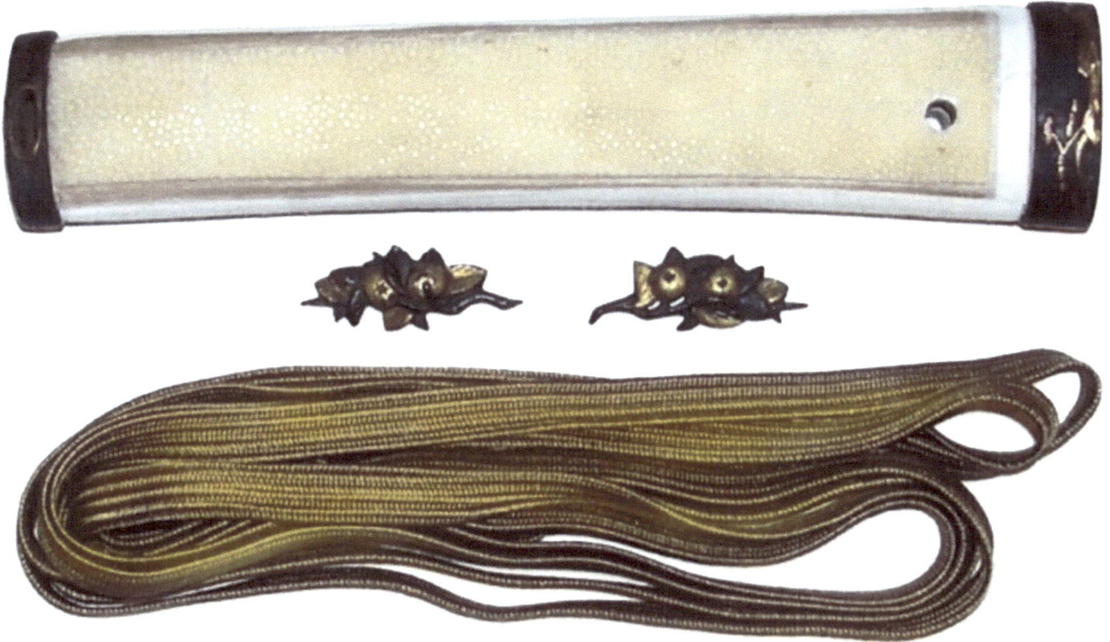

Figure 2.39 Prepared tsuka ready for wrapping, with menuki and ito.

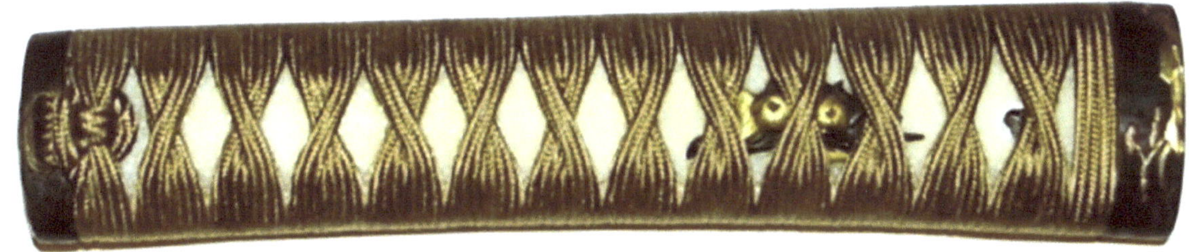

Figure 2.40 Completed tsuka wrapped in the tsumami maki style.

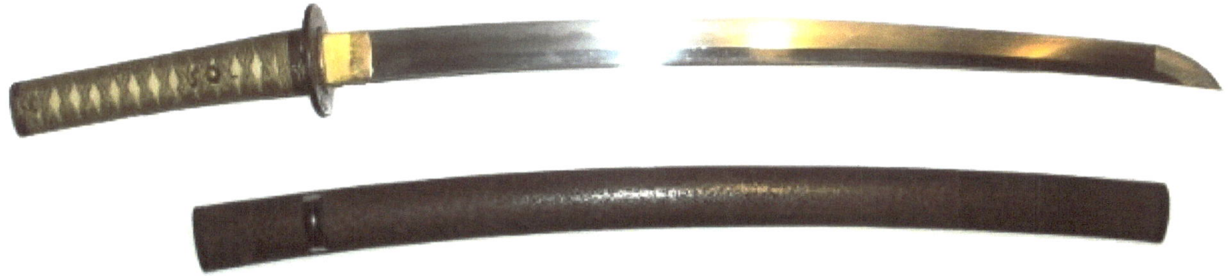

Figure 2.41 The new tsuka mounted on the sword.

The blade this *tsuka* was made for is an Early Edo period *wakizashi* (circa 1624), signed *Sesshu ju Fujiwara Sadakuni*.

Case 3: Restoration of a Koto Period Katana Tsuka

This *tsuka* is from a *koto tachi* blade in Edo period *katana* mounts. The *fuchi* is *shakudo* with an inlaid silver *mon*, the *kashira* is horn with silver *shitodome*, and the *menuki* are copper/*shakudo* with gold *kanji*. At some point, the *tsuka* lost its *ito* and *same*', then was painted gold. The *menuki* were held on with *wire*, and a screw had been put through the *mekugiana*.

As for condition, the tsuka was split down the center and cracked on the side. It also was missing a large section of wood on its *mune* side.

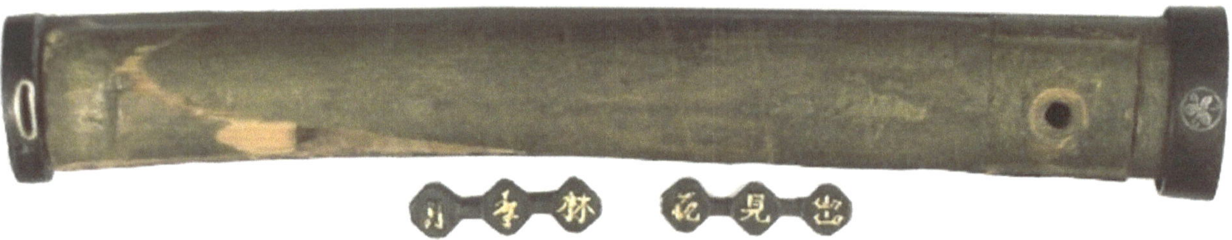

Figure 2.42 The original tsuka, fuchi, kashira and menuki.

Following the same steps as in the previous case, Edo period *wakizashi*, a new handle was constructed using the original *fuchi, kashira* and *menuki*, with new black rayskin.

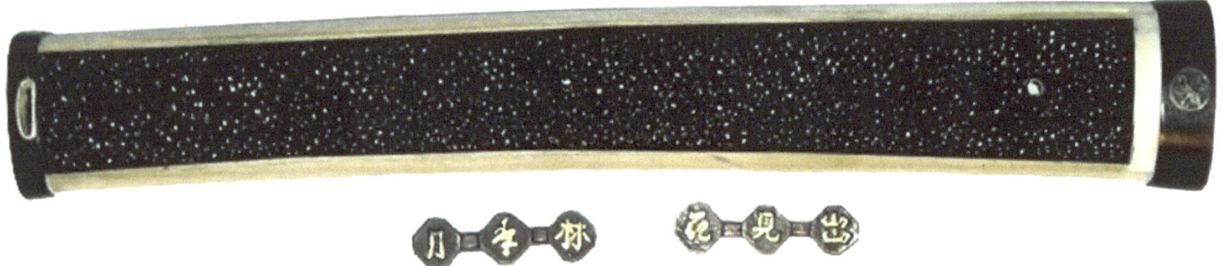

Figure 2.43 The new tsuka, with original fuchi, kashira and menuki.

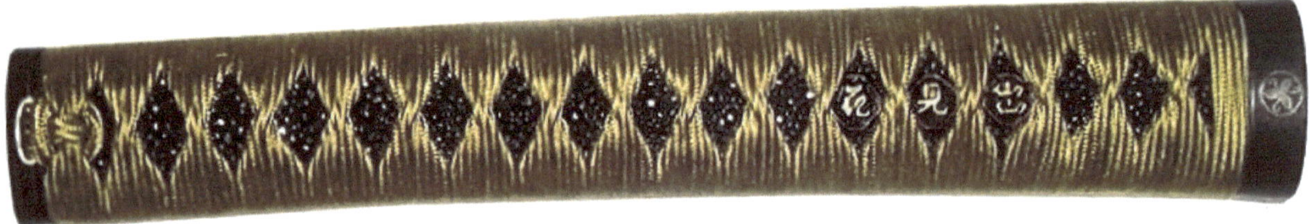

Figure 2.44 Completed tsuka wrapped in the menpumaki style.

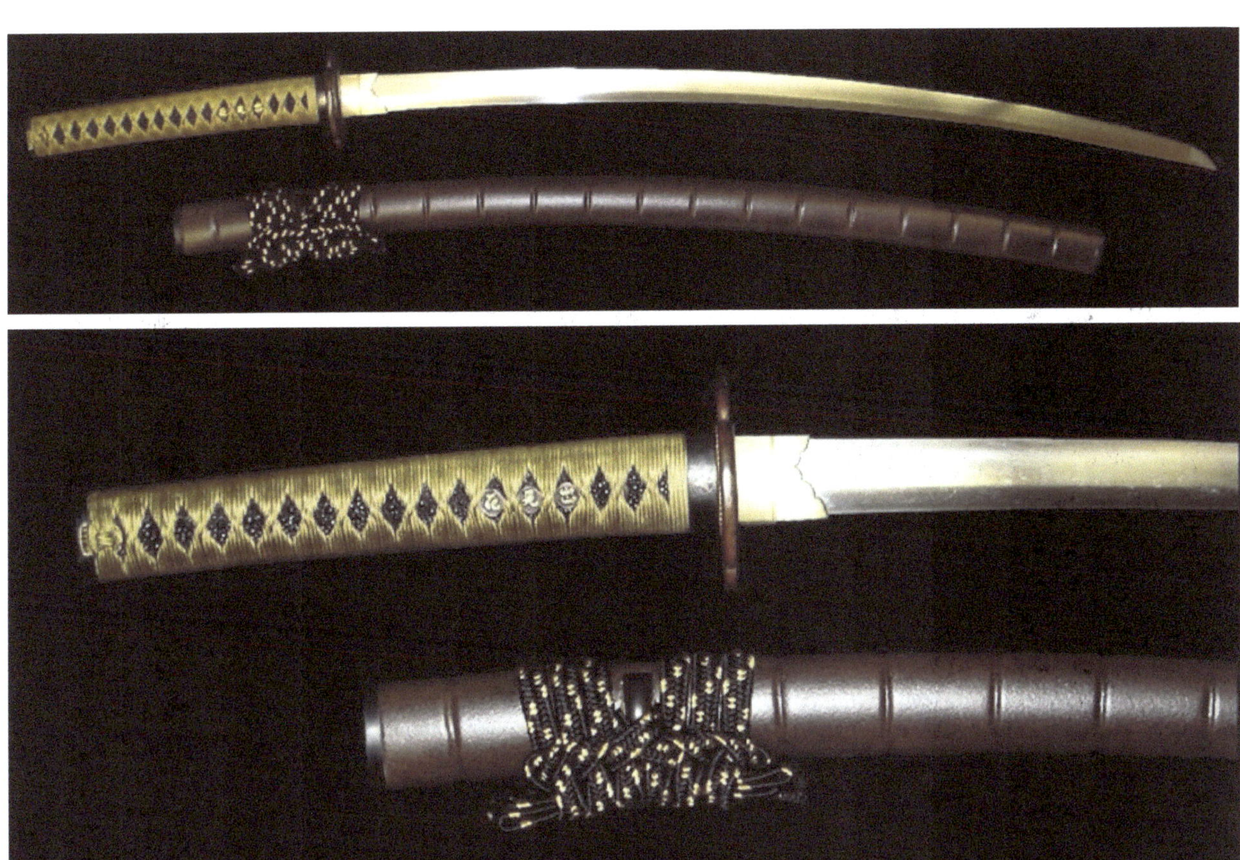

Figure 2.45 The new tsuka mounted on the sword.

The blade this *tsuka* was made for is an Early Kamakura (1185-1225) period *tachi* with a strong *sori*, high *shinogi*, *fumbari*, and a *suguha ko midare hamon* of mixed *nie* and *nioi*.

3 Twenty-five Common Styles of Tsukamaki

3.1 Ganpi Kigami Maki

This is one of a number of *tsukaito* styles that uses paper as a base, which is then usually covered with lacquer. To the right (Fig. 3.1) is an example of *ganpi kigami maki* as it looks before the application of lacquer, done by Takahiro Ichinose.

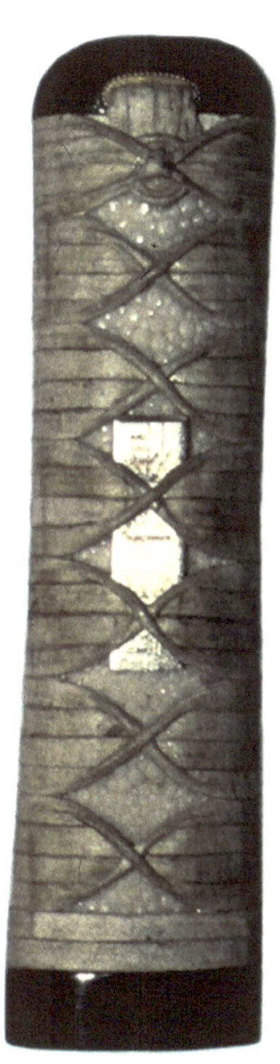

Figure 3.1 A ganpi kigami maki, or paper wrapped, tsuka before the lacquer is applied.

In this type of *maki*, basically paper is applied much like regular *ito*, but then is heavily lacquered.

In some ways this medium is more dynamic than cloth, and allows for more stunning effects through sculpting and shaping. Often the lacquered paper is mistaken for lacquered leather.

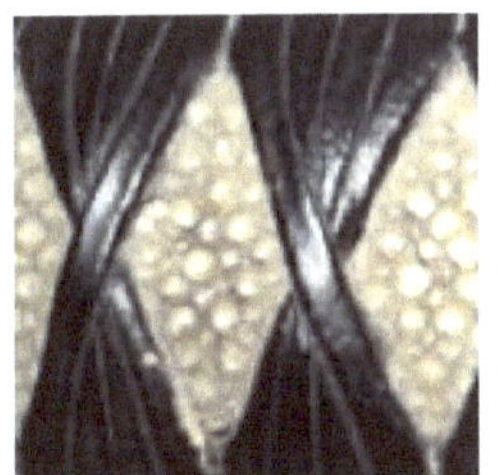
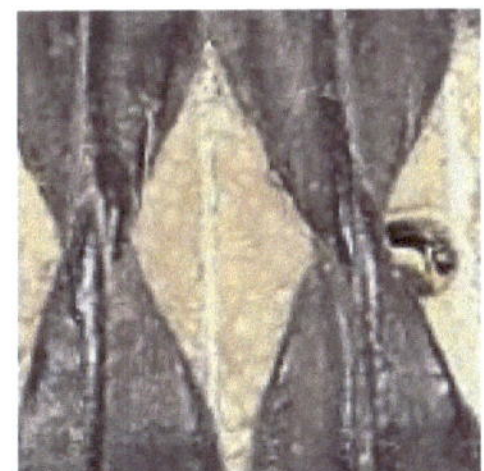
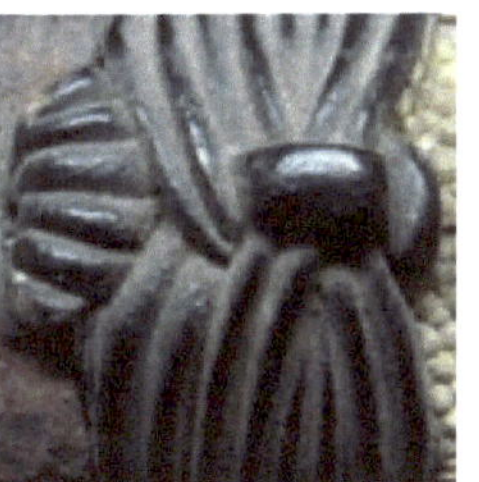

Figure 3.2 Examples of other Edo period paper ito styles.

Although it is one of many styles of paper *ito tsukamaki* (Fig. 3.2), in general, *ganpi kigami maki* shares the same fundamental design in *ito* construction.

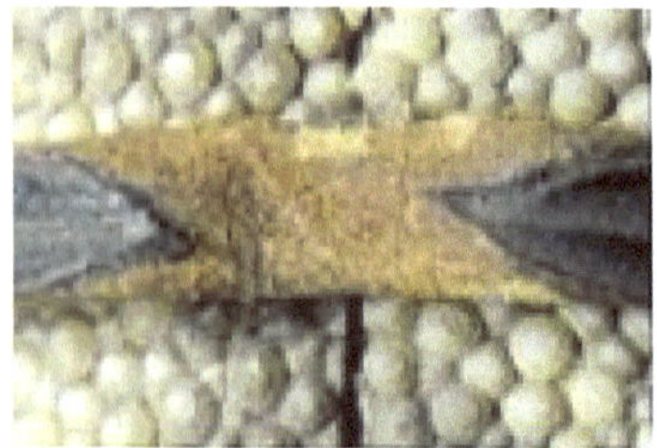

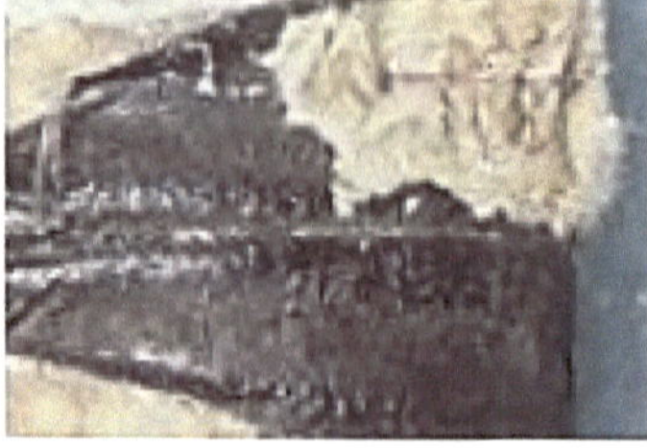

Figure 3.3 Old samples of lacquered paper ito.

Choosing the correct paper density, or weight, is crucial. To gain a better understanding of the spectrum of paper used, I took several samples of paper *ito* from older *tsuka*, like the two in Figure 3.3, to paper conservator Richard Backstrom.

Here is his "best guess" analysis of the weights and thicknesses of the samples in standardized measurements. I am certain that other weights that fit in or out of this spectrum can be used.

Basic Weight (lb)	Caliper (inches)	Thickness (mm)	Grammage (g/ m²)
16	0.0032	0.081	60.20
18	0.0036	0.092	67.72
24	0.0048	0.120	90.30

Figure 3.4 Standardized weights of paper used in ganpi kigami maki.

The process of creating paper *ito* is simple (Fig. 3.5).

- Step 1: Measure and cut strips twice the width of your desired *ito* width.
- Step 2: Fold the edges of the strips in toward the center, measuring the folds a quarter of the way in from either edge.
- Step 3: Join the strips by cutting and pasting small patches where the ends of the

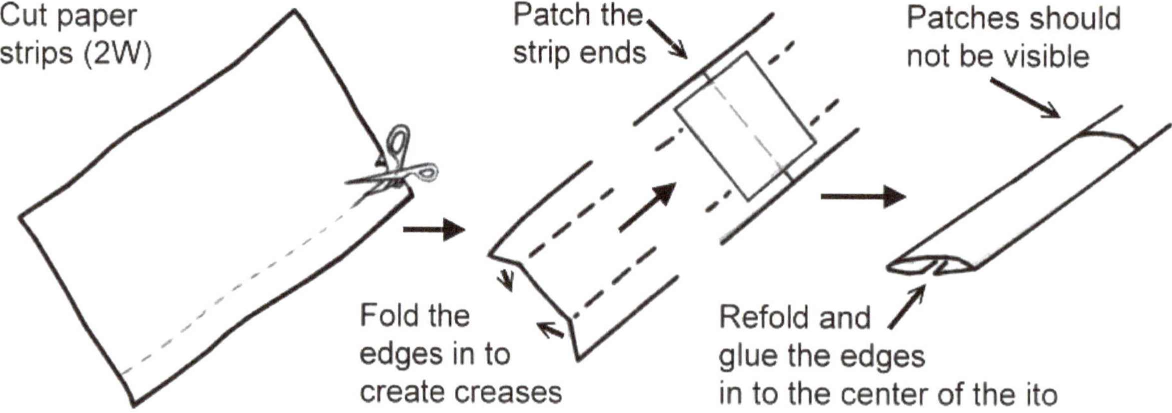

Figure 3.5 Creating paper ito.

strip meet, make a tight seam and have the patches slightly overlapping the folds.

- Step 4: After the patches have completely dried, refold and glue the edges to the center of the paper strip. Remember, the patches should not be visible on the completed *ito*, going on the inside of the fold.

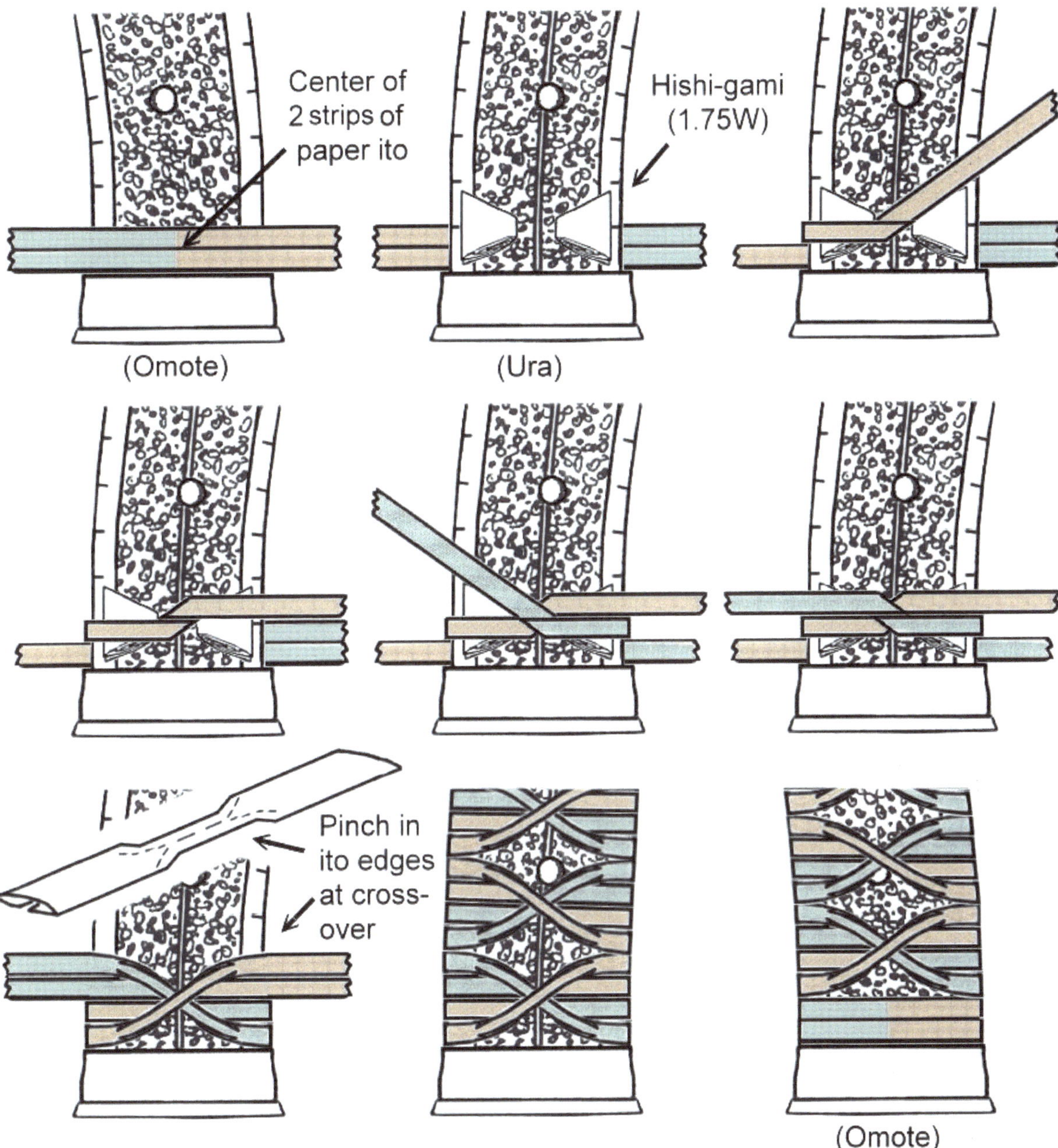

Figure 3.6 Applying the paper ito in the ganpi kigami maki style.

Once you have finished preparing the paper *ito*, to complete the *ganpi kigami maki* follow the directions below (Fig. 3.6).

3.2 Gyu Kawa Kumiage Maki

This style of *tsukamaki* uses *tsukagawa* (a relatively smooth leather *ito*) primarily in a gloss black, a black mat, or a dark brown.

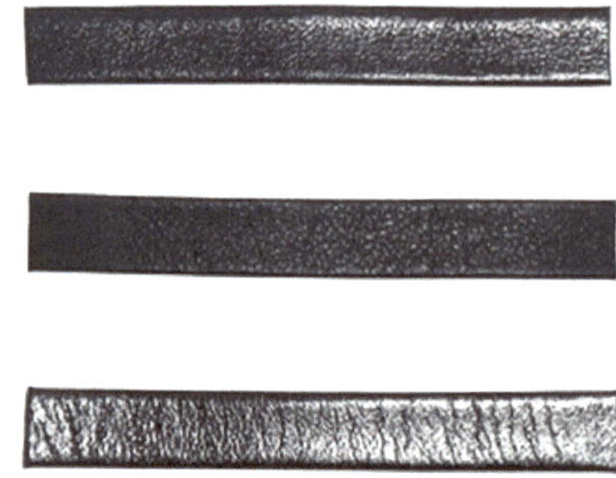

Figure 3.7 Tsukagawa.

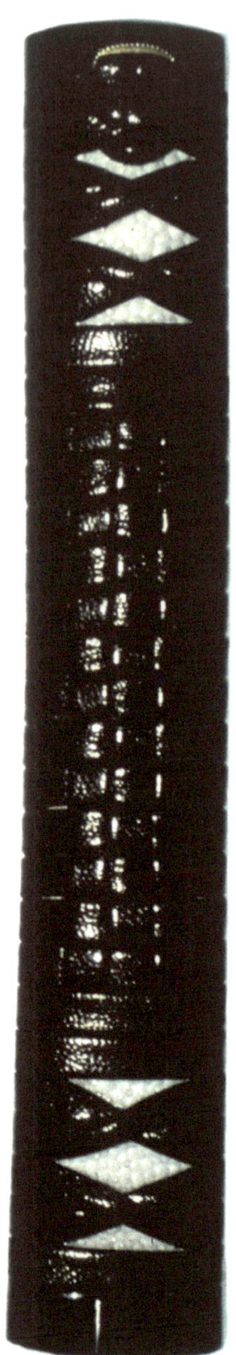

Figure 3.8 Above is a tsuka wrapped in the gyu kawa kumiage maki style.

The *maki* techniques combine ones generally found in *tsumami maki* and *katate maki*. One of the more unique aspects of this style is that it is void of *menuki*, having woven stips of *ito* (three per side) in their place.

The beginning steps, and the ending knots use the same basic techniques as *tsumami maki*, using the twisting crossovers with the start and finish on the *omote* side.

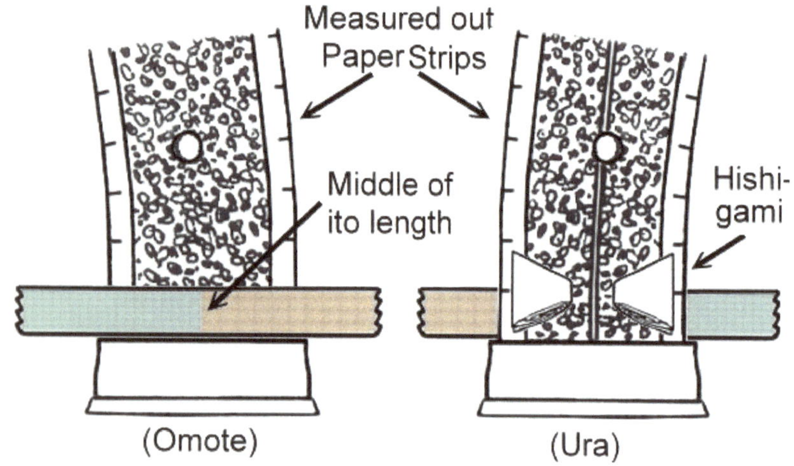

Figure 3.9a Beginning steps.

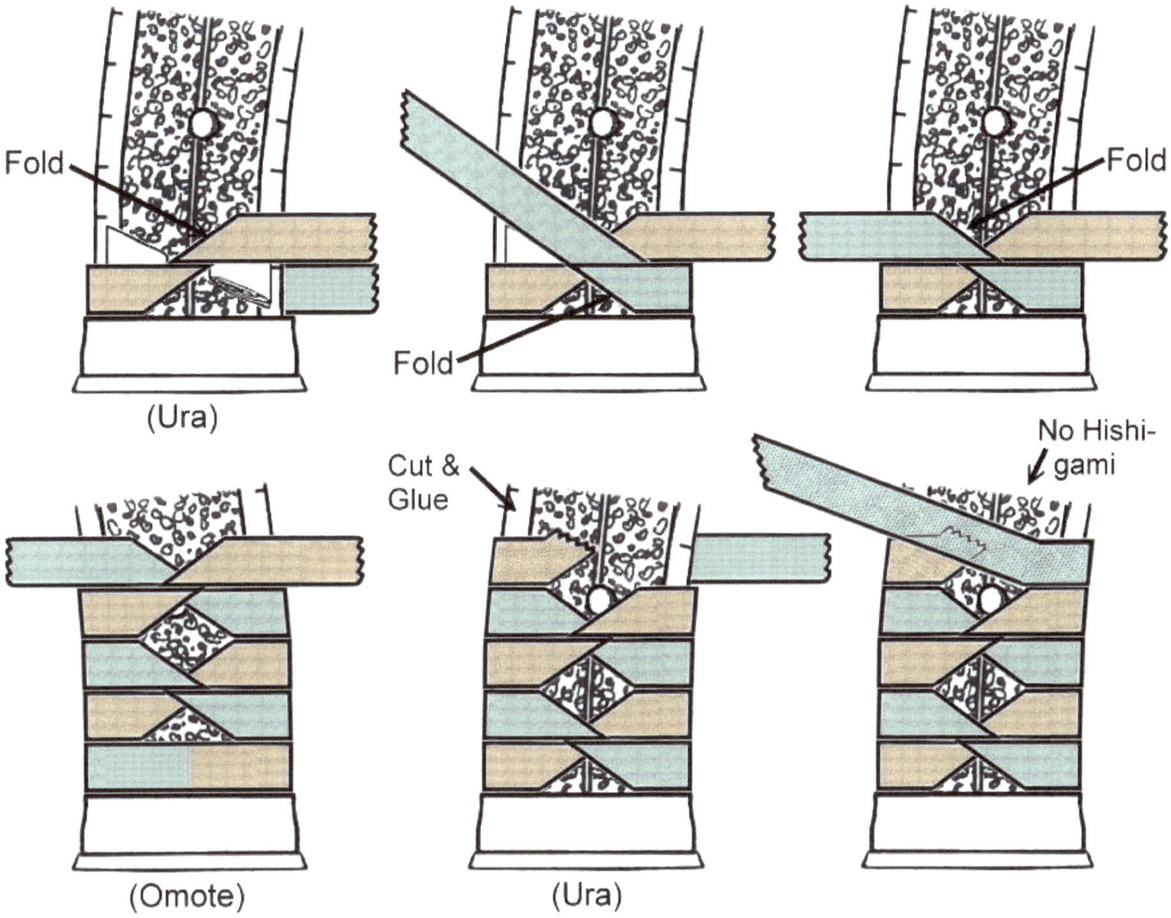

Fold
Fold
Fold
(Ura)
Cut & Glue
No Hishi-gami
(Omote)
(Ura)

Figure 3.9b Beginning steps (continued)

Above, Figure 3.9b shows the initial crossover pattern, as well as how the transition is made from wrapping with two ends to using a single strip. Figure 3.11 shows the correct method for inserting the *ito* strips used in the weaving.

Figure 3.11 also shows views of a woven section and the finished end knots on both the *ura* and *omote* sides. Notice how the woven section is separated by two plain strips from the more traditional section, the same as when they were initially inserted. Simularly, the *ito* is inserted at the resumption of the crossover pattern in the same way it was ended at the beginning of the woven section.

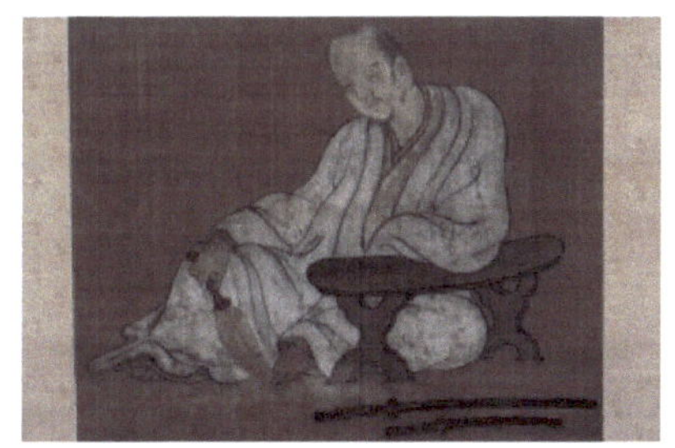

Figure 3.10 Omura Suitada, the Christian ("Kirishitan") daimyo.

This is one of the more interesting styles of *tsukamaki* because it directly reflects the influence of Christianity, and more specifically the Jesuits in medieval Japan. In it, the *ito*'s perpendicular lines represent the cross, and the three woven strips of *ito* are emblematic of the Christian Trinity. This style was most notably popular among supporters of the two *Kirishitan daimyo*, Omura Sumitada and Arima Harunobu, from the mid-16th century until the early 17th century.

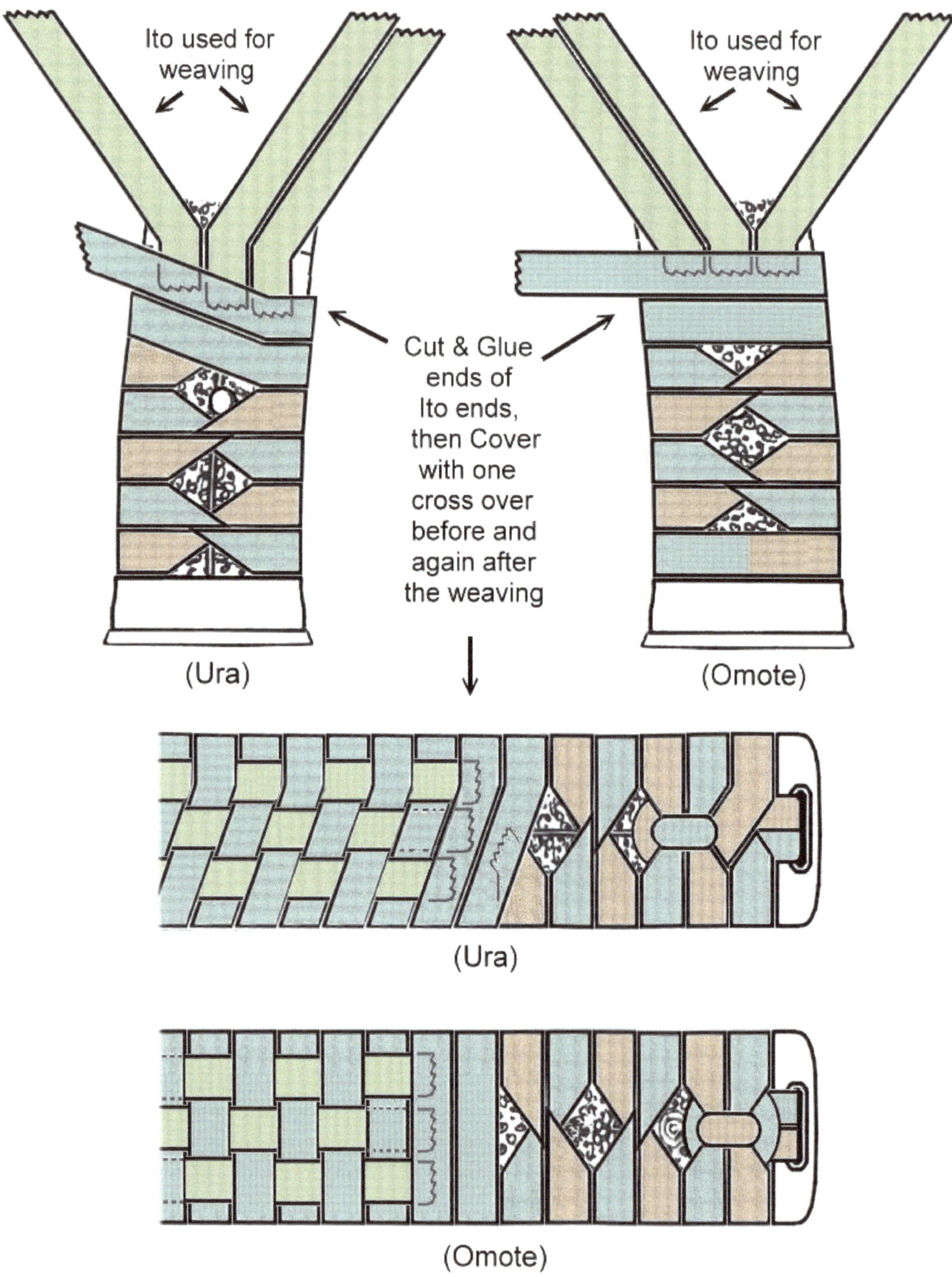

Figure 3.11 Inserting the ito strips used for weaving and finished end knots.

3.3 Handachi Zuka

The term *handachi* literally means half-*tachi*, or swords that had mounts simular to a *tachi* minus the *ashi*, but were worn edge up (Fig. 3.13).

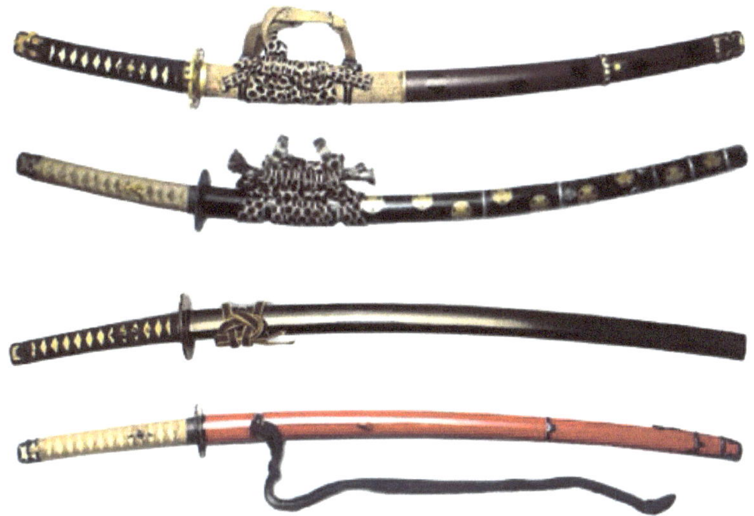

Figure 3.13 Tachi (top two) and handachi (bottom two) koshirae.

In addition to the *tachi,* like *fuchi/ kashira,* a significant hallmark of the *handachi zuka tsukamaki* is its pinched crossover, as opposed to the *tsumami maki* twist.

The beginning steps, and the ending knots use the same basic techniques as *tsumami maki.*

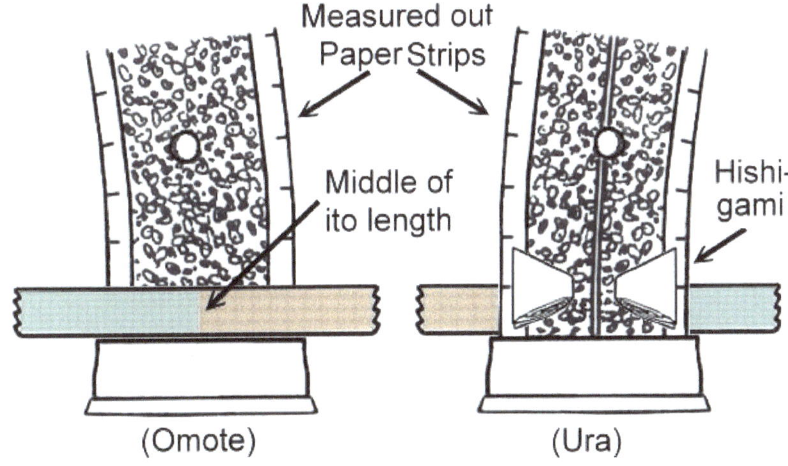

Figure 3.14 The beginning steps.

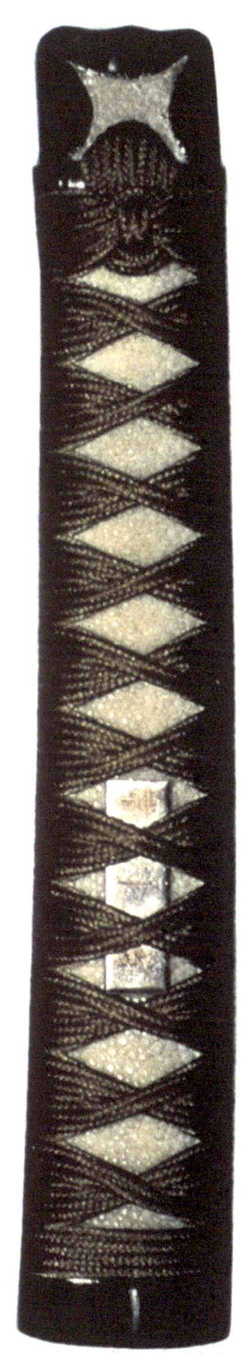

Figure 3.12 Above is a tsuka wrapped in the handachi style.

Figure 3.15 (Right) Cross over techniques & finished end knots.

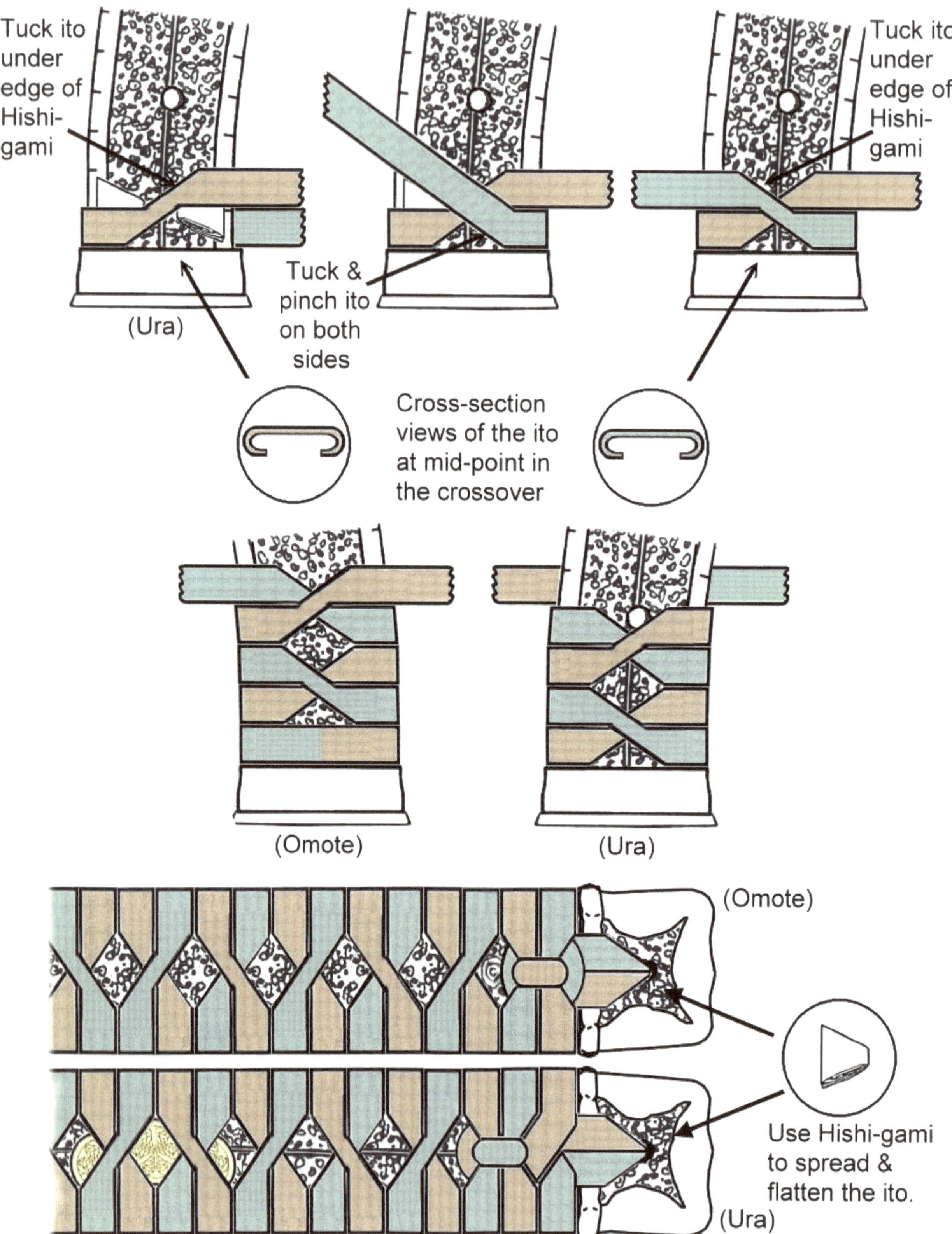
Tuck ito
under
edge of
Hishi-
gami
Tuck ito
under
edge of
Hishi-
gami
(Ura)
Tuck &
pinch ito
on both
sides
Cross-section
views of the ito
at mid-point in
the crossover
(Omote)
(Ura)
(Omote)
Use Hishi-gami
to spread &
flatten the ito.
(Ura)

3.4 HEBIGAWA TSUMAMI MAKI

The only significant difference between the *hebigawa tsumami maki* and the classic *tsumami maki* is the *ito*, which in this case is made from a combination of snakeskin and leather. To construct the *ito*, apply sections of thin dried snakeskin to lengths of leather

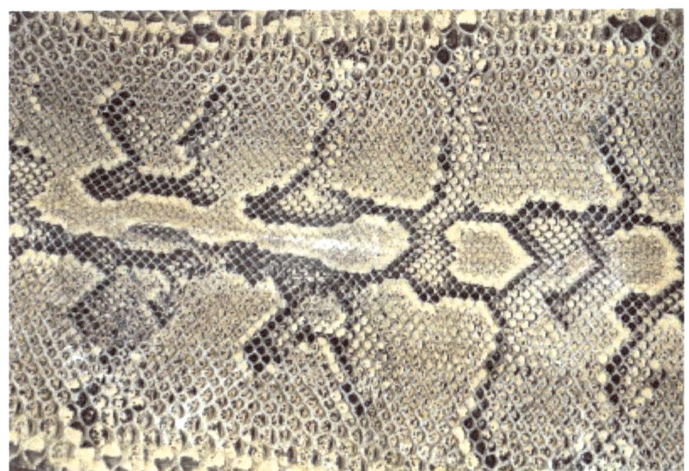

Figure 3.17 A sample of dried snakeskin.

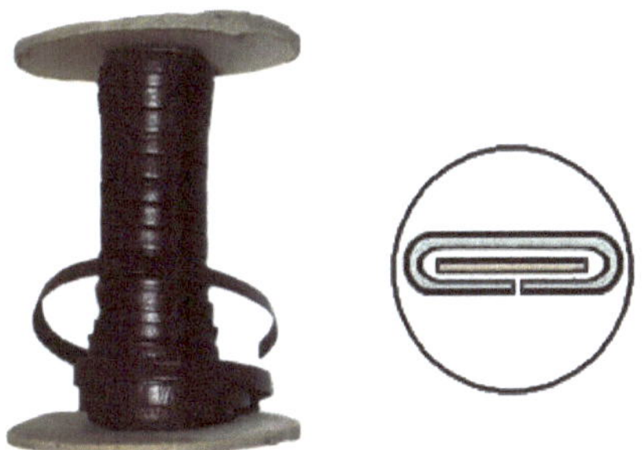

Figure 3.18 A length of leather ito, and a cross section view of the applied snake skin.

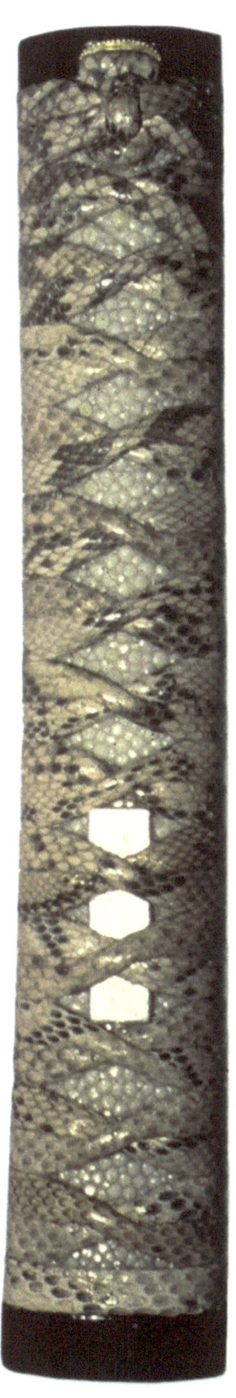

Figure 3.16 Above is a tsuka wrapped in the hebigawa tsumami maki style.

ito by cutting the skin into strips twice the width of the leather and wrapping it around to create a seam on its underside (see cross section view in Fig. 3.18), applying glue regularly and evenly throughout the process. All of these materials, including the glue, should be available at leather supply, craft or fabrics stores.

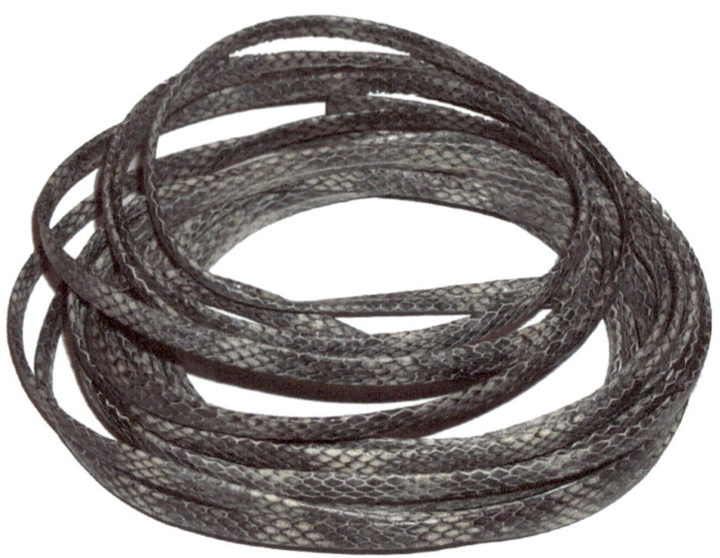

Figure 3.19 The finished product - snake skin ito.

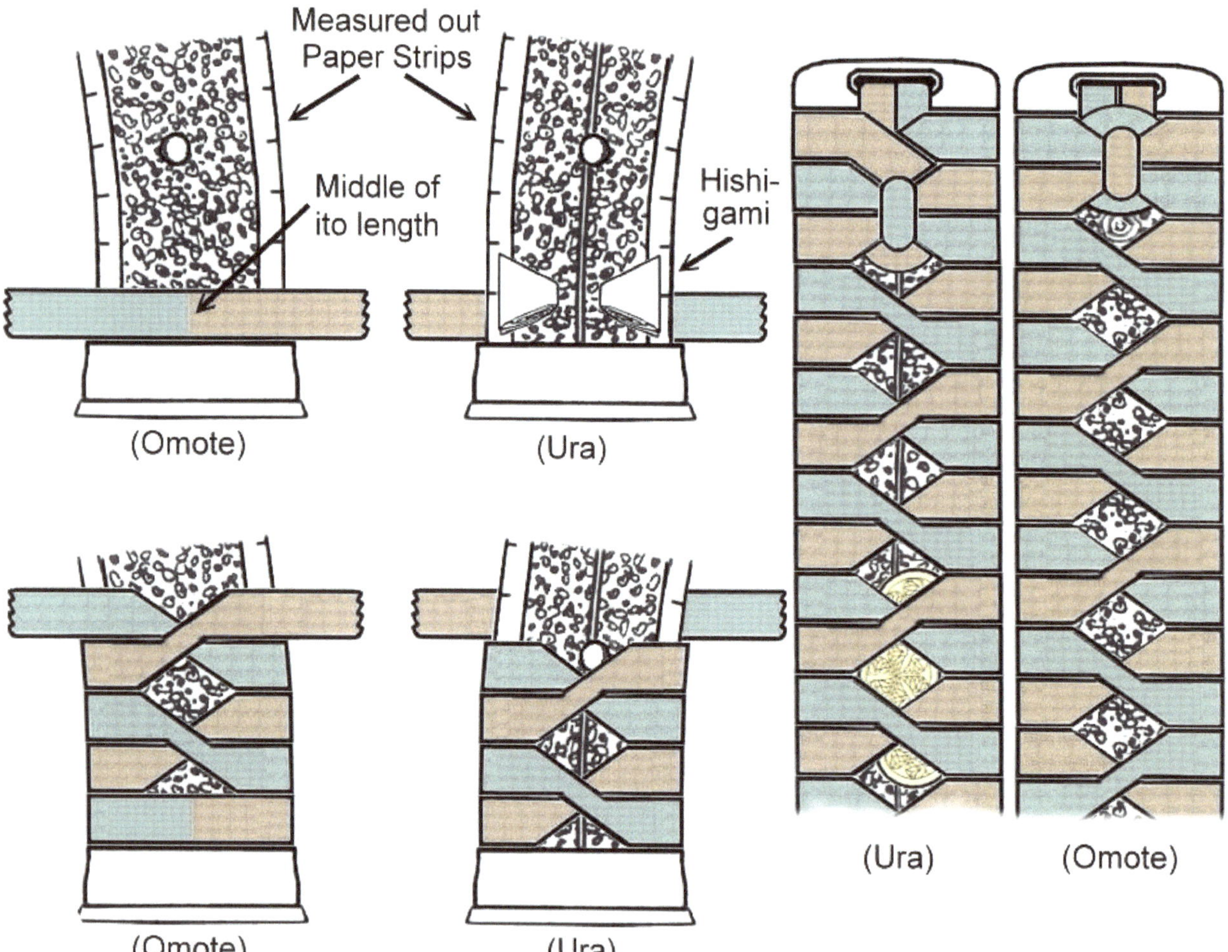

Measured out Paper Strips

Middle of ito length

Hishi-gami

(Omote)

(Ura)

(Omote)

(Ura)

(Ura)

(Omote)

Figure 3.20 The beginning and end steps, crossover technique, and finishing knots.

3.5 Higo Kusube Maki

The *higo kusube maki* is the hallmark standard for works from the Higo province. Its characteristics include the rounded *kashira* with a single switchback line or groove crossing both sides, a tapering *fuchi*, and black *same'*, or rayskin.

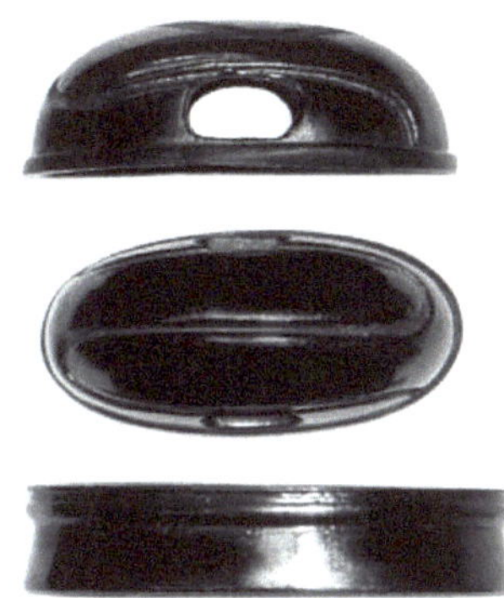

Figure 3.22 Higo style fuchi / kashira.

The *saya* have *samenuri*, or *same'* filled with lacquer, and the *tsuka* are covered with doeskin *tsukagawa ito.*

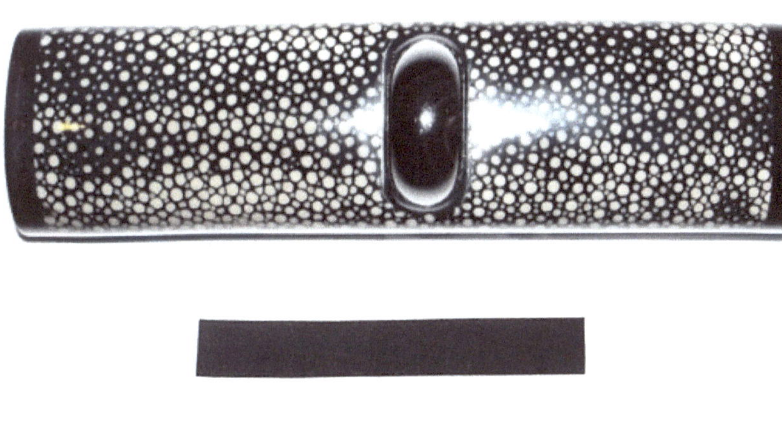

Figure 3.23 Top is a saya with samenuri – the "valleys" in the *same'* filled with lacquer, and the "mountains" are polished flush. Below saya, examples of tsukagawa ito.

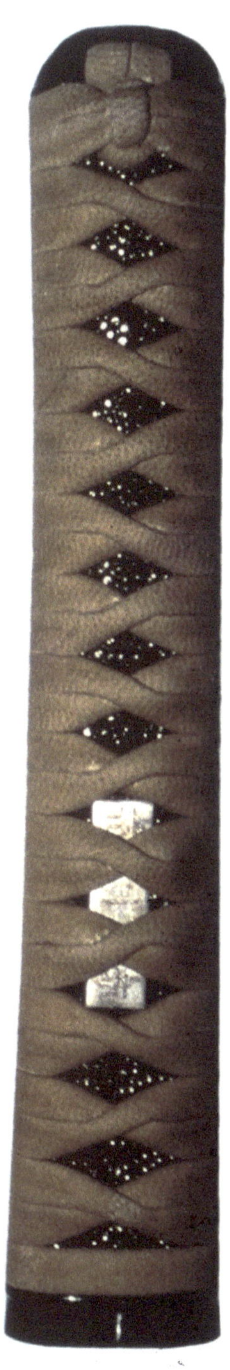

Figure 3.21 Above is a tsuka wrapped in the higo kusube maki.

The origins of the Higo style came primarily from the support of the *daimyo* Hosokawa Tadaoki (d. 1645), followed by Hayashi Matashichi Shigeharu (1608-91), who founded a school for *higo koshirae* at Kasuga.

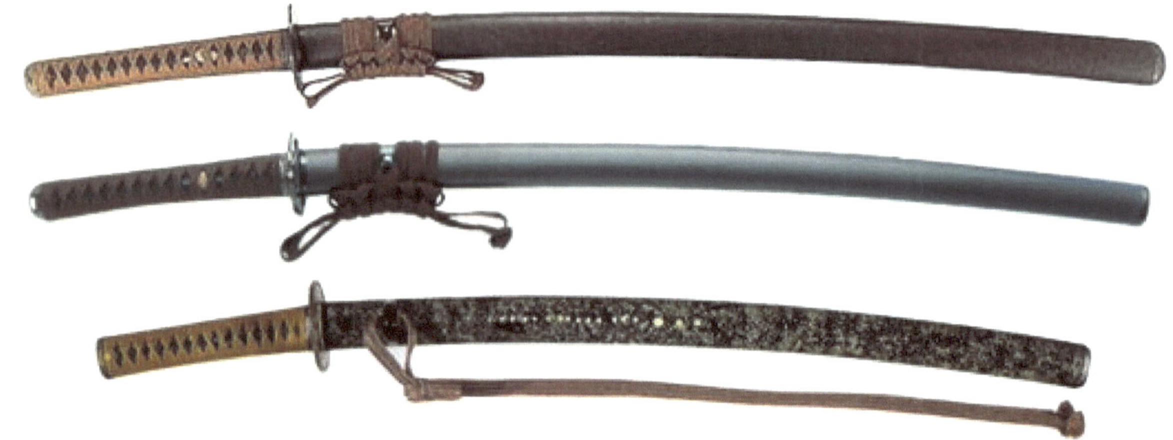

Figure 3.24 (Above) Three examples of higo kusube maki style koshirae.

Figure 3.25 (Below) The beginning and end steps, and crossover technique.

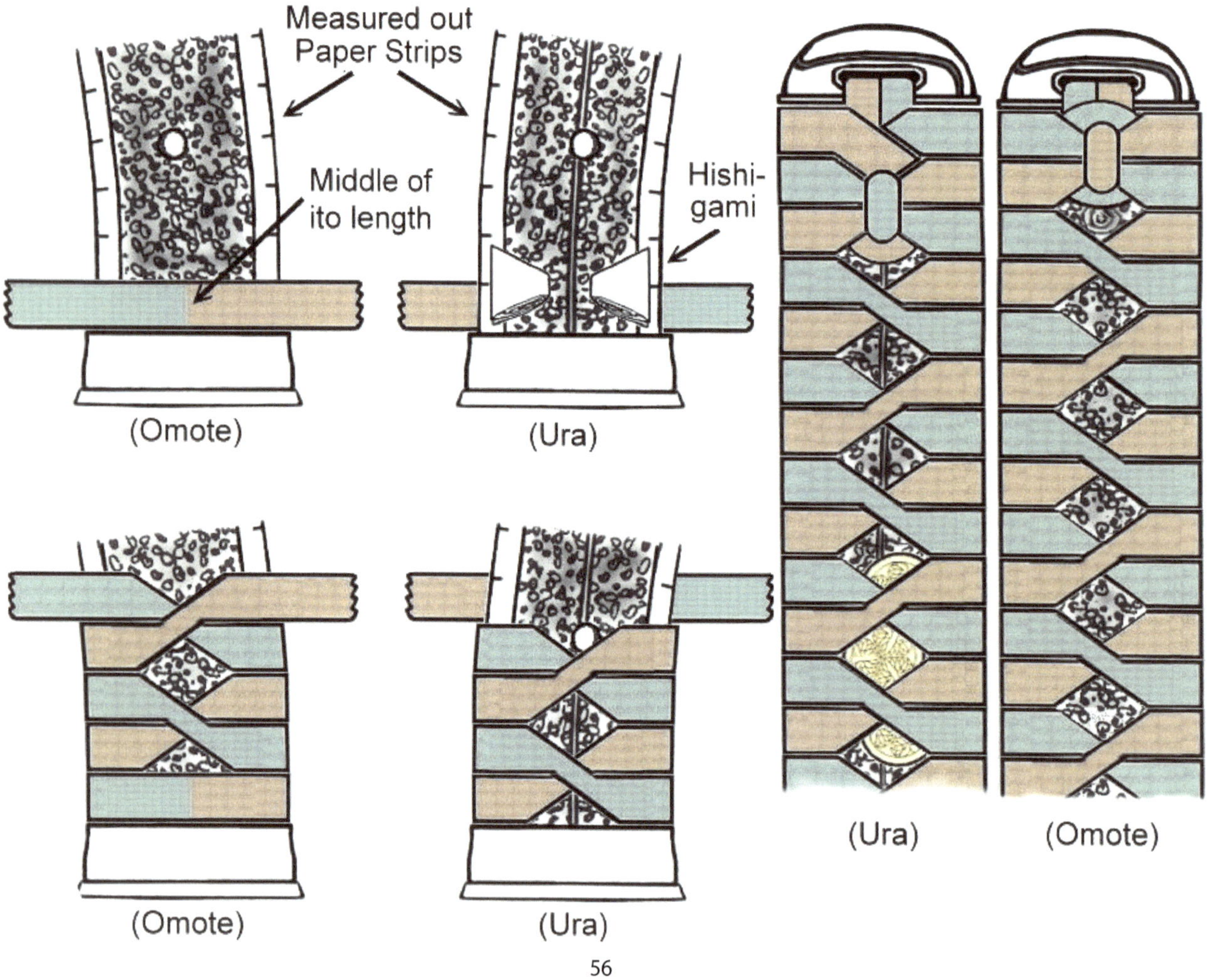

Measured out Paper Strips

Middle of ito length

Hishi-gami

(Omote)

(Ura)

(Ura)

(Omote)

(Omote)

(Ura)

3.6 HIRAMAKI

Hiramaki, or flat wrap, is one of the oldest known styles of *tsukamaki*. Originally used on *tachi* (Style 3.22 Tachi Tsukagashira Kakemaki), it remained popular until the end of the Edo period.

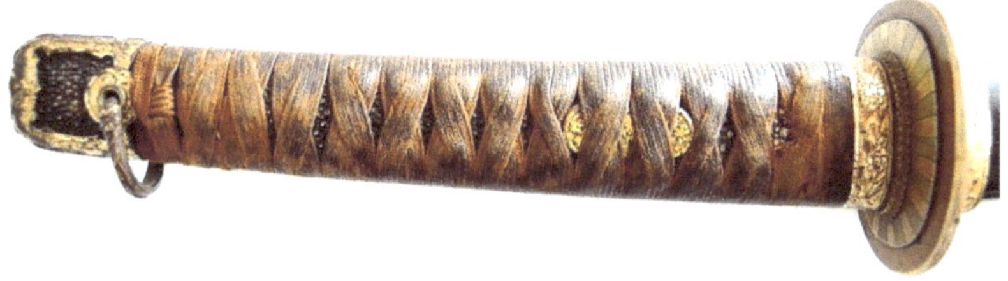

Figure 3.27 A World War II naval officer's sword wrapped in the hiramaki style.

In addition, during World War II, several forms of military sword mounts used the *hiramaki* style.

The beginning steps are basically the same as other styles, except *hiramaki* can be done either with or without the use of *hishi-gami*, or paper wedges.

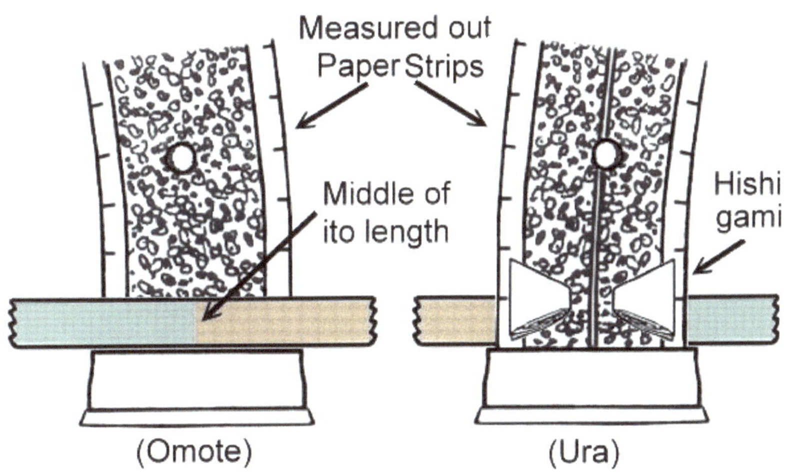

Figure 3.28 The beginning steps.

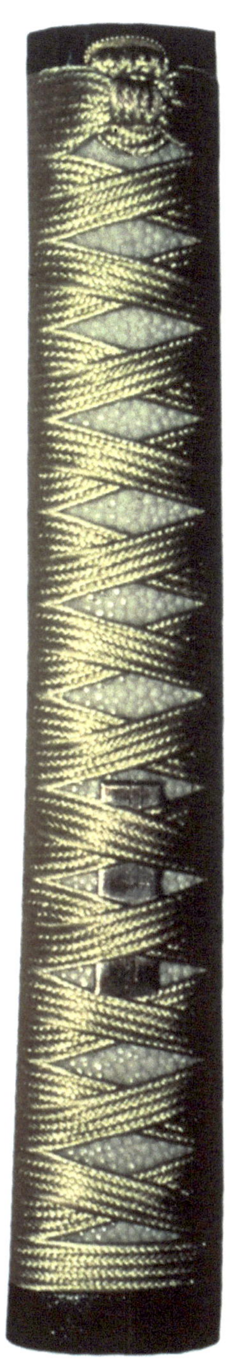

Figure 3.26 Above is a tsuka wrapped in hiramaki style.

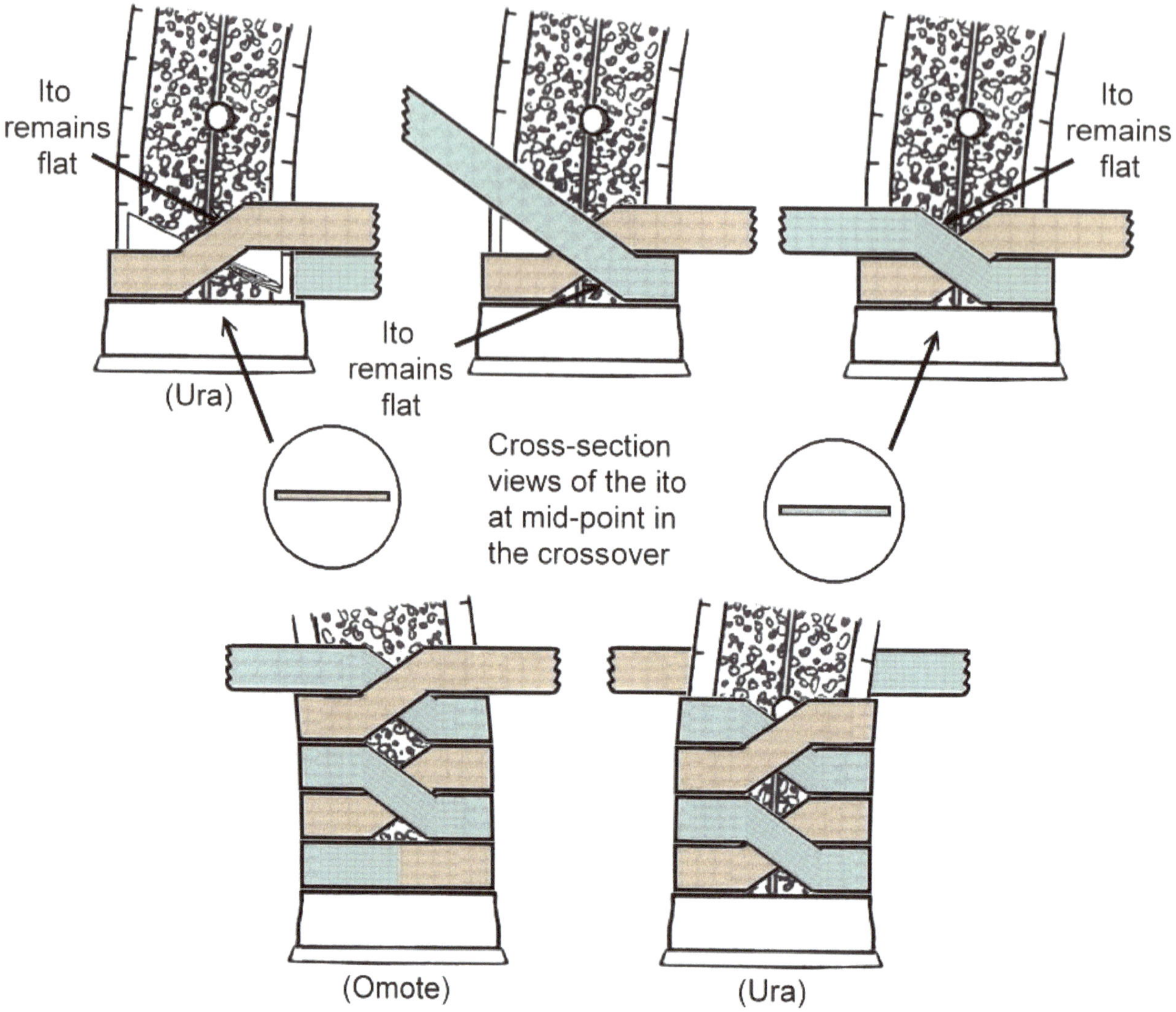

Ito remains flat

Ito remains flat

Ito remains flat

(Ura)

Cross-section views of the ito at mid-point in the crossover

(Omote)

(Ura)

Figure 3.29 (Above) & Figure 3.30 (Below) The beginning & ending steps and crossover technique.

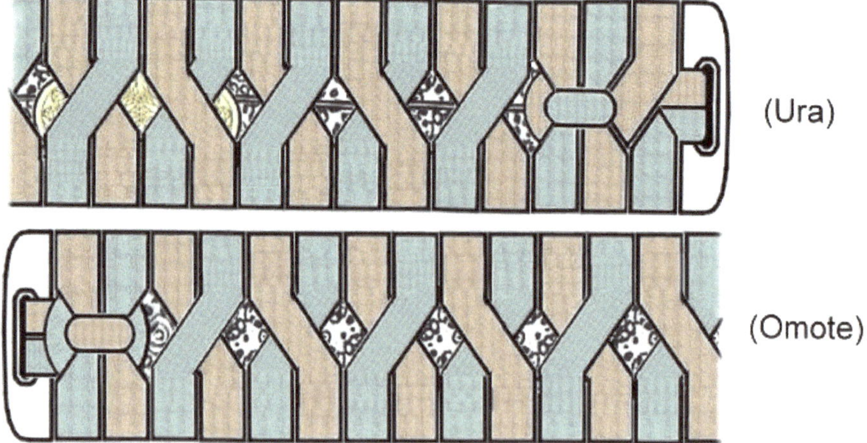

3.7 Hoso Jabaraito Kumi Zura

Jabaraito is made of eight or more individual strands of *ito* braided, woven and/or sewn together, and is considered a decorative pattern of the highest quality.

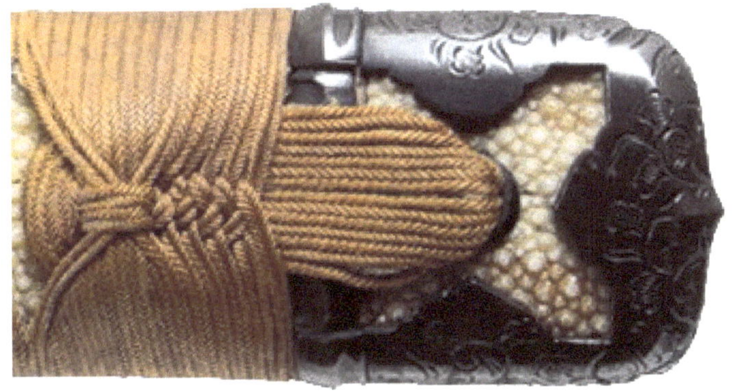

Figure 3.32 A close-up of a hoso jabaraito ura knot.

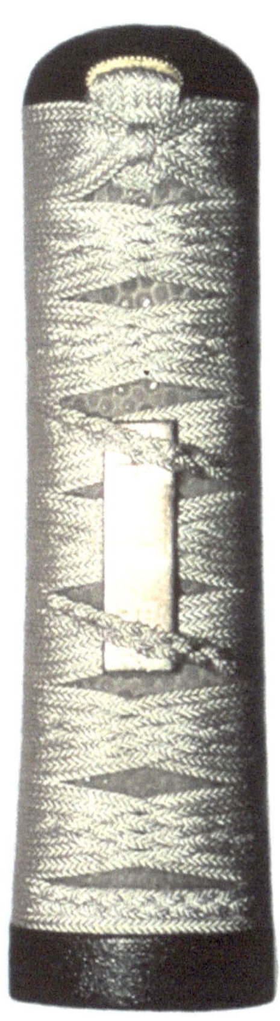

Figure 3.31 Above is a tsuka wrapped in the hoso jabara-ito kumiage zuka style.

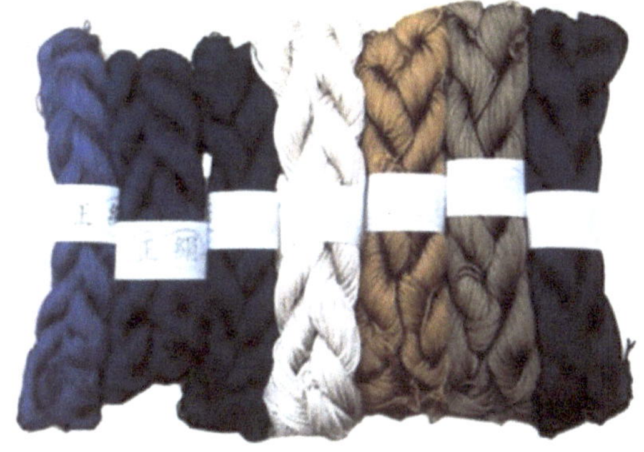

Figure3.33 An assortment of jabaraito.

Figure 3.34 (Below) The beginning steps and crossover technique.

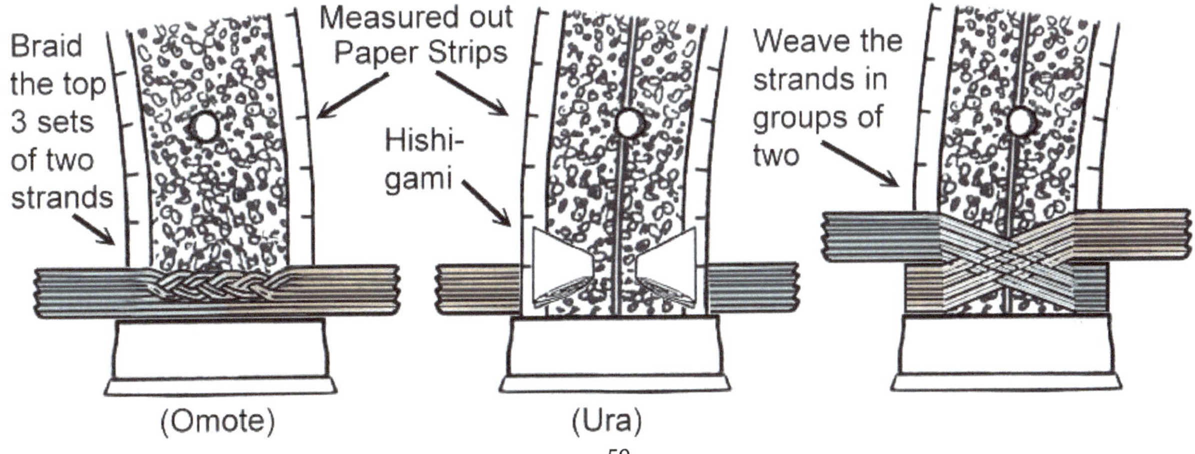

Hoso jabaraito kumiage zuka is done by primarly weaving the strands in groups of two at crossover, and braiding strands in three sets of two at the beginning crossing, and in securing the *menuki.*

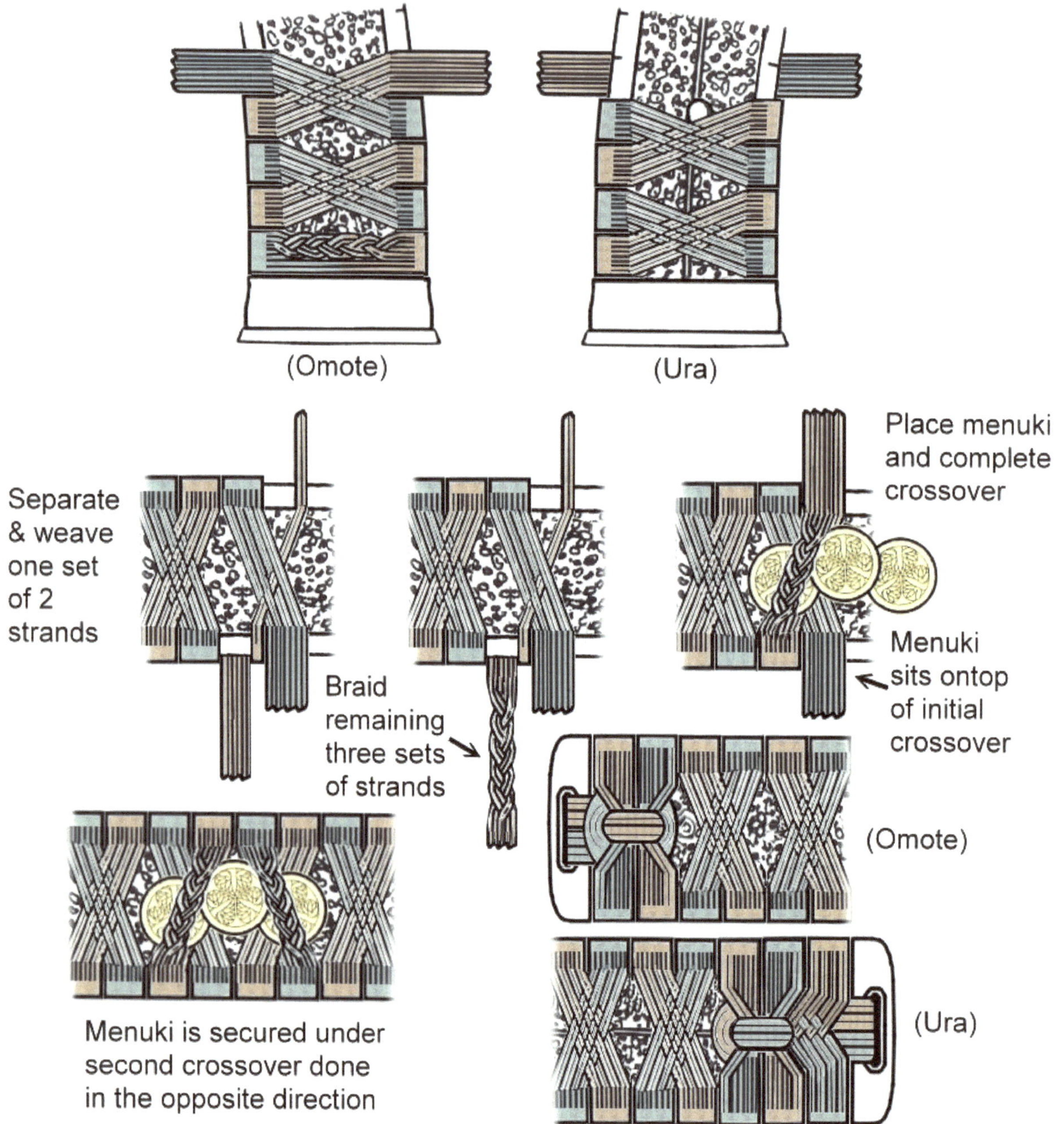

Figure 3.35 The crossover techniques, securing the menuki and the finishing knots.

3.8 Hoso To Katate Maki

This is one of several versions of the *katate maki*, or battle wrap, in which the *same'* is exposed only at the ends, and the majority of the *tsuka* is covered by the *ito* wound around it. The unique aspect of *hoso to katate maki* comes from the size and material of the *ito*, which is usually done in 4 mm wide leather *ito*.

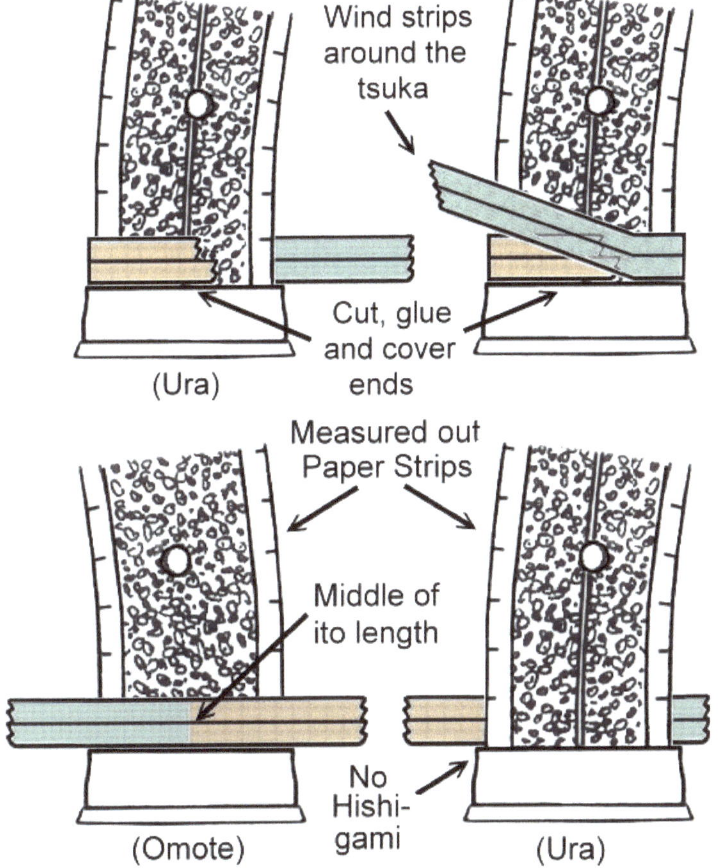

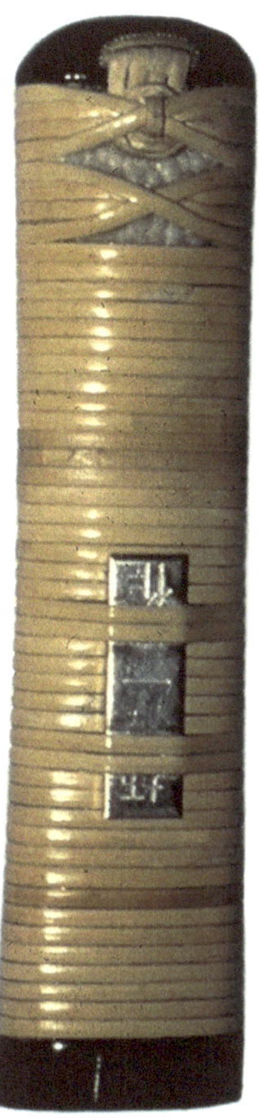

Figure 3.36 Above is a tsuka wrapped in the hoso to katate maki.

Figure 3.37 (Left) The beginning steps and the initial crossover.

Figure 3.38a (Below) Menuki placement and openings for mekugiana.

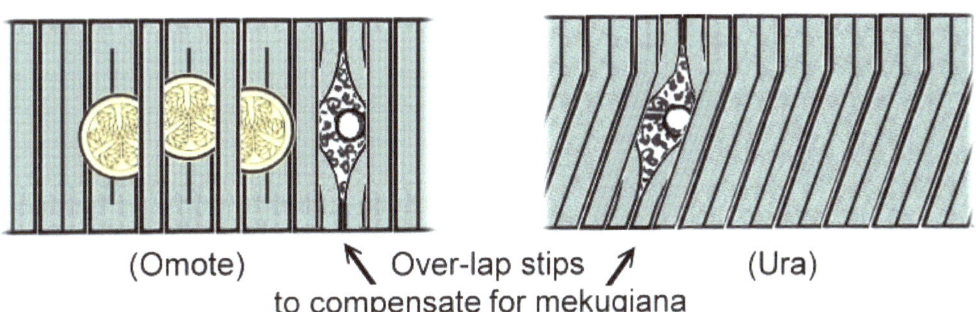

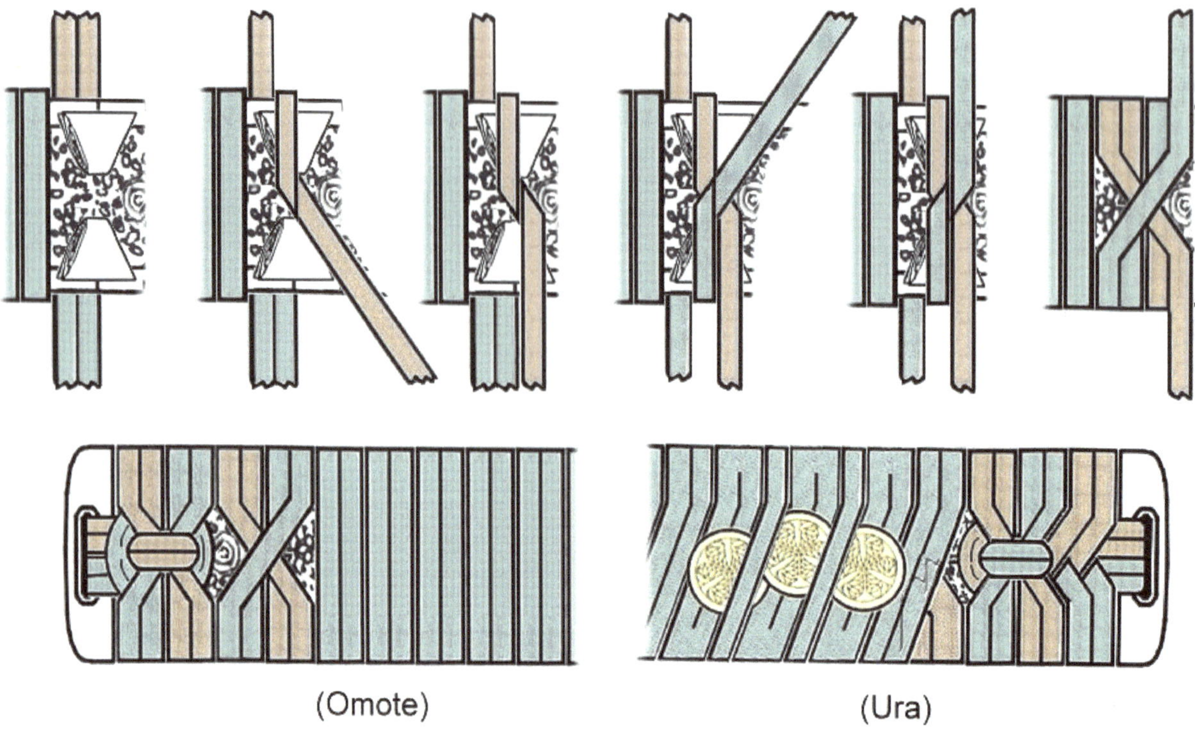

Figure 3.38b First crossover and finished knots. Notice the second set of two strips of ito is secured under both menuki as well as the first set of strips.

Hoso to katate maki (narrow battle wrap) refers to both the size of the *ito*, as well as the *tsuka* itself. Below is an example of *hoso to katate maki* done using silk *ito* instead of leather. Note the compensation technique for the *mekugiana*, or peg hole.

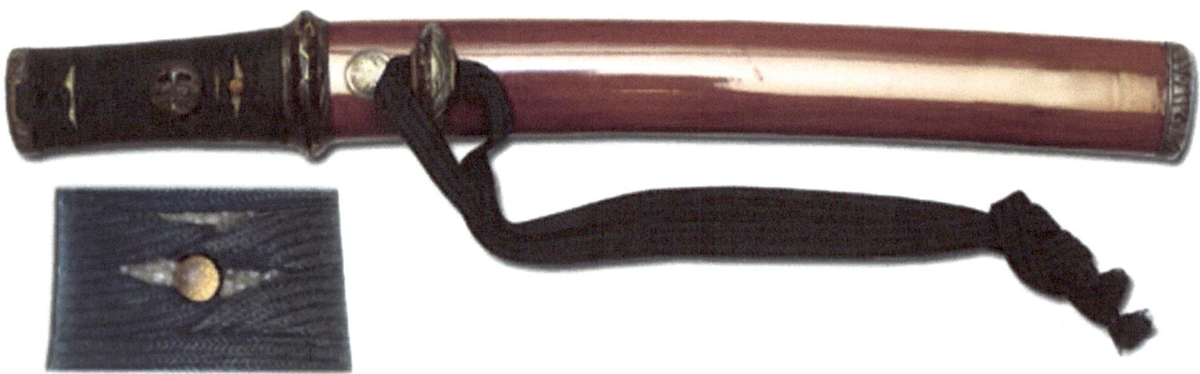

Figure 3.39 A tanto with a variation of the hoso to katate maki tsuka. Note the twists in the ito on either side of the mekugiana.

3.9 Jabara Kumiage Shiho Maki

The *jabara kumiage shiho maki* uses a type of silk *ito* that is one quarter the width of regular silk *ito*, and combines *hoso jabaraito* and *menpumaki* techniques.

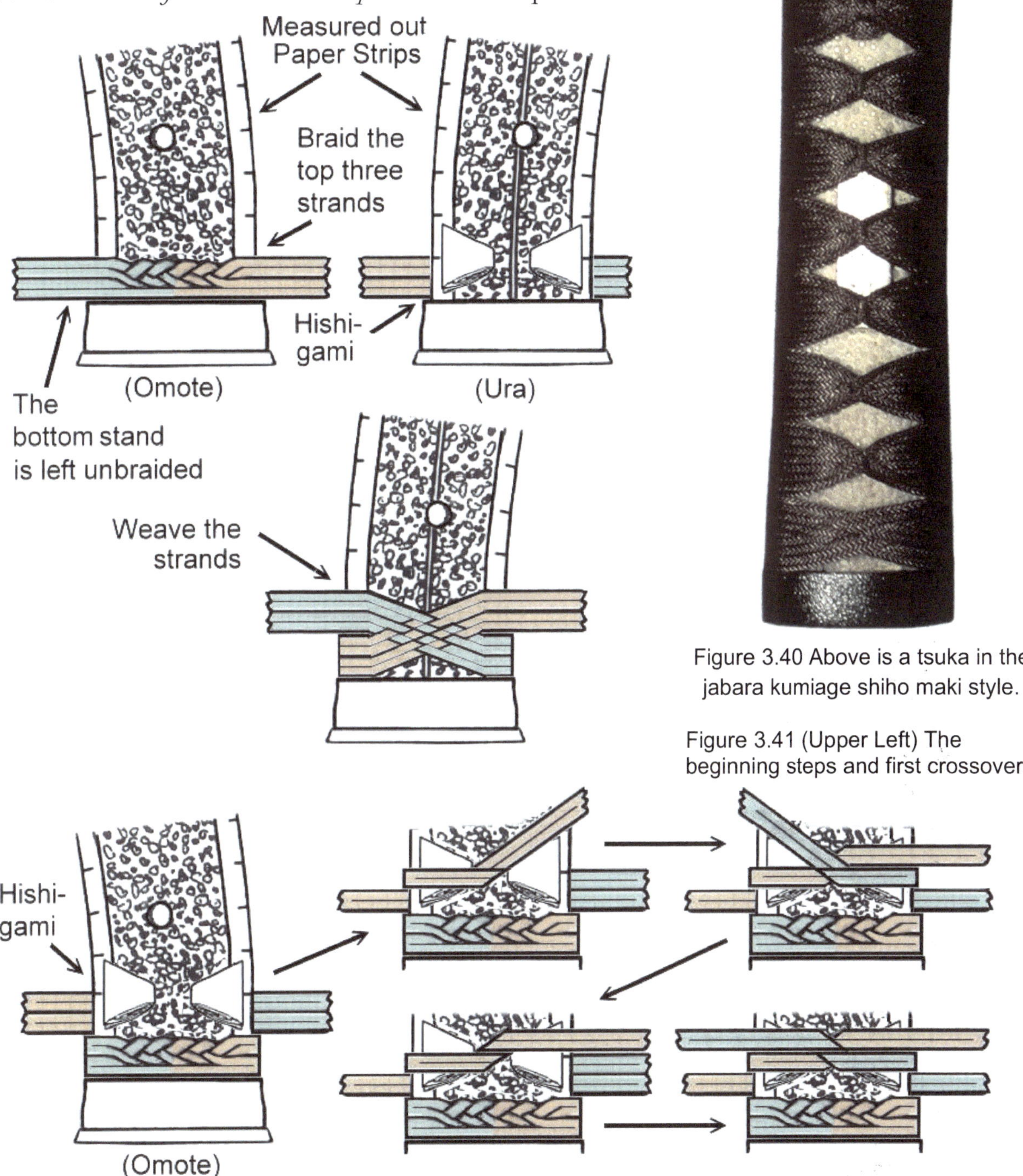

Figure 3.40 Above is a tsuka in the jabara kumiage shiho maki style.

Figure 3.41 (Upper Left) The beginning steps and first crossover.

Figure 3.42a The second crossover technique using strands in sets of two.

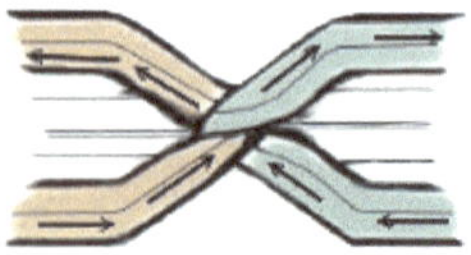

The final step in the second cross-over technique loops the ito through its opposite strand, then switches back in the direction it came.

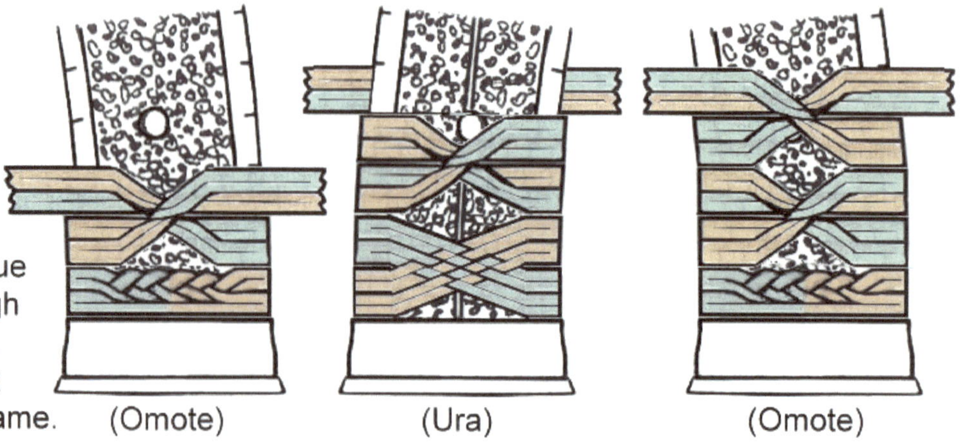

(Omote) (Ura) (Omote)

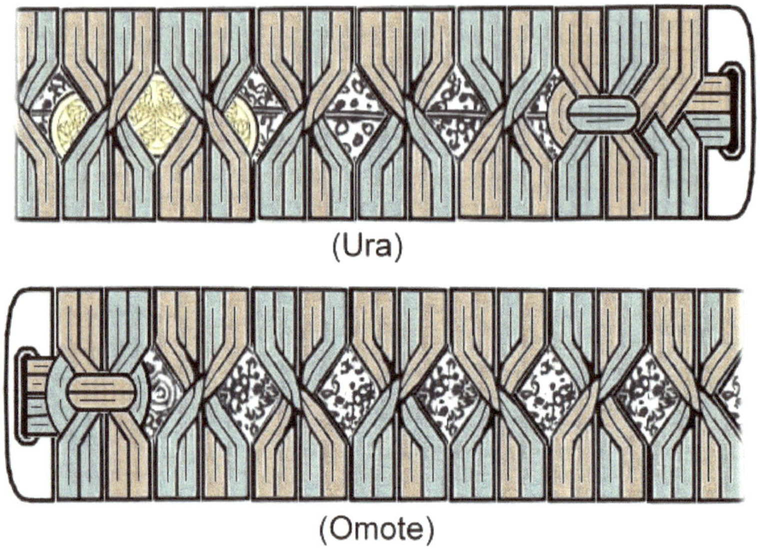

(Ura)

(Omote)

Figure 3.43b The finished second crossover technique, and knots.

Below is a variation in *menuki* placement, where the primary crossover technique is the same, but the *menuki* are secured using a braided crossover simular to *hoso jabaraito kumiage zuka.*

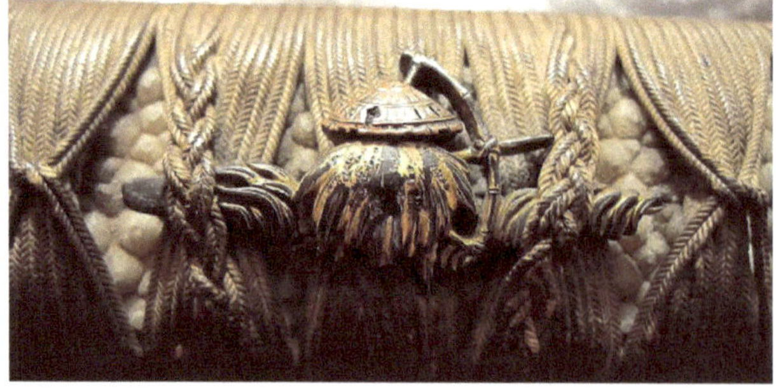

Figure 3.43 Braided crossover menuki placement.

3.10 Kami Hosoyori Hiramaki Zuka

The *kami hosoyori hiramaki zuka*, or string-wrapped *tsuka*, is wrapped using *jabaraito* in matching sets of two to four strings.

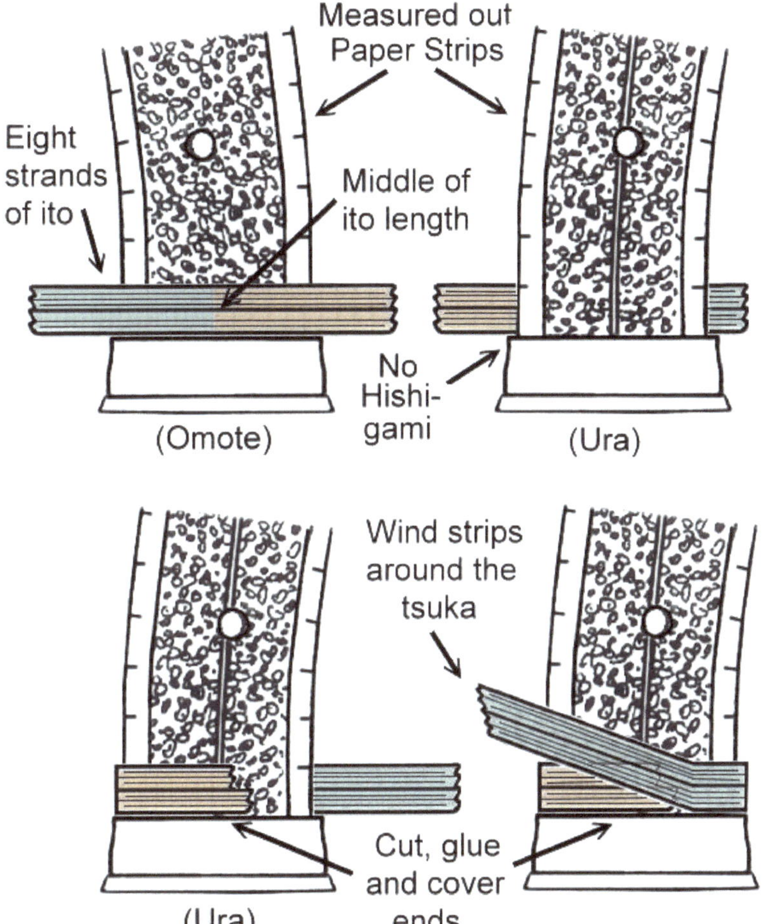

Figure 3.45 The beginning maki steps.

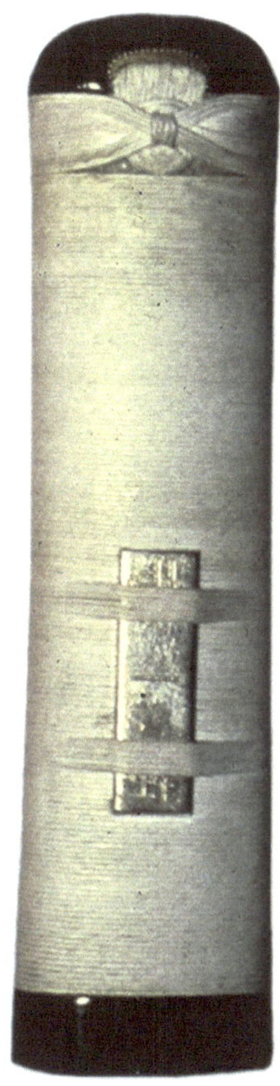

Figure 3.44 Above is a tsuka wrapped in the kami hosoyori hiramaki zuka style.

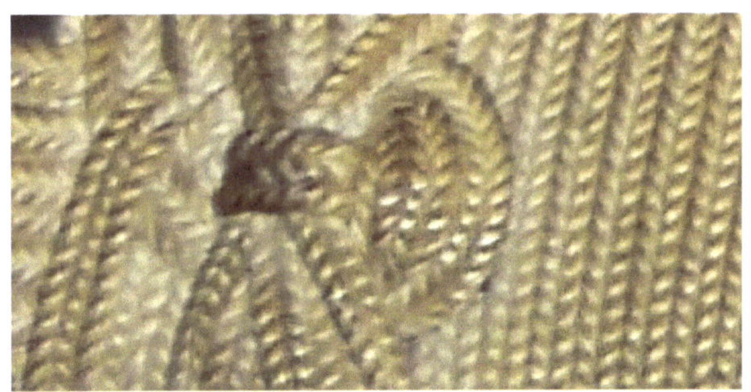

One of the more notable hallmarks of this style is how each string is paired with a matching string that twists in the opposite direction.

Figure 3.46 Close-up of the ura knot and ito.

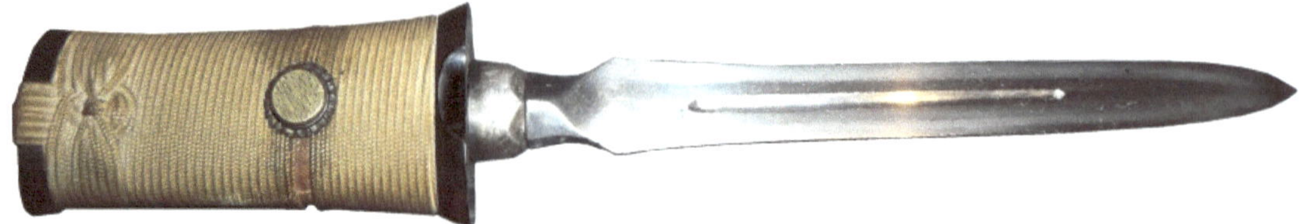

Figure 3.47 The ura side view of a yari tanto with a kami hosoyori hiramaki zuka style tsuka.

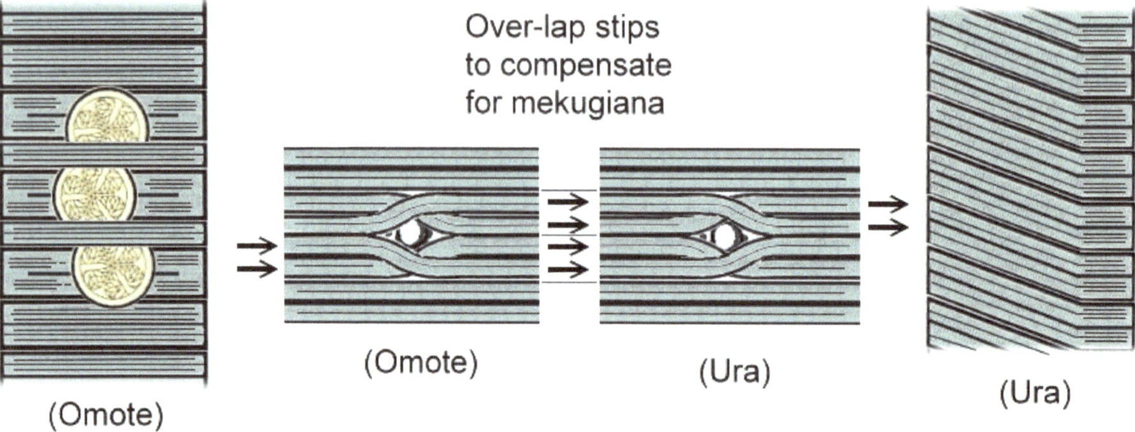

Figure 3.48 Securing the menuki, and compensating for the mekugiana.

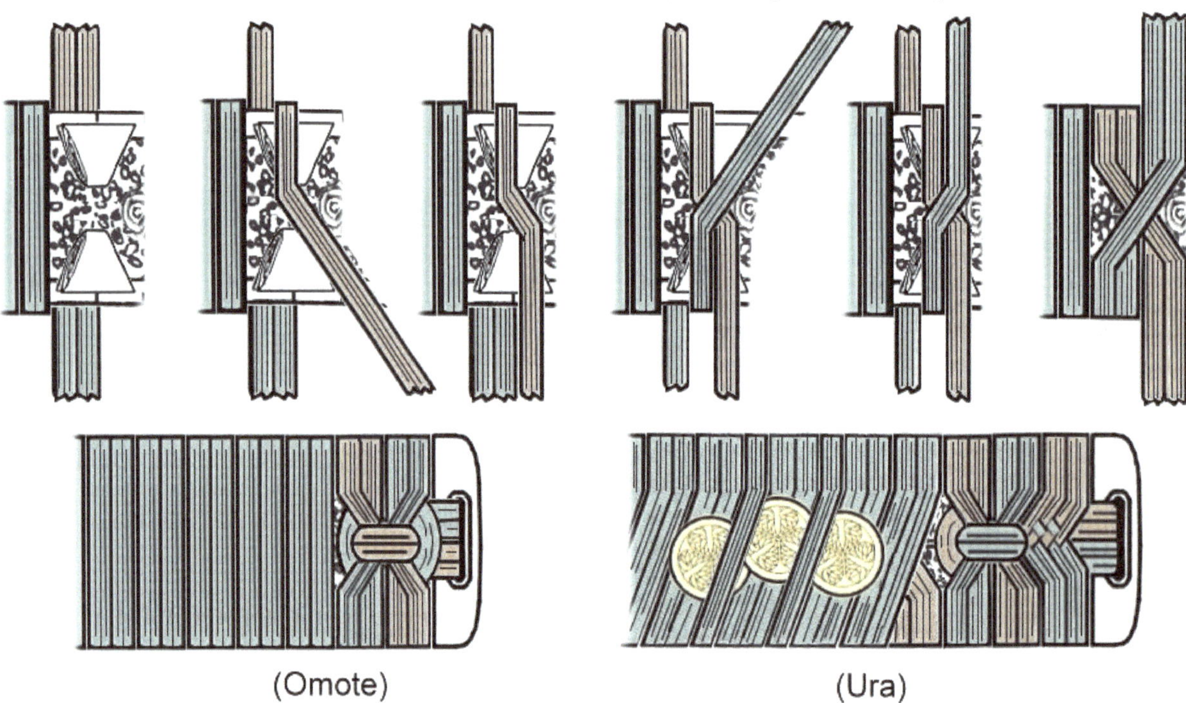

Figure 3.49 The first crossover and the finished knots.

Although there may seem to be a discrepency between lining up the *omote* and *ura* knots, if you look closely (see Fig. 3.46) you will see how the *ura* knot actually overlaps the preceding *ito*.

3.11 KATAHINERI MAKI

The *Katahineri maki* combines elements of two of the more popular styles, *tsumami maki*, or pinched, and *menpumaki*, or folded, crossover.

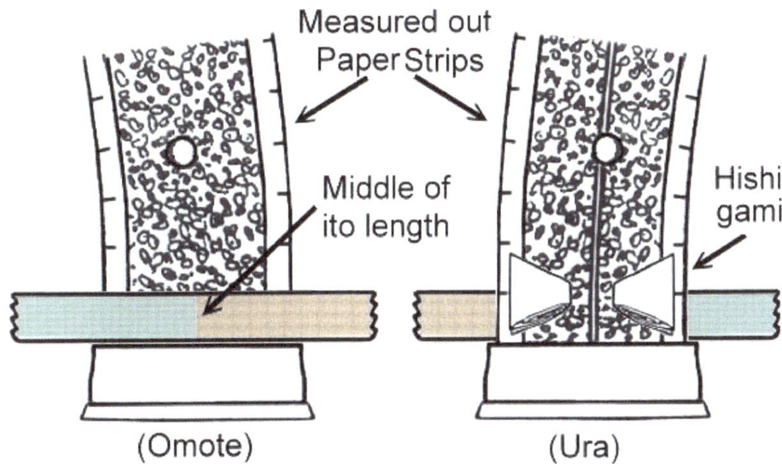

Figure 3.51 The beginning maki steps.

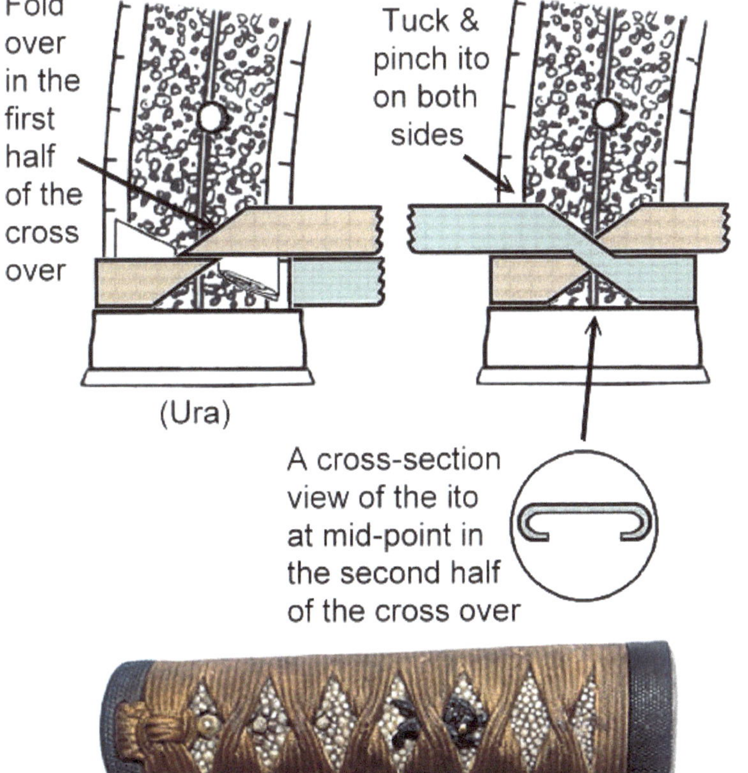

Figure 3.53 Wakizashi tsuka wrapped in the katahineri maki style.

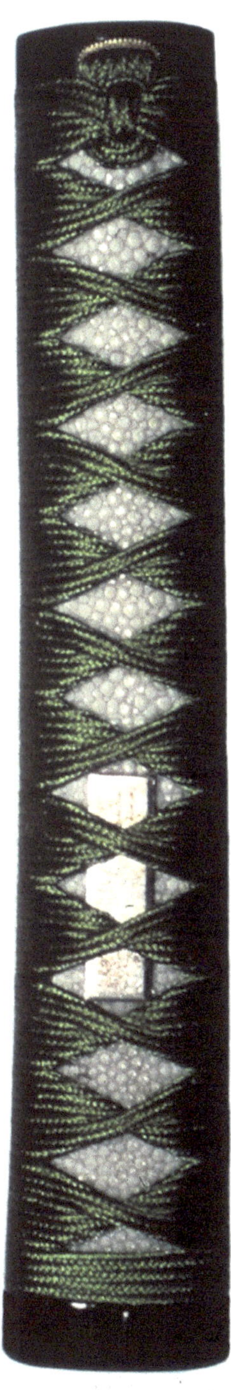

Figure 3.50 Above is a tsuka wrapped in the katahineri maki.

Figure 3.52 (Middle Left) The crossover technique.

3.12 Katate Maki

There are several variations of this style, including *kawa hoso maki buyotsuka* (Style 3.13), *kawakasane katate maki* (Style 3.14), *gyu kawa kumiage maki* (Style 3.2). Their common trait is a starting and an ending of

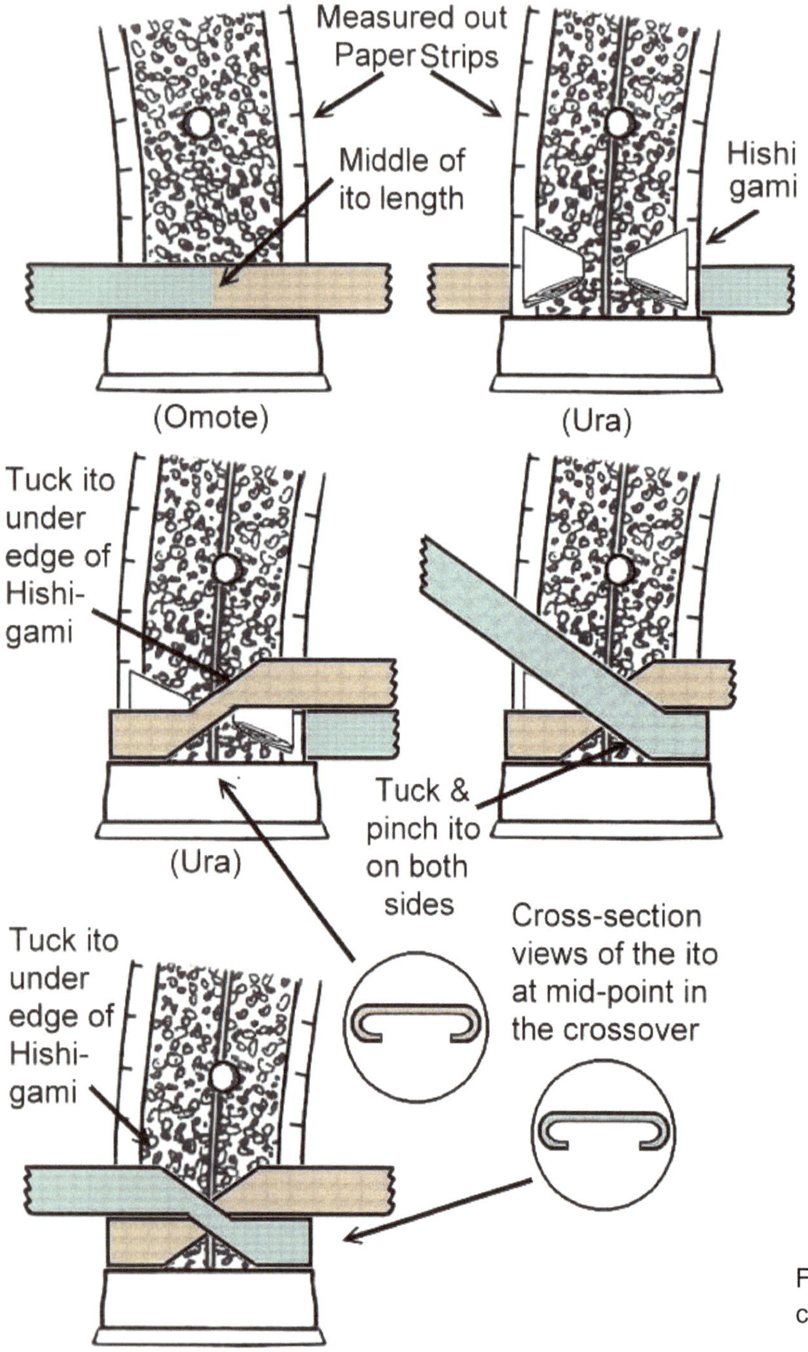

Measured out Paper Strips
Middle of ito length
Hishi gami
(Omote)
(Ura)
Tuck ito under edge of Hishi-gami
(Ura)
Tuck & pinch ito on both sides
Tuck ito under edge of Hishi-gami
Cross-section views of the ito at mid-point in the crossover

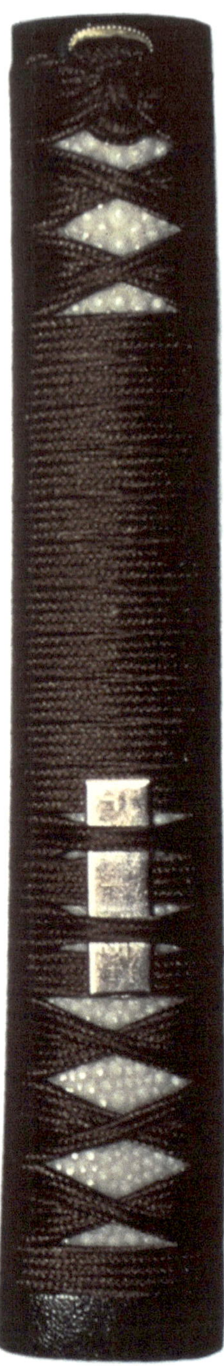

Figure 3.54 Above is a tsuka wrapped in the katate maki style.

Figure 3.55 (Left) The crossover technique.

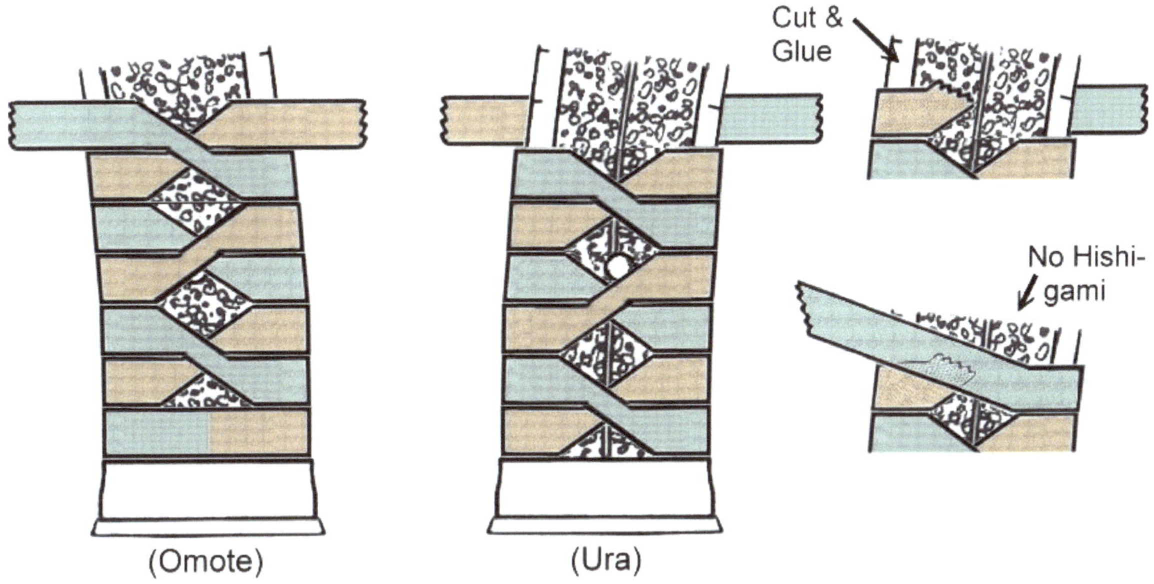

Figure 3.56 Beginning crossovers and transition to spiral.

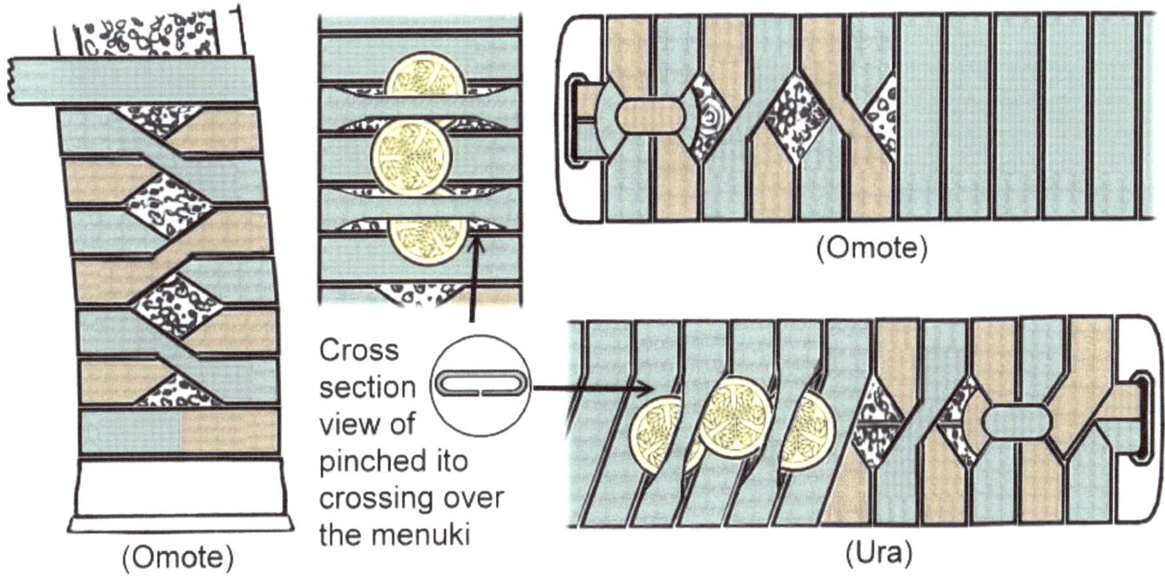

Figure 3.57 Menuki placement and end knots.

diamond-shaped openings, divided by a spiraling wrap of *ito*. Some interesting research has been done into the origins of this style. In particular, Dr. Takeuchi has identified two separate and historically unique styles of katate maki, or battle wrap (Takeuchi, 2003). The first style was popular during the Muromachi Period (Fig. 1.19), also known as *akechi tsukamaki;* and the second, displayed here, became widely used during the late Edo period, then reappeared on some late war gunto koshirae in 1944.

3.13 Kawa Hoso Maki Buyotsuka

The *kawa hoso maki buyotsuka* is like the *katate maki*, but instead of cloth *ito*, it uses two to four thin strips of lacquered leather *ito*.

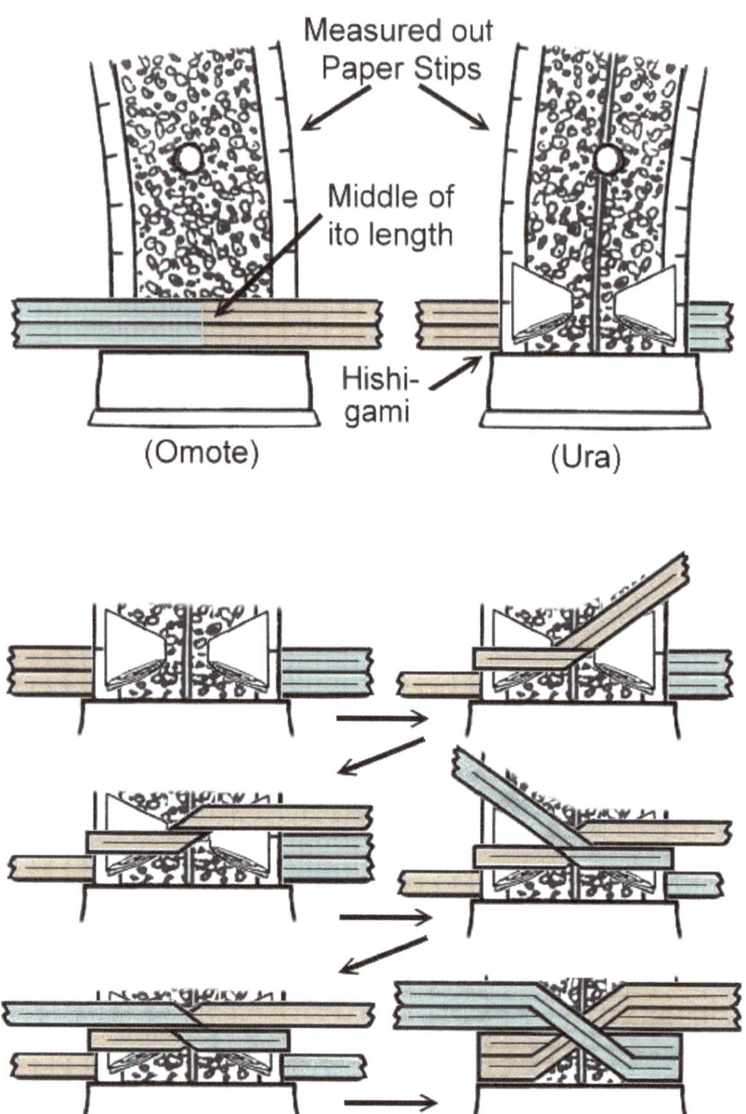

Figure 3.59a The crossover technique.

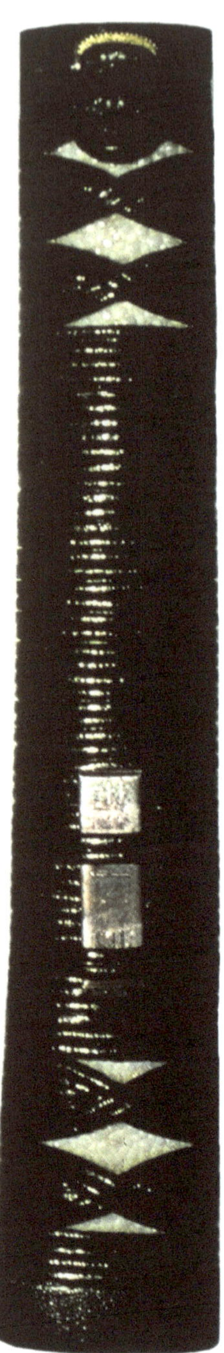

Figure 3.58 Above is a tsuka wrapped in the kawa hoso maki buyotsuka style.

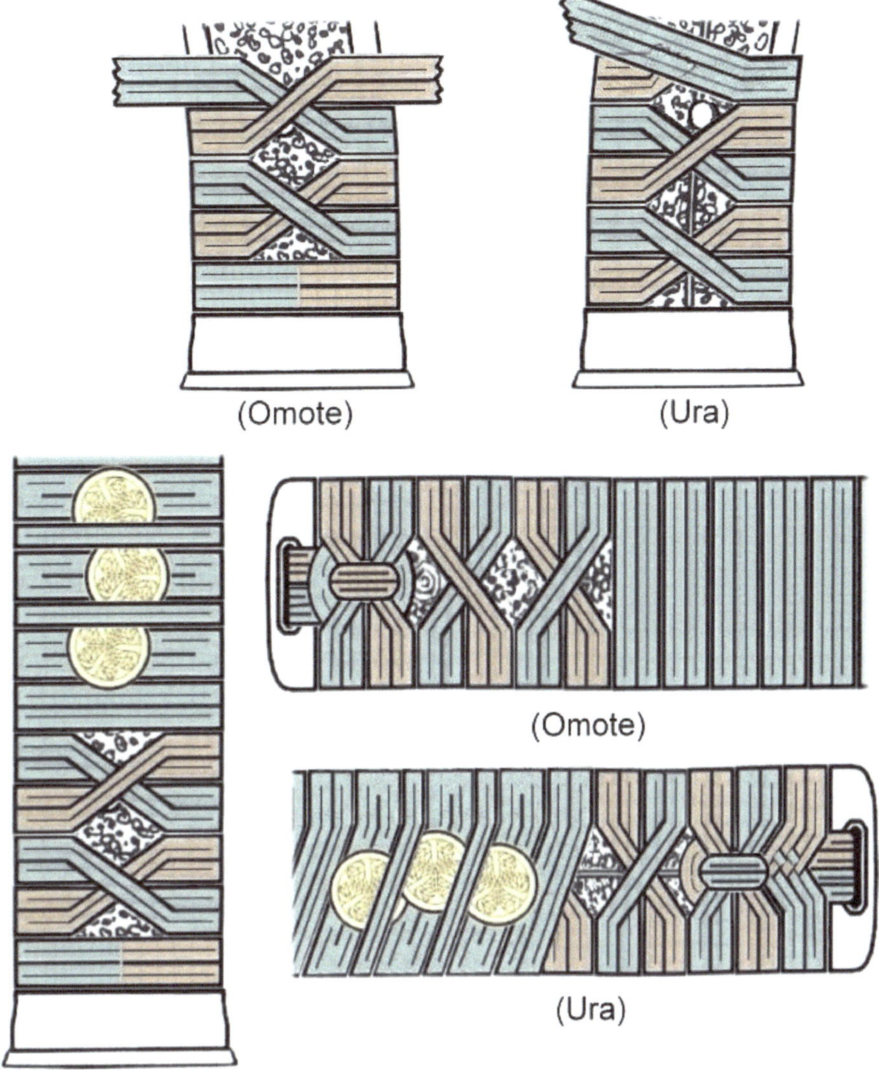

Figure 3.59b Crossover technique continued, as well as menuki placement and end knots.

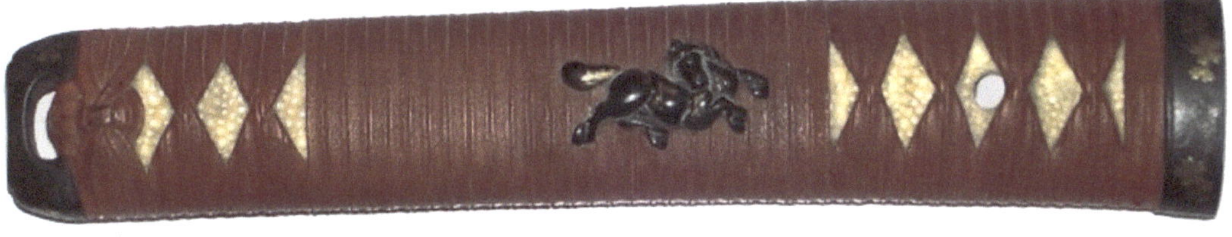

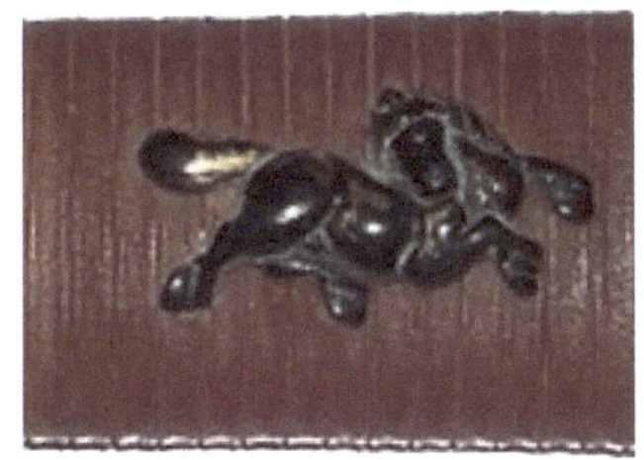

Figure 3.60 A variation of this style, wrapped with two strips of leather and having the menuki secured by a stud projecting from its back, instead of by crossovers.

3.14 Kojidai Asaito Makiage Zuka

Literally meaning to wrap with hemp, *kojidai asaito makiage zuka* is basically just that, a plain *tsuka* with a horn *kashira* wrapped with a hemp cord *ito*.

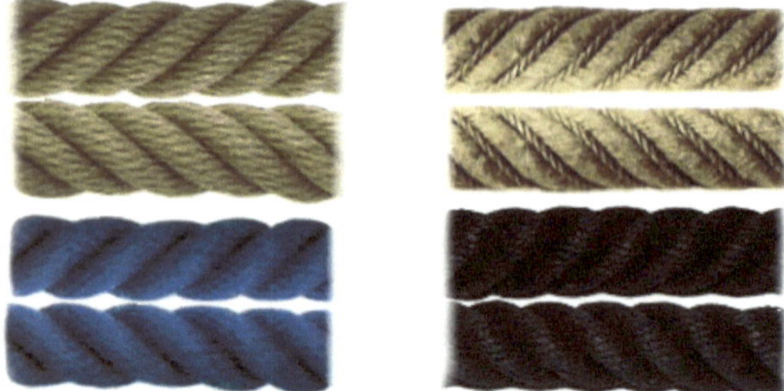

Figure 3.62 Four pairs of Japanese hemp cord ito.

Although this style generally uses pairs of twisted cord, it can be done with a single cord, or a more flat braided hemp *ito*.

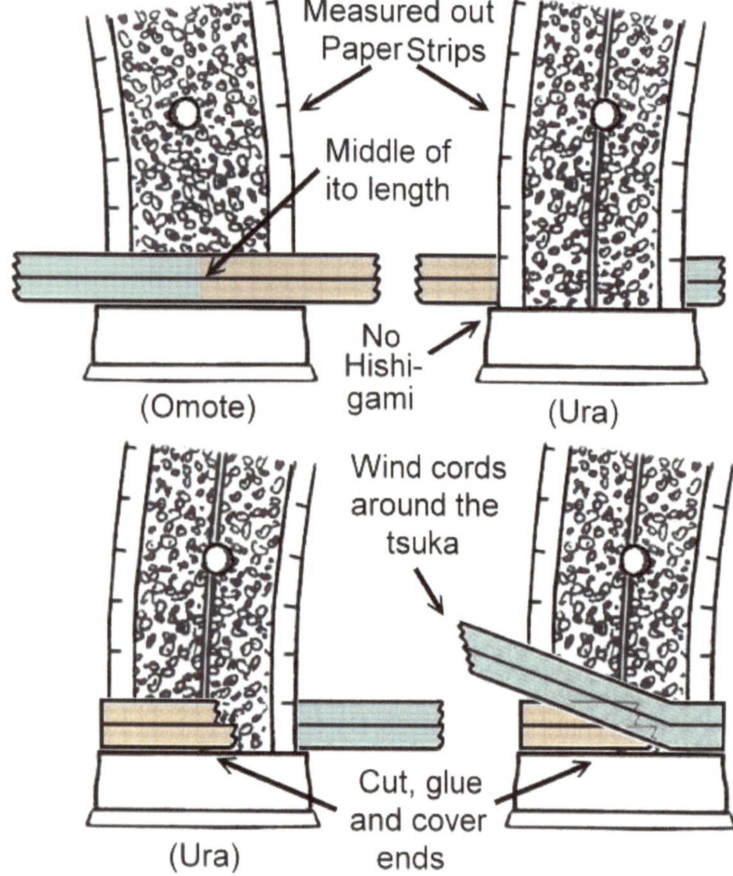

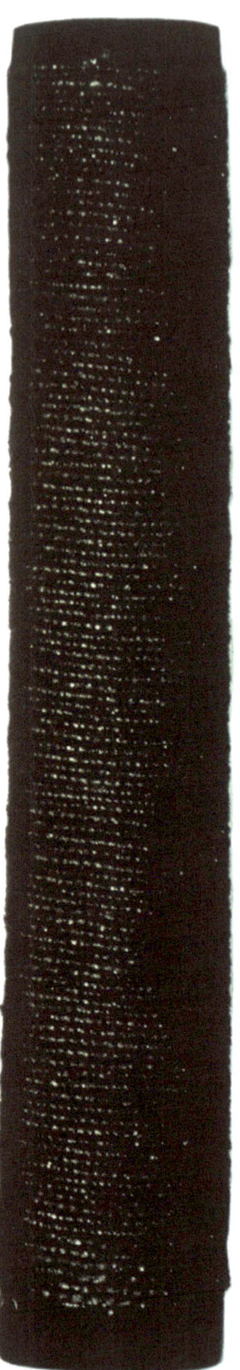

Figure 3.61 Above is a tsuka wrapped in the kojidai asaito makiage zuka.

Figure 3.63 (Left) The beginning steps.

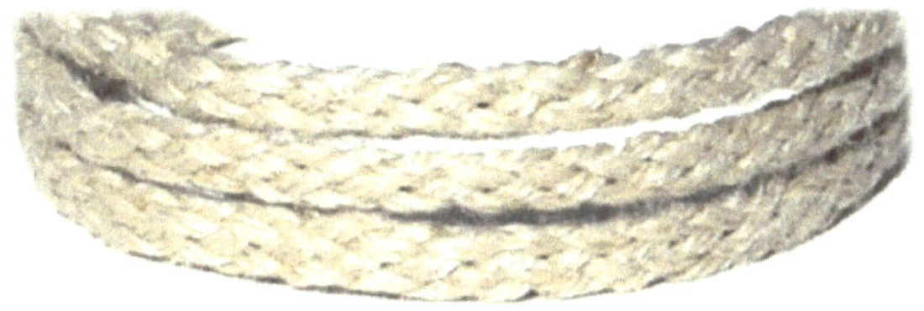

Figure 3.64 An example of braided hemp ito.

Often this style of *tsukamaki* would use a braided hemp *ito*, pictured above, which was then coated with as many as 12 layers of lacquer.

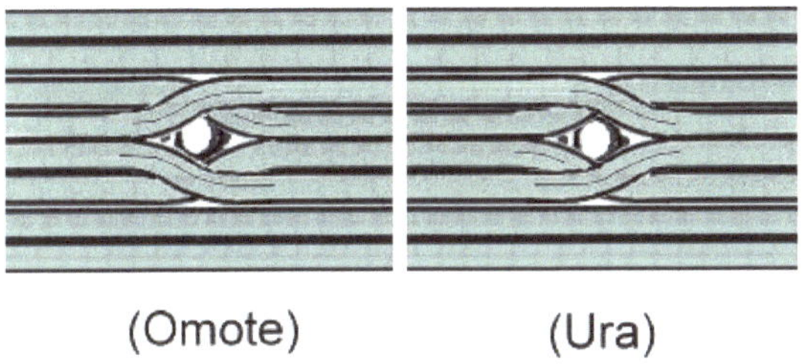

(Omote) (Ura)

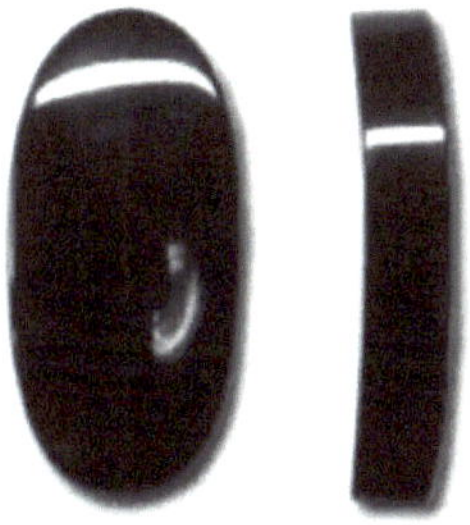

(example of a horn kashira)

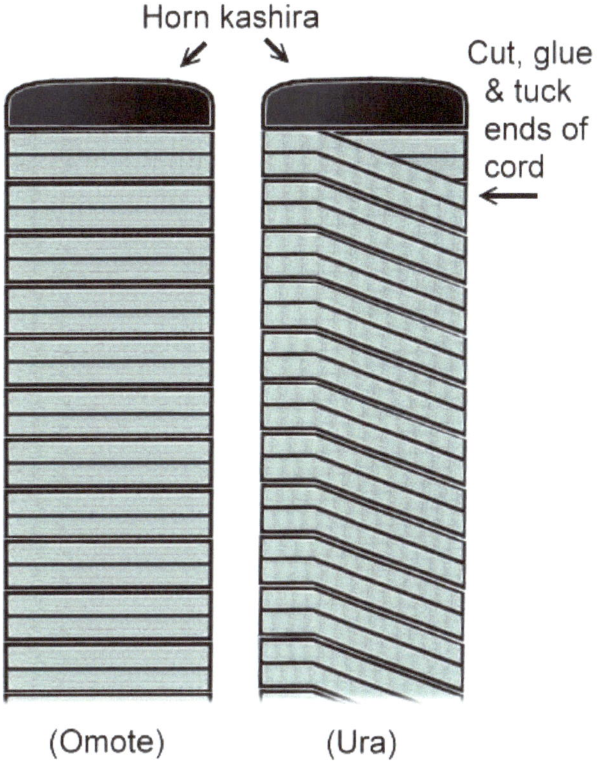

Horn kashira

Cut, glue & tuck ends of cord

(Omote) (Ura)

Figure 3.65 (Above) Compensation for mekugiana, and finishing tuck of ito.

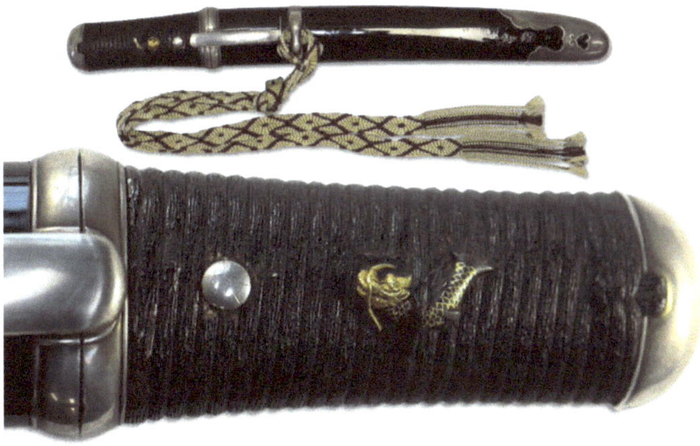

Figure 3.66 (Left) A variation of hemp maki. Note the adding of second strand & knot.

3.15 Kigami Ganpi Maki

Basically, *kigami ganpi maki* is the paper version of *menpumaki*. As was discussed in *ganpi kigami maki,* the finished *maki* is covered with lacquer of varying thicknesses and weights (see Style 3.1 for the making of paper *ito*).

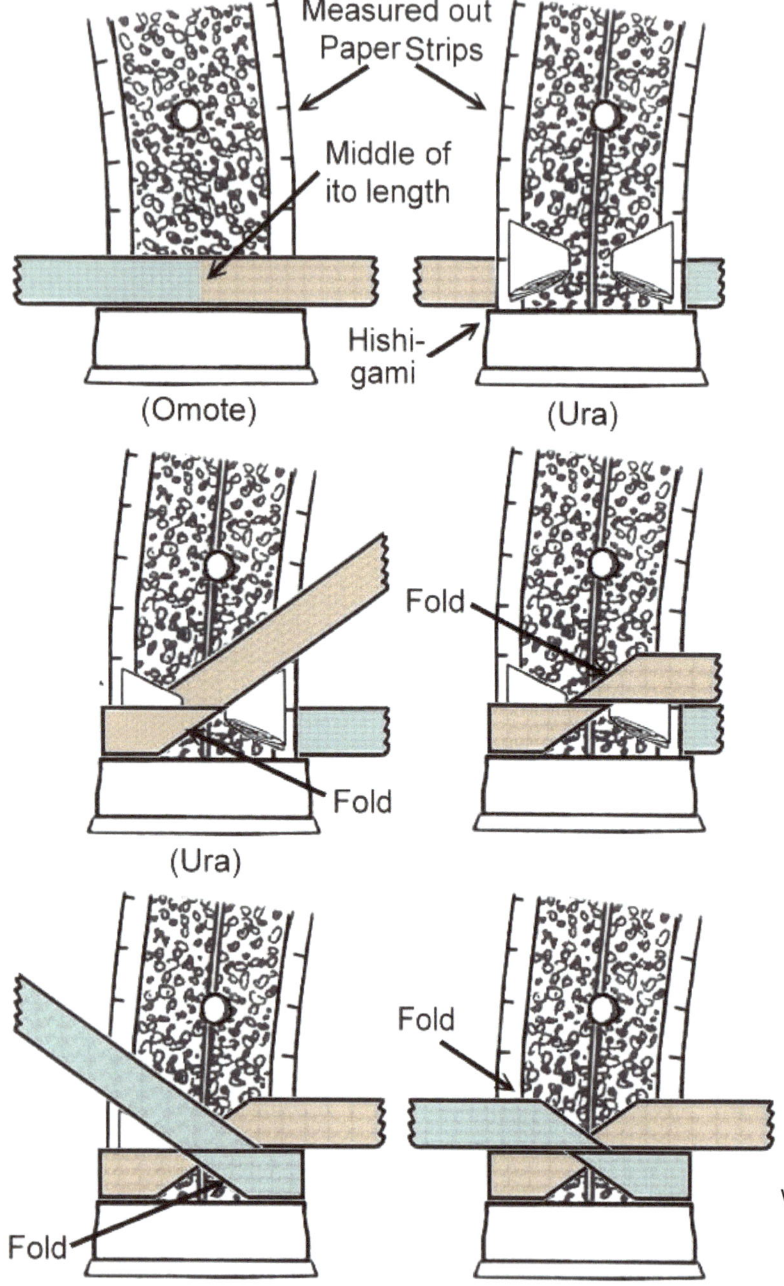

Figure 3.68 The beginning steps and first crossover.

Figure 3.67 Above is a tsuka wrapped in the kigami ganpi maki style before the lacquer is applied to the paper ito.

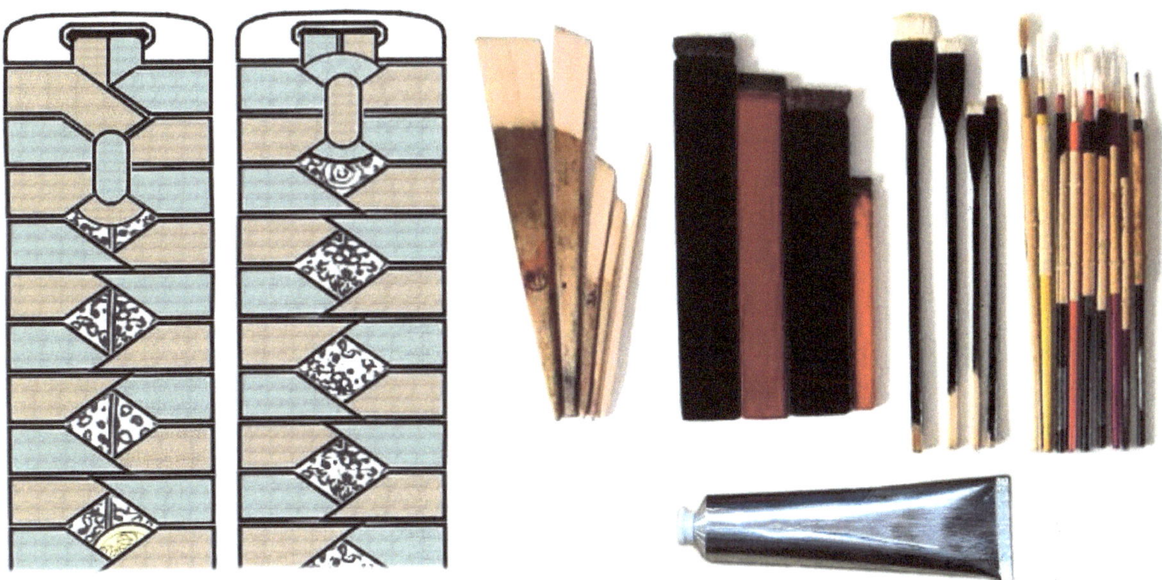

Figure 3.69a Finished knots and examples of lacquering tools and supplies.

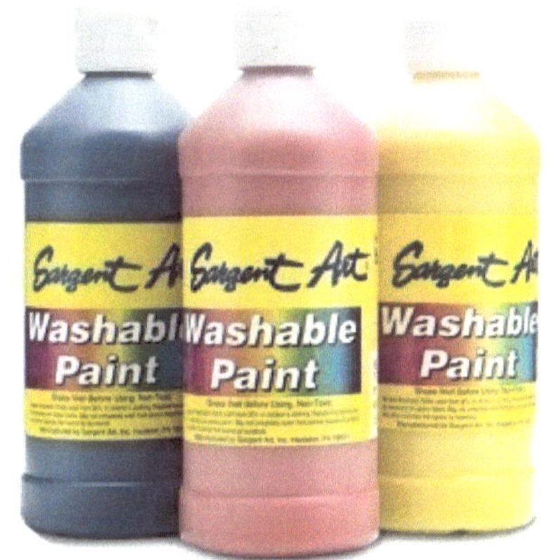

Figure 3.69b Dry pigment for coloring lacquer base.

Lacquer finishing on a *tsuka* is time-consuming and demanding. It requires precise surface preparation and a carefully followed schedule of application, with constant examination and correction along the way. Lacquer, or *urishi*, is a low-wetting finish, which means it does not noticeably saturate the paper, but lies on it as a film. The surface tension of this film will draw it away from any sharp edges of the folds and the seams, leaving little, especially if they are uneven or not flush. Therefore, as part of your pre-finishing surface preparation, soften and flatten all edges of the *ito* to be sure they will remain flush and adequately coated. To color the lacquer base, use only japan paints or dry poster paint (flat opaque pigments in an oil-free varnish), toning it down with lampblack and burnt umber to suit whatever effect you are trying to achieve. Keep in mind that when varying pigments are mixed, if the tonal value is below medium, it will appear darker when dry; if above medium value, it will appear lighter. The lacquer usually is diluted with an equal volume of thinner and is applied at the same rate as the sealer, a coat every hour or two, no more than three coats per day until finished.

3.16 KIODAI MURASAKI JABARA MAKI

This is done with two sets of two 1.5-2.0 mm wide *jabaraito*, initially braided, then done in crossovers that combine *tsumami maki* and *menpumaki* techniques.

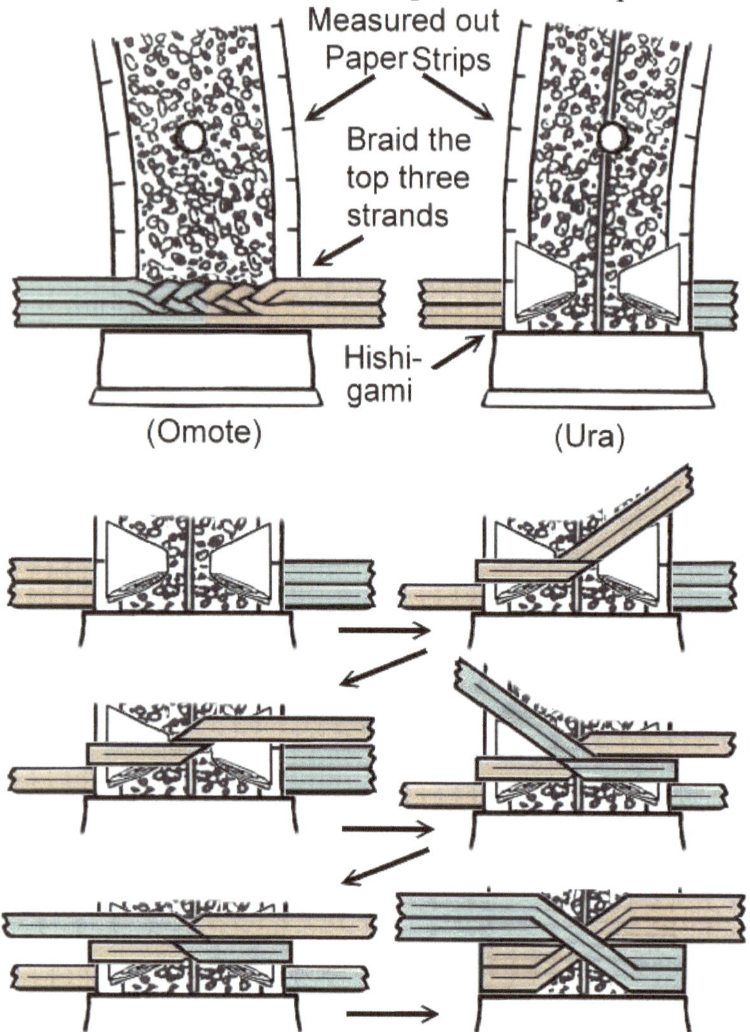

Figure 3.71The beginning steps and crossover technique.

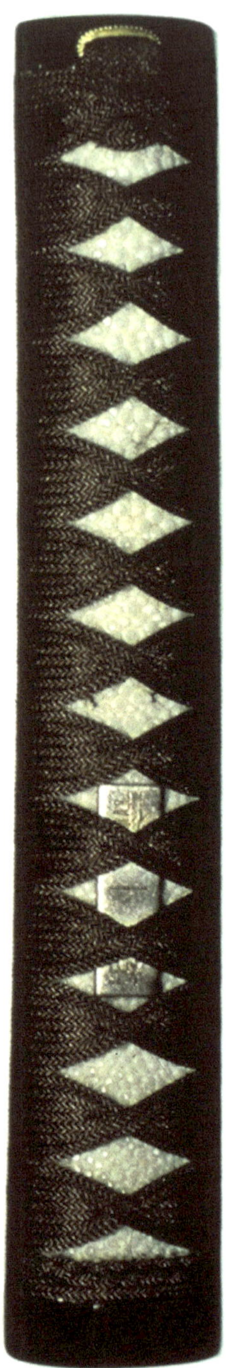

Figure 3.70 Above, an example of kodai murasaki jabara maki.

As with most things relating to Japanese swords, when it comes to *tsukamaki* styles, there are no rigid absolutes, but more simply guidelines. A good example can be seen in Fig. 3.73 where the *maki* fits the general rules of *kodai murasaki*, yet its finishing knot is on the *ura* side.

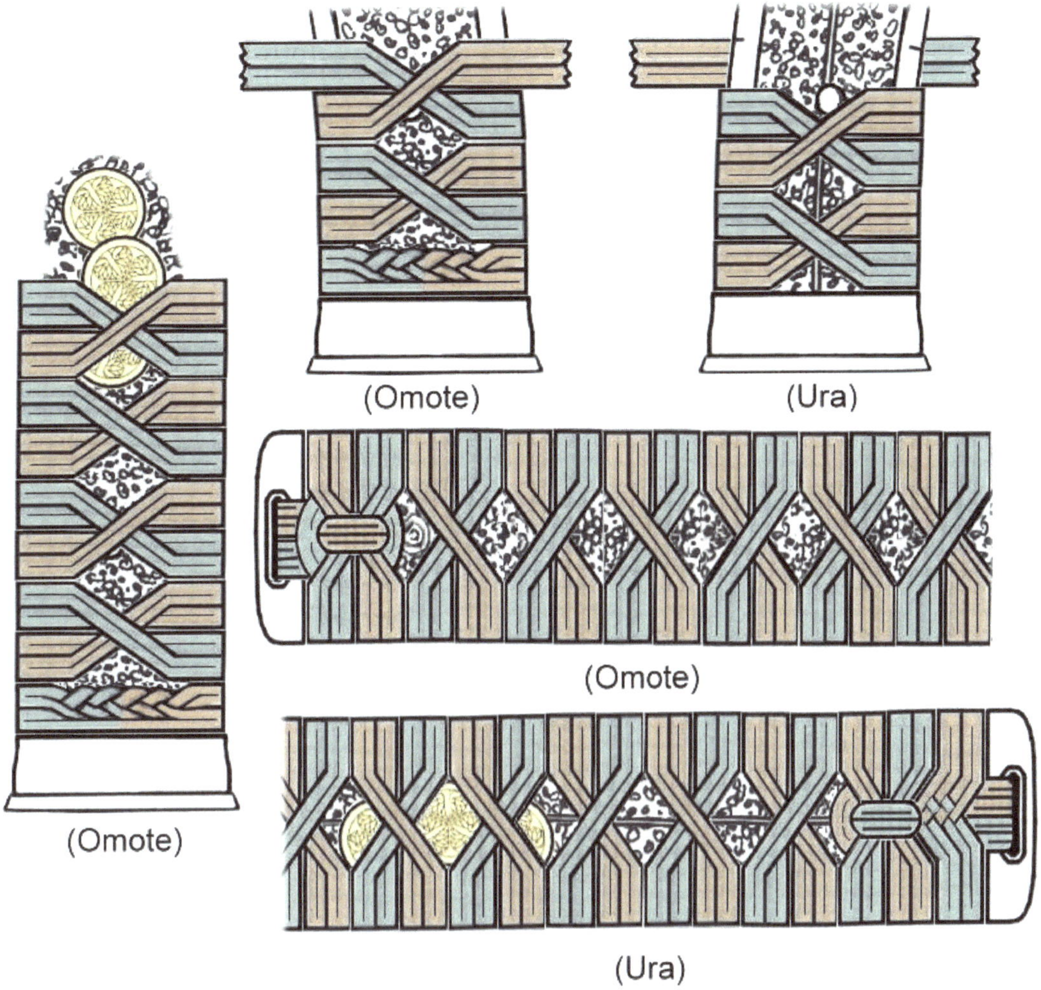

(Omote)

(Ura)

(Omote)

(Omote)

(Ura)

Figure 3.72 Crossover technique continued, as well as menuki placement and finishing knots.

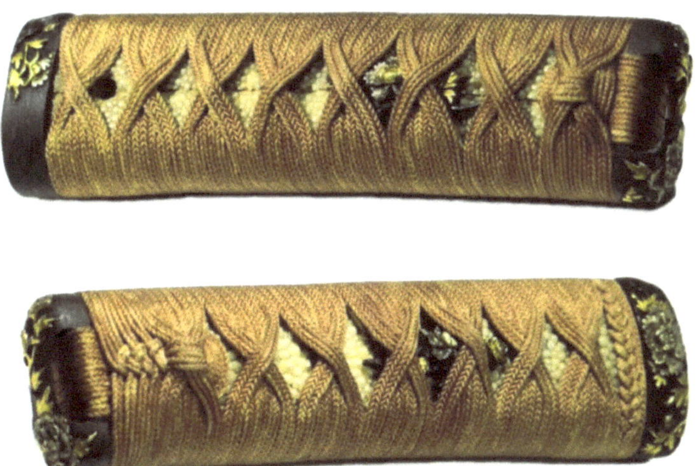

Figure 3.73 Front and back views of a wakizashi wrapped in a variation of kodai murasaki jabara maki.

3.17 KUJIRAHIRE AJIROMAKI ZUKA

This type of *tsukamaki* is traditionally done in a woven pattern using 4 to 8 strands of lacquered baleen, or *kujira* (whale) hair.

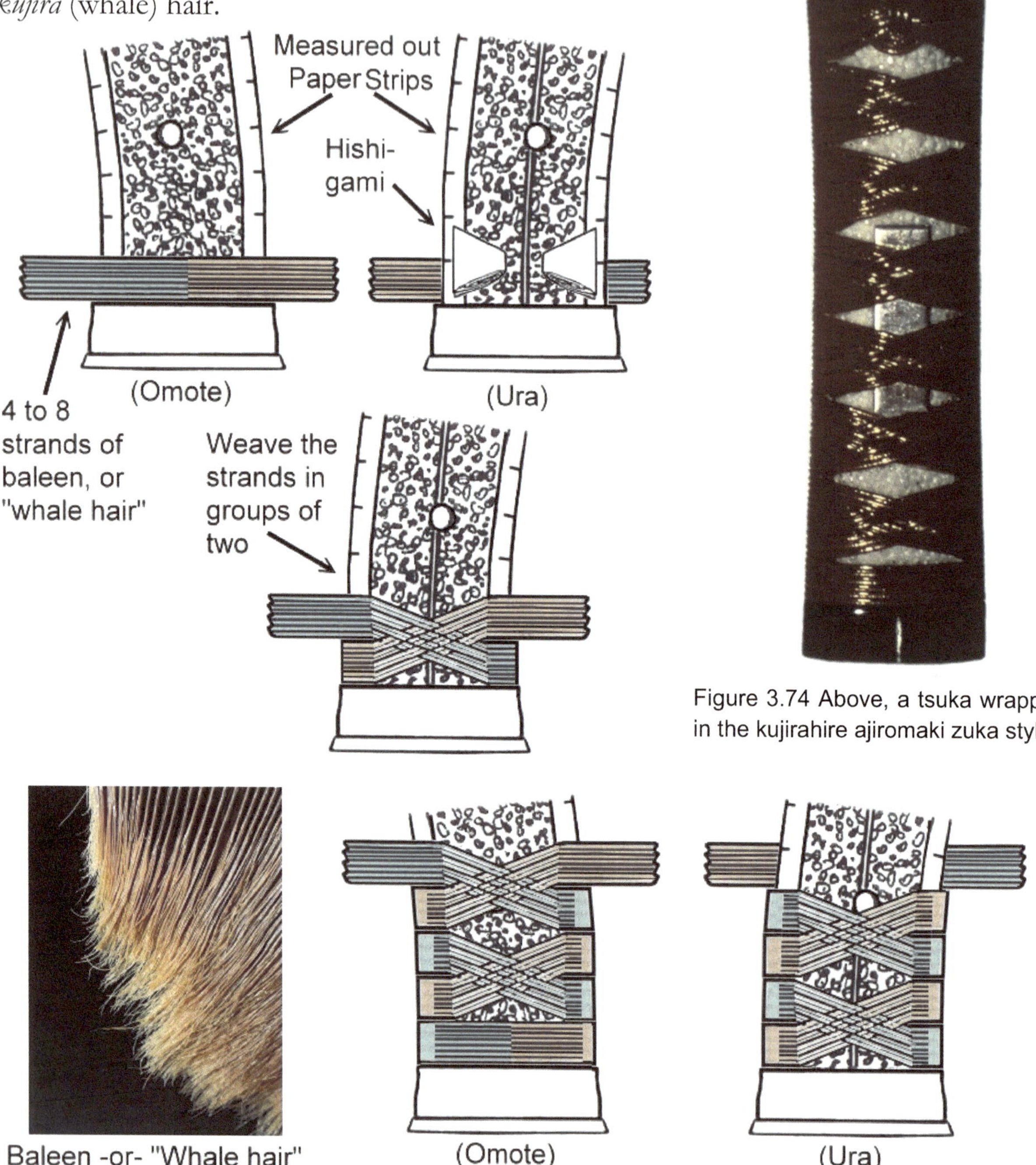

Figure 3.74 Above, a tsuka wrapped in the kujirahire ajiromaki zuka style.

Figure 3.75 The opening steps, crossover techniques, and examples of baleen.

3.18 SHONAI UESUGI ZUKA

The town of Shonai, now known as Tsurugaoka, was the castle-town of the Sakai Clan and *daimyo* from 1622 to 1864. Among other things the *daimyo's* retainers were known for maintaining a relatively strict hierarchy of authority, both in dress and manners, as well as in their sword *koshirae*, and are described by such phrases as "boldness of design" and "having great strength." They also are remembered for presenting significant resistance to the Mikado's troops in 1868. *Tsukamaki* styles 3.18 thru 3.21 are examples of this hierarchical tradition.

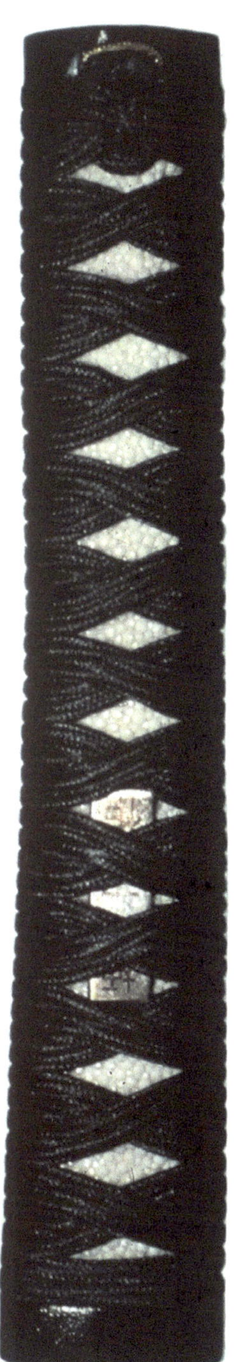

Figure 3.76 Above is a tsuka wrapped in the shonai uesugi zuka style.

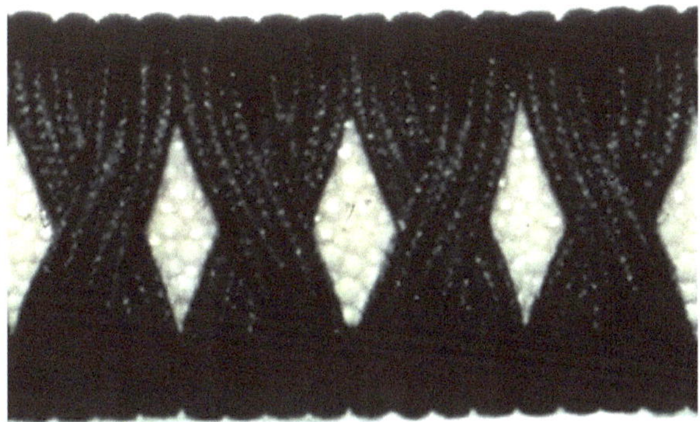

Figure 3.77 A close-up of the shonai uesugi zuka style.

The first of these, *shonai uesugi zuka*, can be done in a number of ways, but the most common is with two lengths of narrow (4 mm) yet heavy *ito*, giving it a

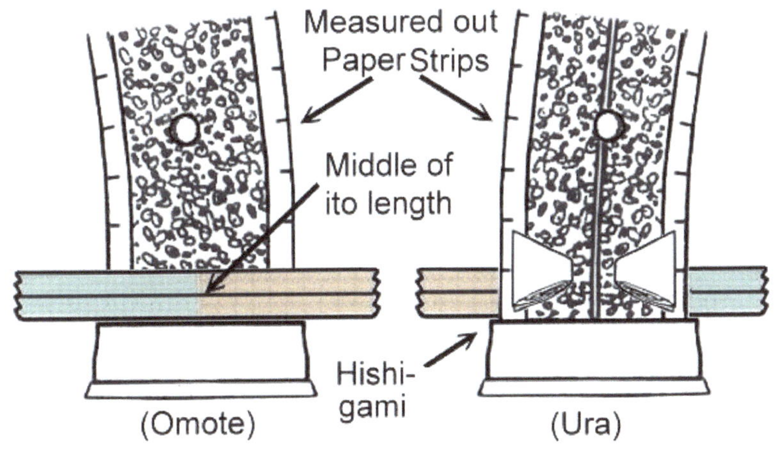

Figure 3.78a (Left)
The opening steps.

distinctive rib like surface, wrapped in a variation of the *hiramaki* style. Occasionally this rib is enhanced with paper ribs, wads or strips under the *ito*.

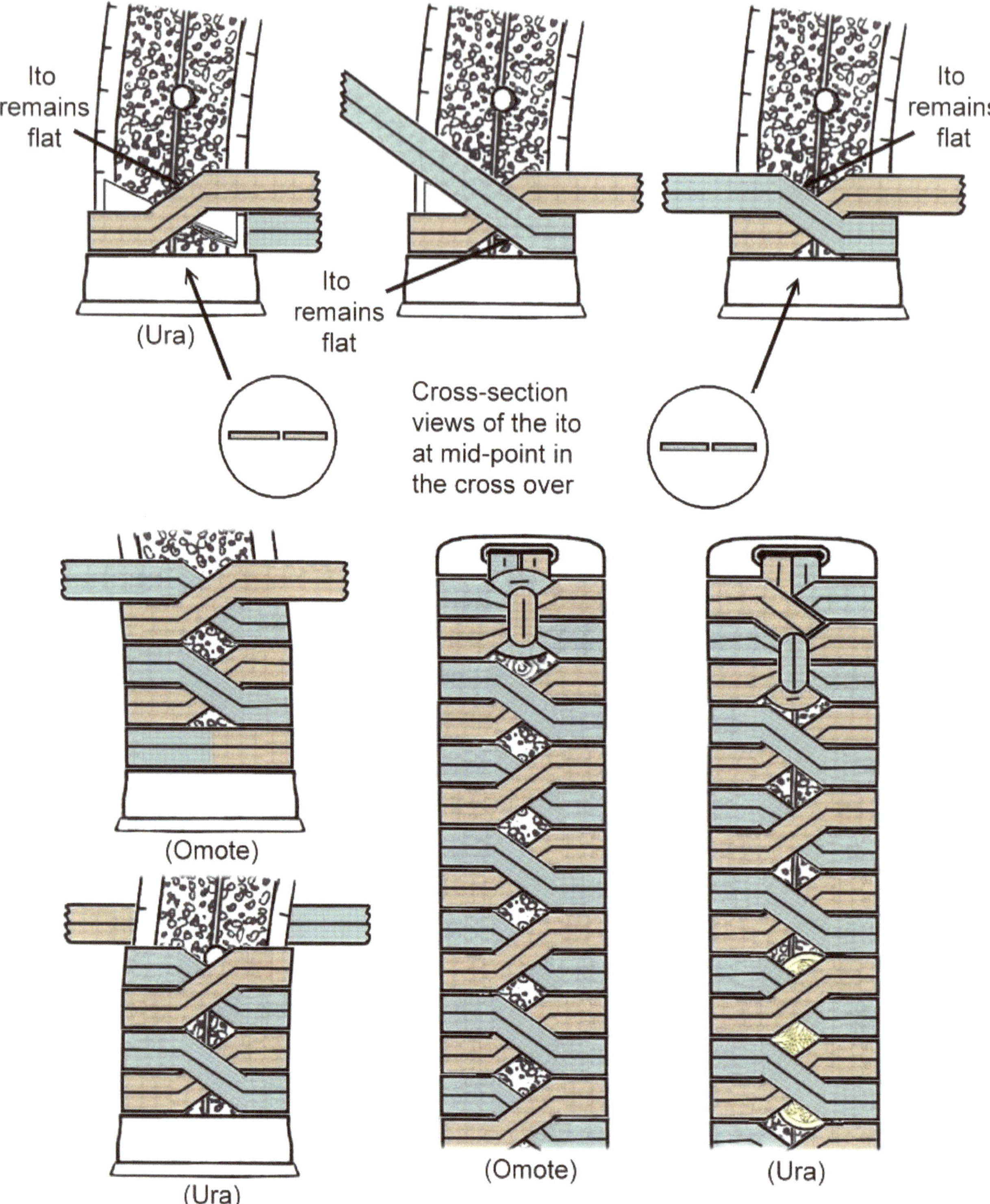

Figure 3.78b The crossover technique, menuki placement and final knots.

3.19 Shonai Zuka – High Rank

The high rank *shonai zuka* is very much like the *katate maki* in design, and follows the same basic steps.

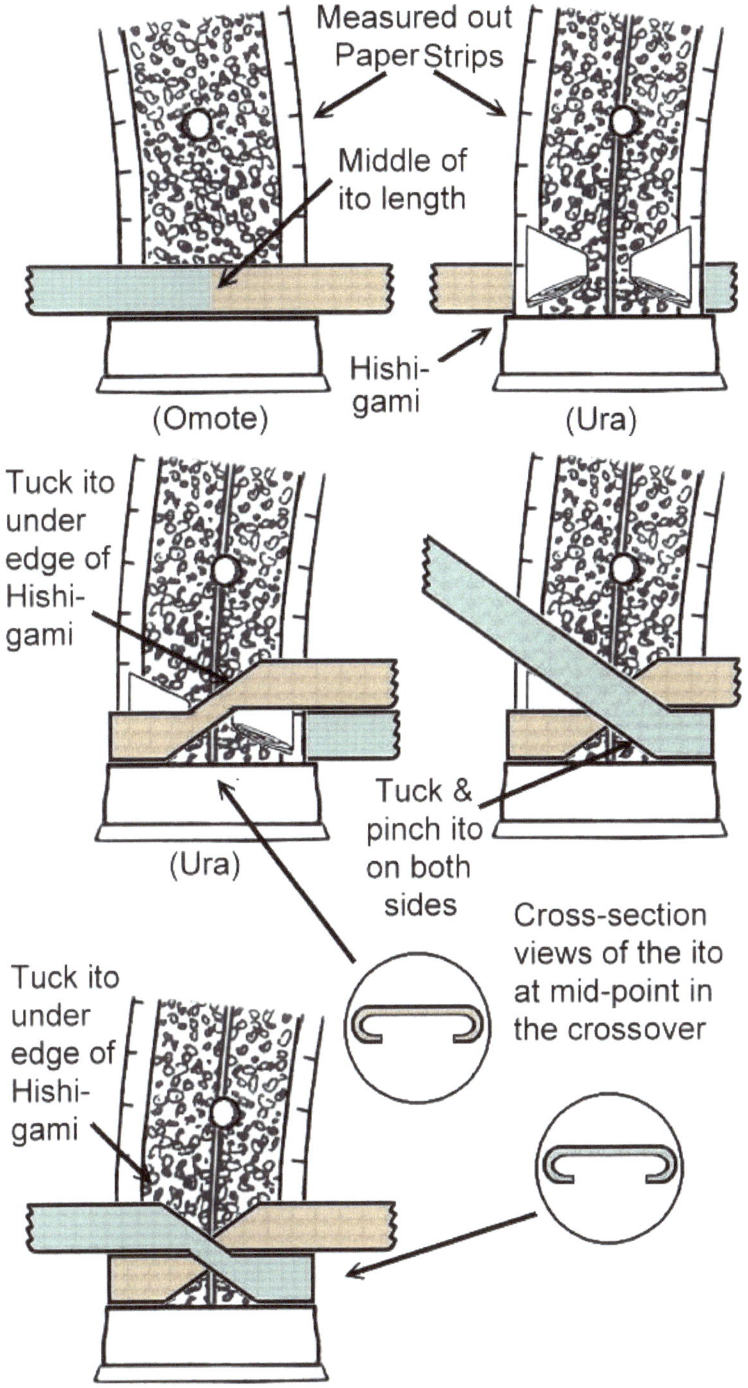

Measured out Paper Strips

Middle of ito length

Hishi-gami

(Omote)

(Ura)

Tuck ito under edge of Hishi-gami

(Ura)

Tuck & pinch ito on both sides

Cross-section views of the ito at mid-point in the crossover

Tuck ito under edge of Hishi-gami

Figure 3.80 The first crossover technique.

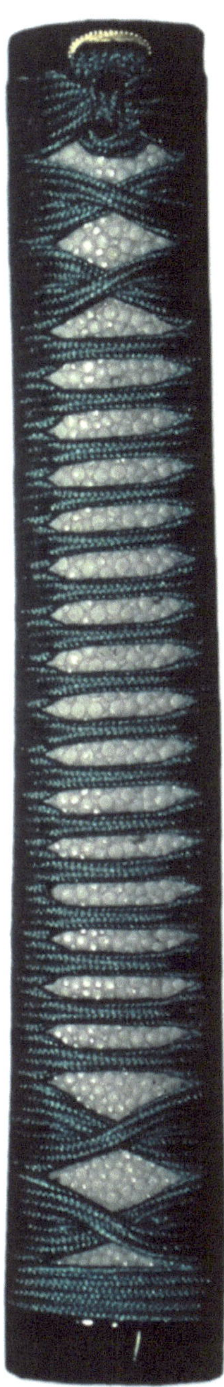

Figure 3.79 Above, a tsuka wrapped in the shonai zuka (high rank) style.

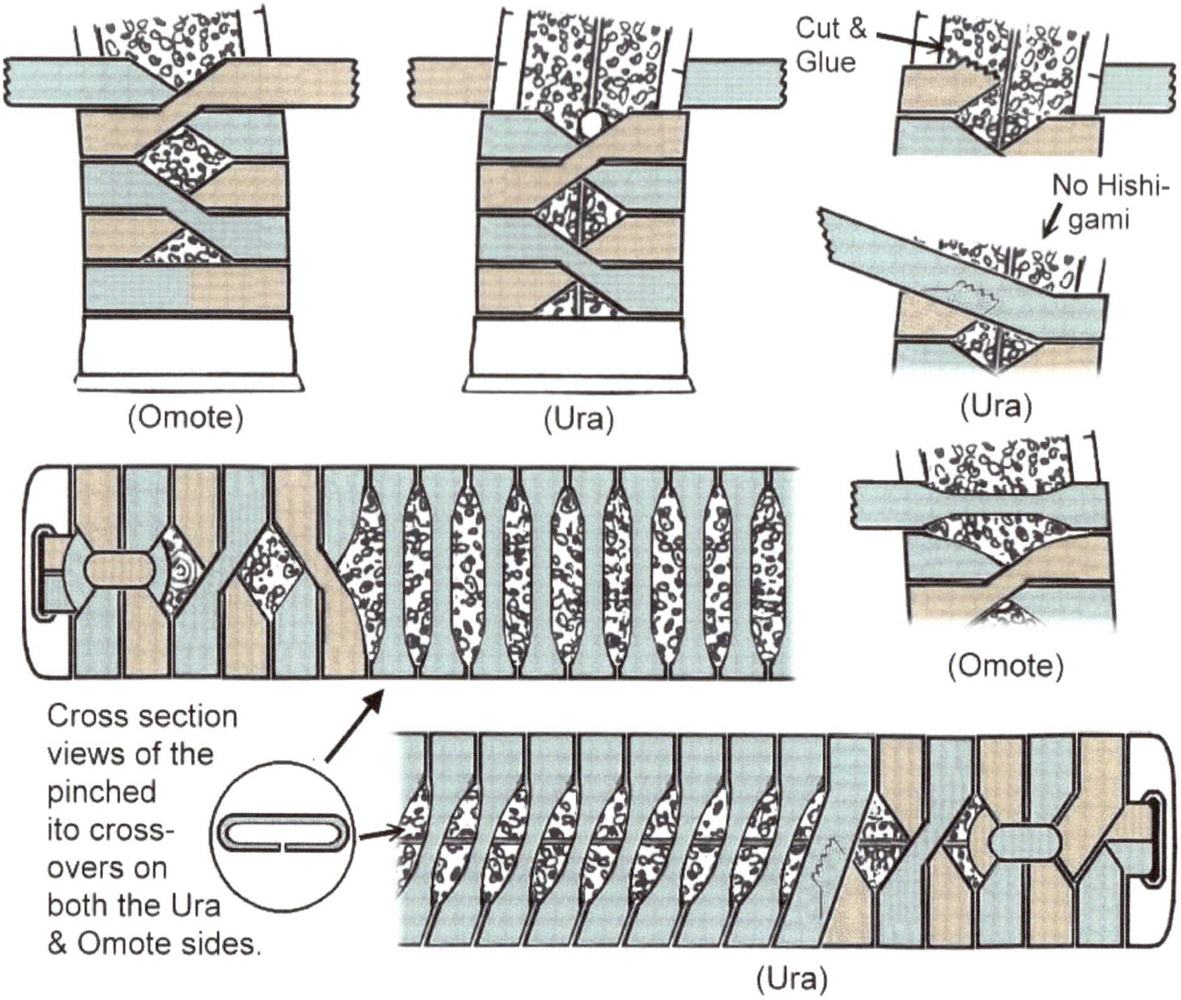

Cut & Glue

No Hishi-gami

(Omote)

(Ura)

(Ura)

(Omote)

Cross section views of the pinched ito cross-overs on both the Ura & Omote sides.

(Ura)

Figure 3.81 (Above) The transition from the first crossover to the second, then back to the first.

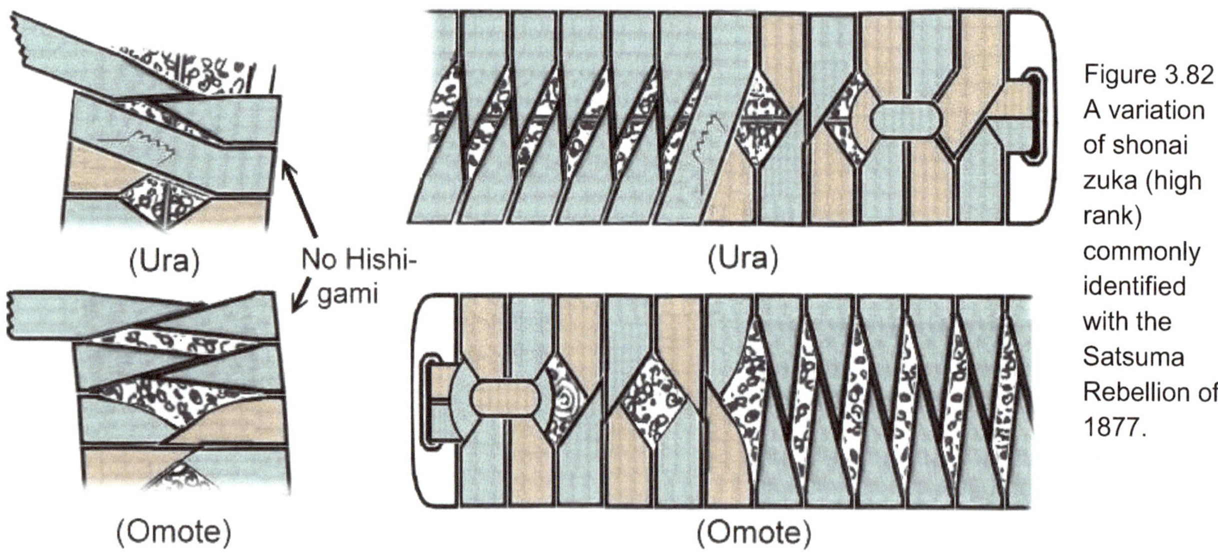

Figure 3.82 A variation of shonai zuka (high rank) commonly identified with the Satsuma Rebellion of 1877.

3.20 Shonai Zuka – Low Rank

The low rank *Shonai Zuka* uses loops for its primary crossover technique.

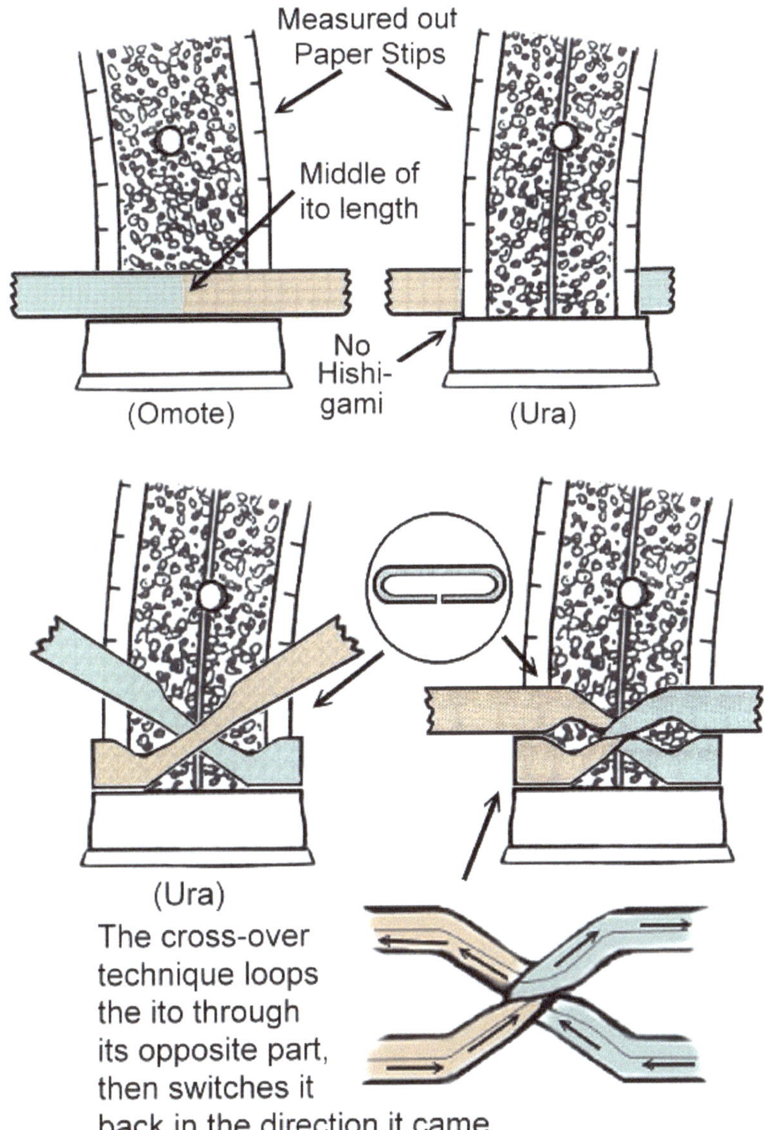

Figure 3.84 The beginning steps and crossover technique.

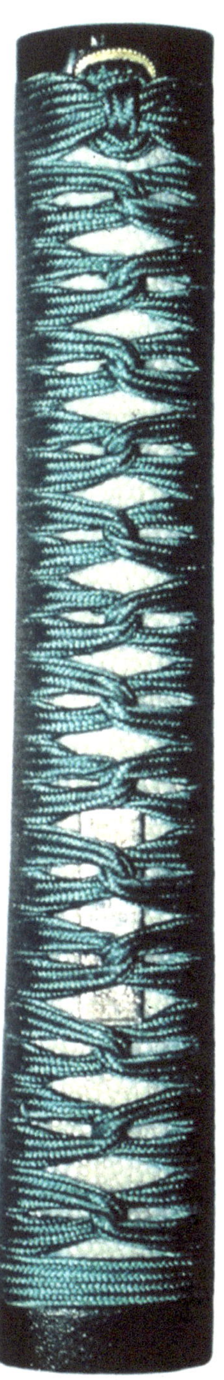

Figure 3.83 Above is a tsuka wrapped in the shonai zuka (low rank) style.

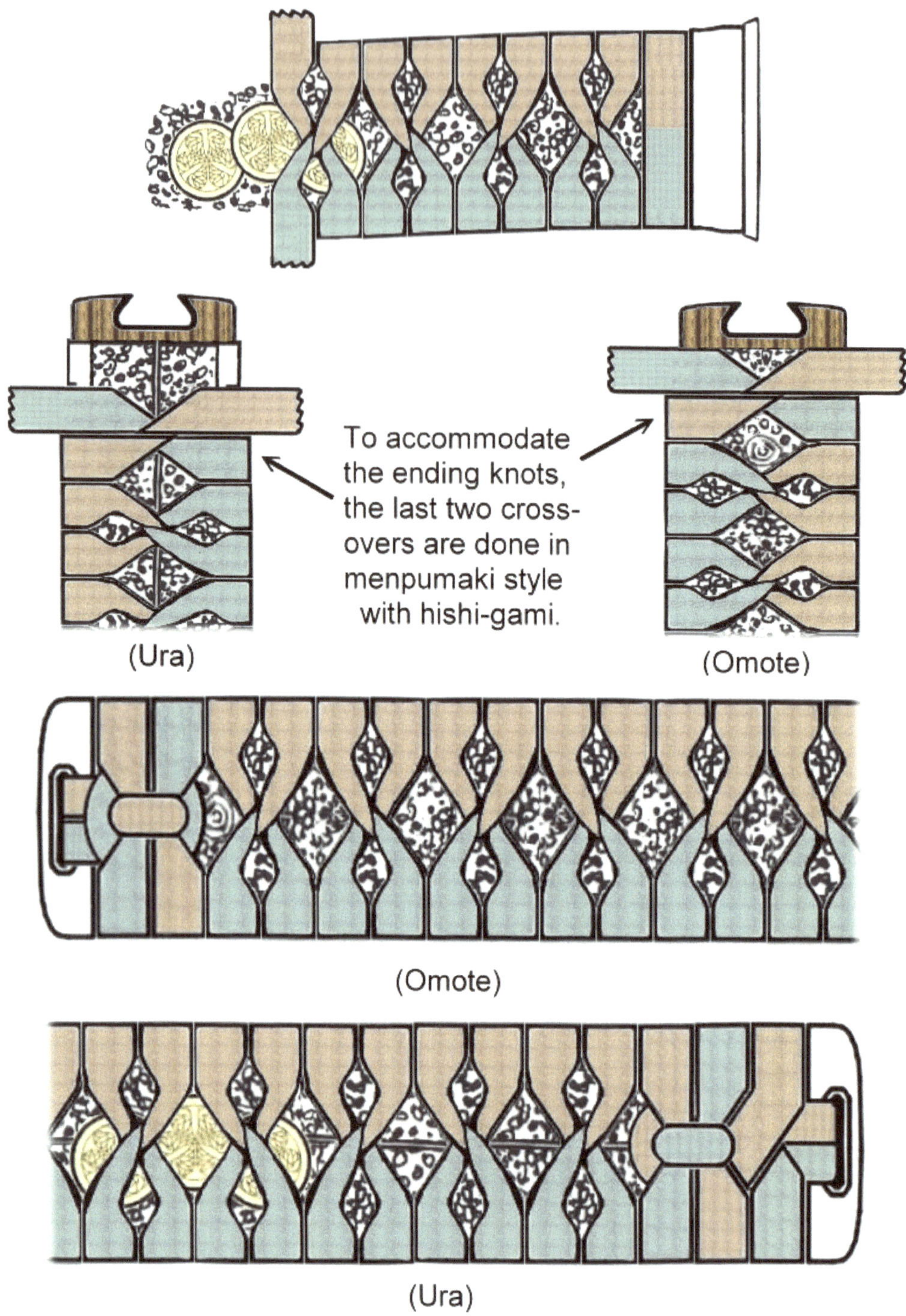

Figure 3.85 Menuki placement, the transition to menpumaki crossover technique and the final knots.

3.21 Shonai Zuka – Common

This *tsukamaki* is primarily a *menpumaki*, with the only exception being the placement of the *menuki*, which rest, at least in part, on top of the *ito*.

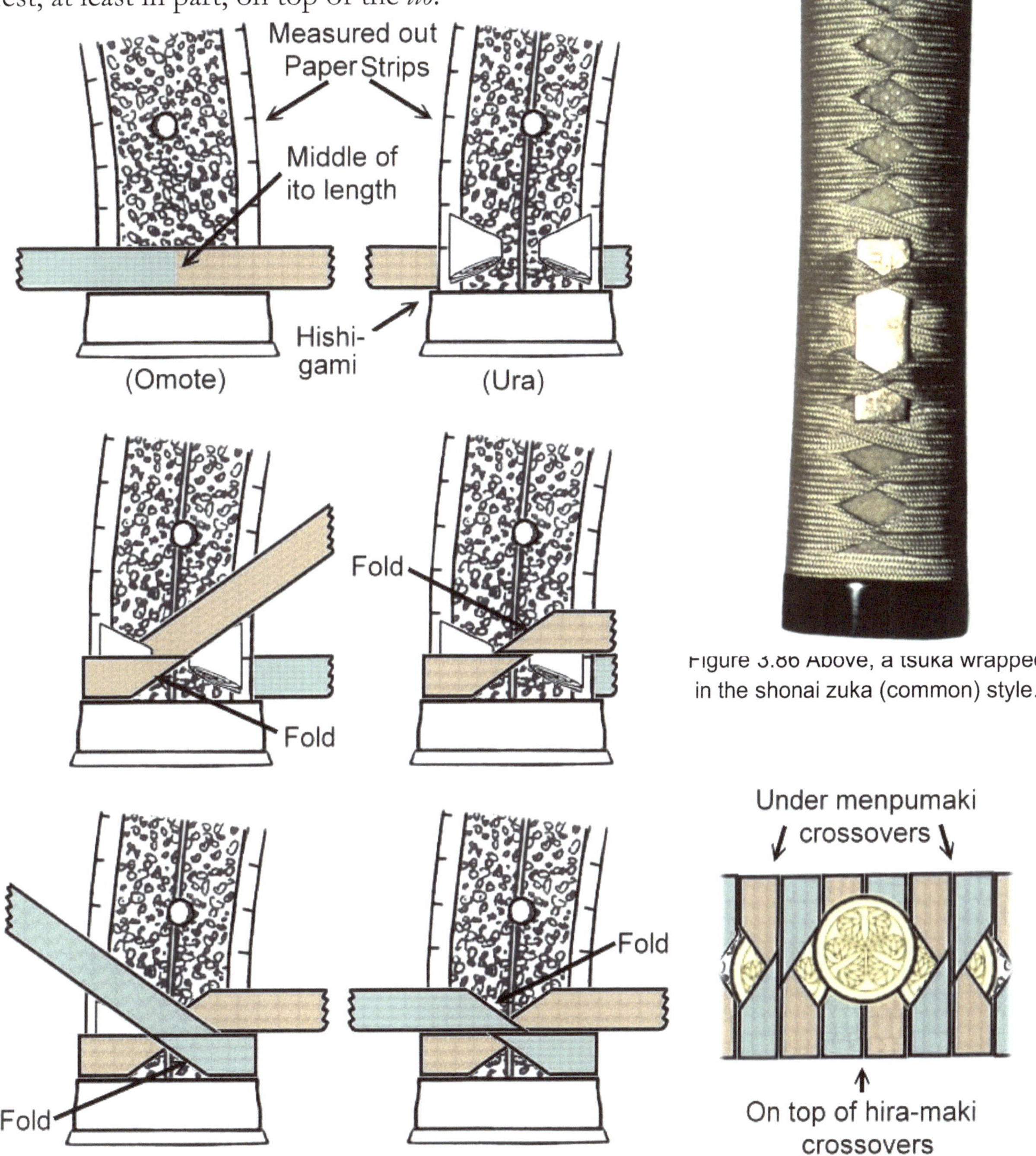

Figure 3.86 Above, a tsuka wrapped in the shonai zuka (common) style.

Figure 3.87 The opening steps, crossover technique and menuki placement.

3.22 Tachi Tsukagashira Kakemaki

This is a variation on the *hiramaki*, or flat wrap, specifically for *tachi*. Aside from the flat *ito*, the key distinguishing factors are the beginning side and the finishing knots.

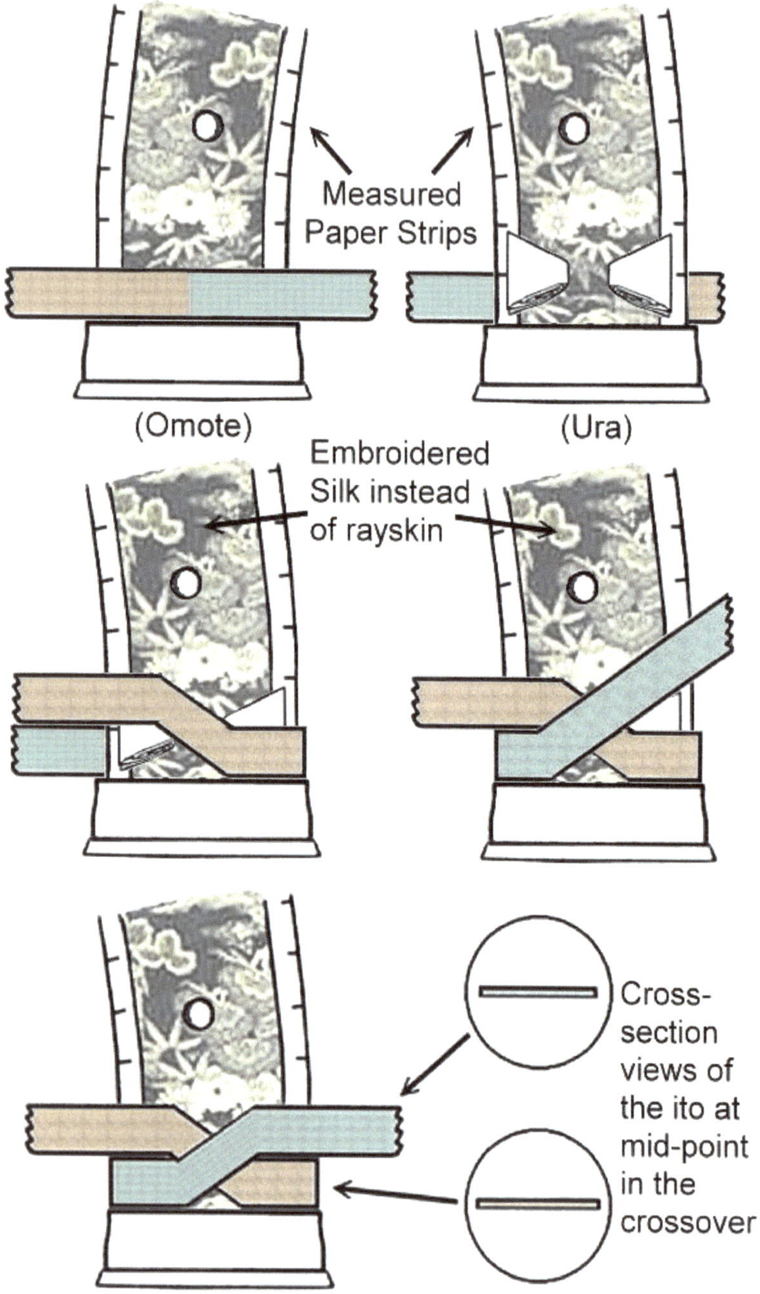

Measured Paper Strips

(Omote)

(Ura)

Embroidered Silk instead of rayskin

Cross-section views of the ito at mid-point in the crossover

Figure 3.89 The opening steps and crossover technique.

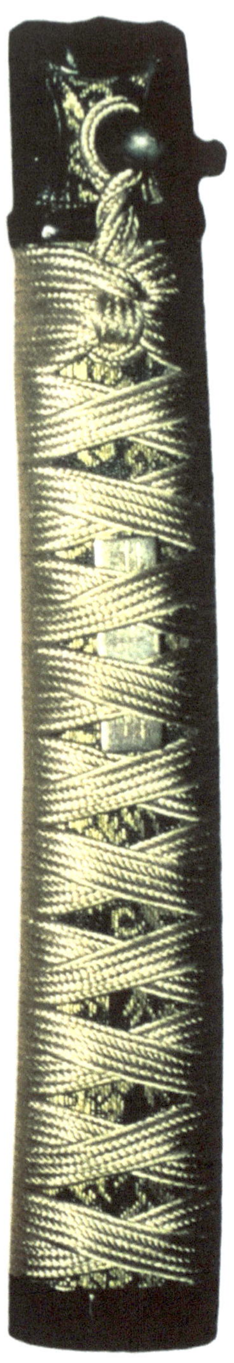

tsukagashira kakemaki tsuka.

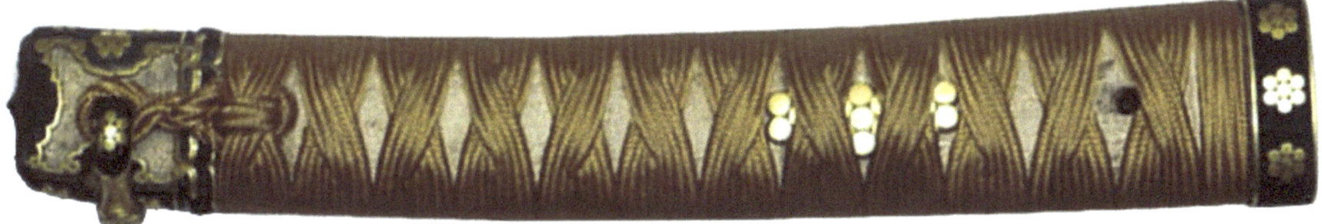

Figure 3.90 An example of a tachi tsuka with same' instead of an embroidered silk base.

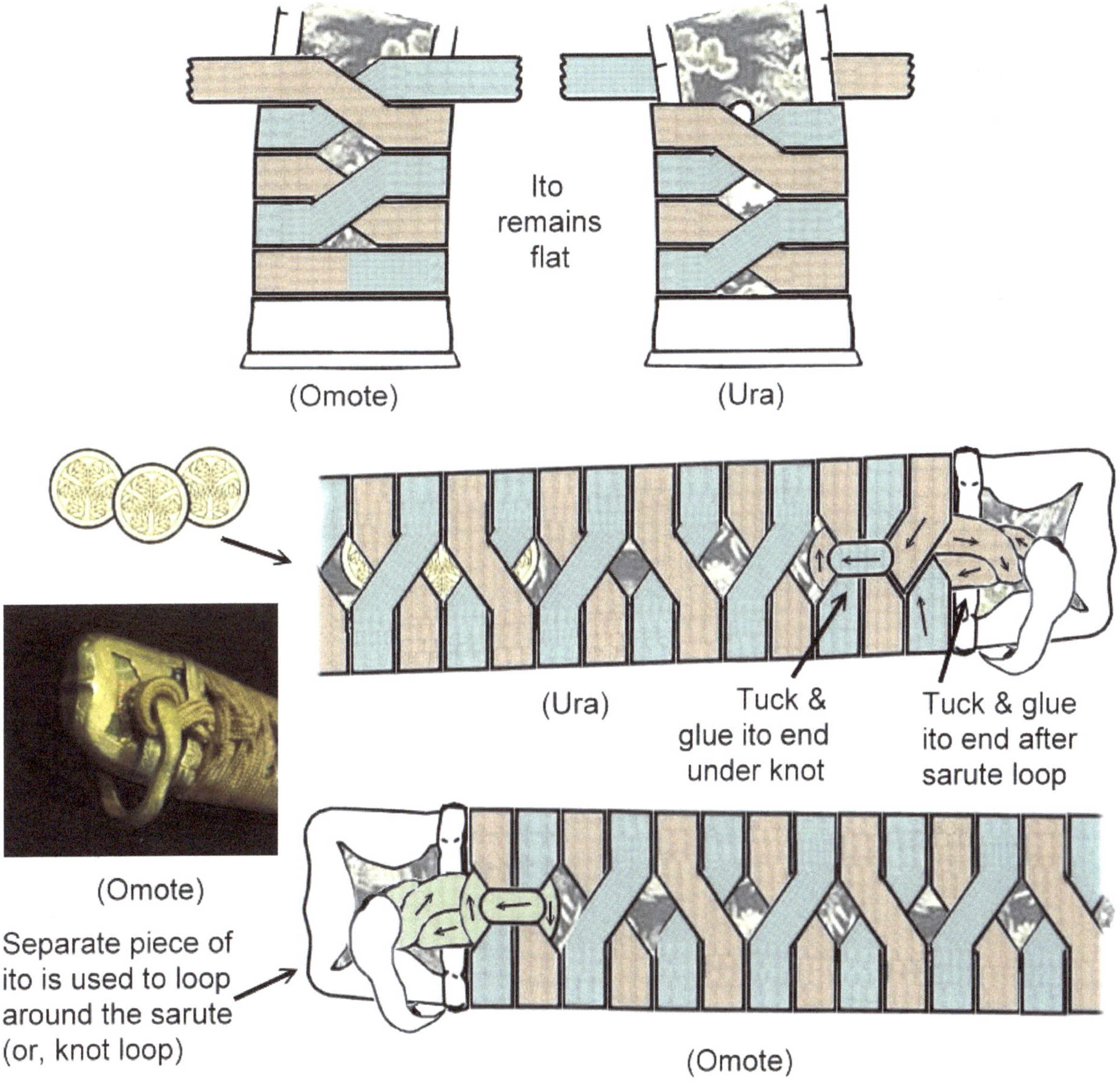

Ito remains flat

(Omote)

(Ura)

(Ura)

Tuck & glue ito end under knot

Tuck & glue ito end after sarute loop

(Omote)

Separate piece of ito is used to loop around the sarute (or, knot loop)

(Omote)

Figure 3.91 Menuki placement, final steps & ito looping around sarute.

3.23 Tomaki Nihon Kumiage Zuka

This style of *tsukamaki* is done using two narrow (4 mm) strips of leather *ito*, and follows the same basic pattern as a *kodai murasaku tsuka.*

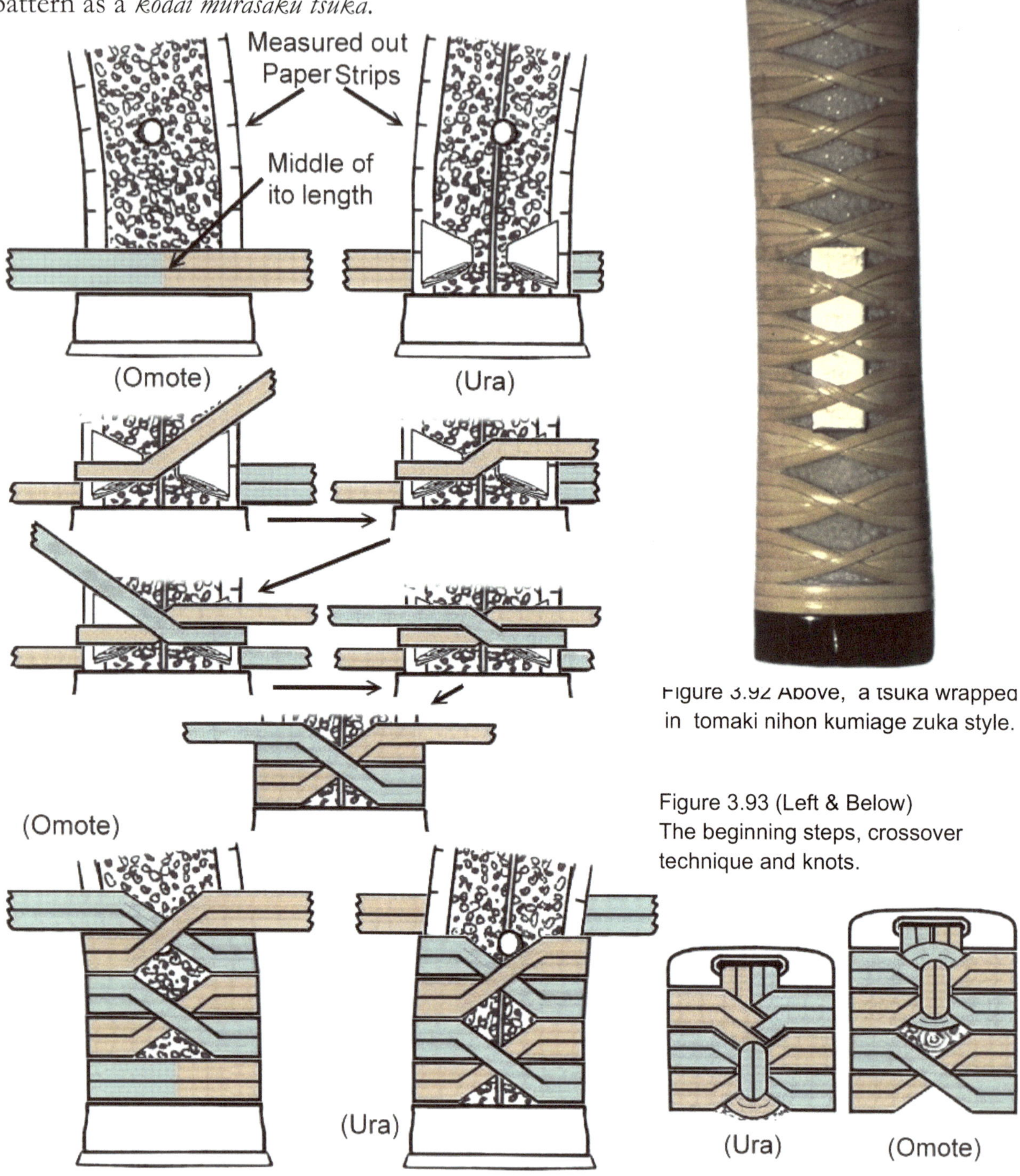

Figure 3.92 Above, a tsuka wrapped in tomaki nihon kumiage zuka style.

Figure 3.93 (Left & Below) The beginning steps, crossover technique and knots.

3.24 Tsumami Maki

Tsumami maki is one of the most common styles of *tsukamaki*. Although it is relatively simple in design, it is difficult to maintain even and uniform openings.

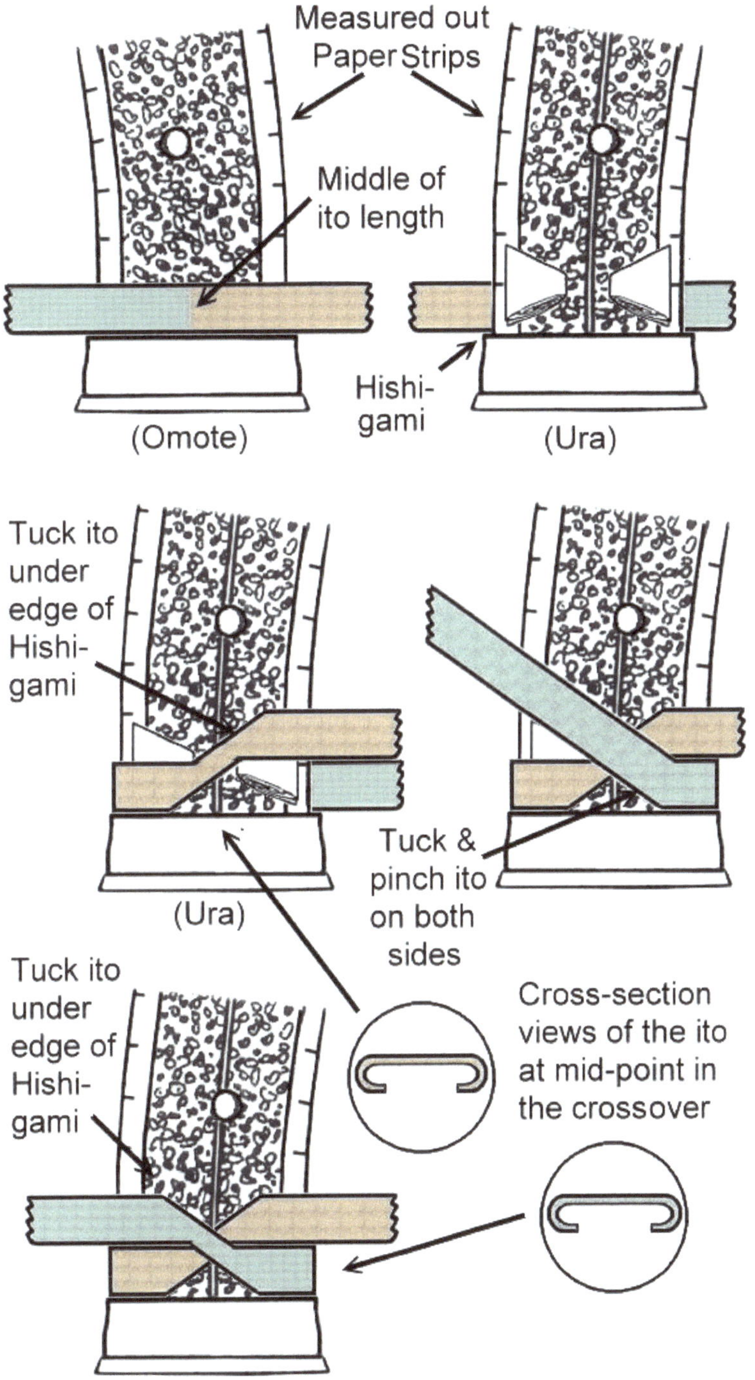

Measured out Paper Strips

Middle of ito length

Hishi-gami

(Omote)

(Ura)

Tuck ito under edge of Hishi-gami

(Ura)

Tuck & pinch ito on both sides

Tuck ito under edge of Hishi-gami

Cross-section views of the ito at mid-point in the crossover

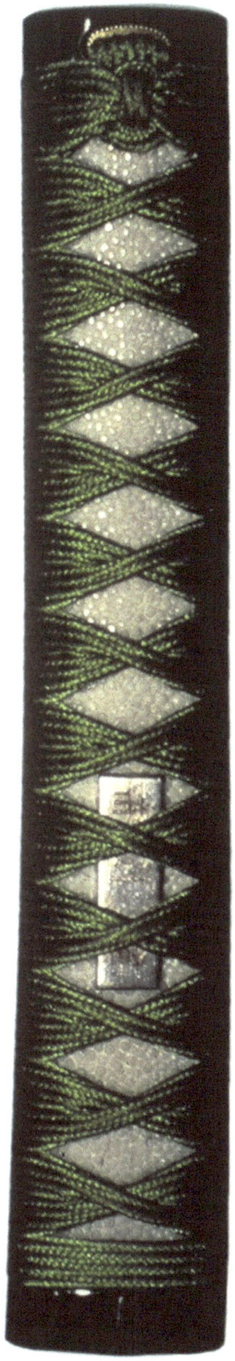

Figure 3.94 Above, a tsuka wrapped in tsumami maki.

Figure 3.95 (Left) The beginning steps and crossover technique.

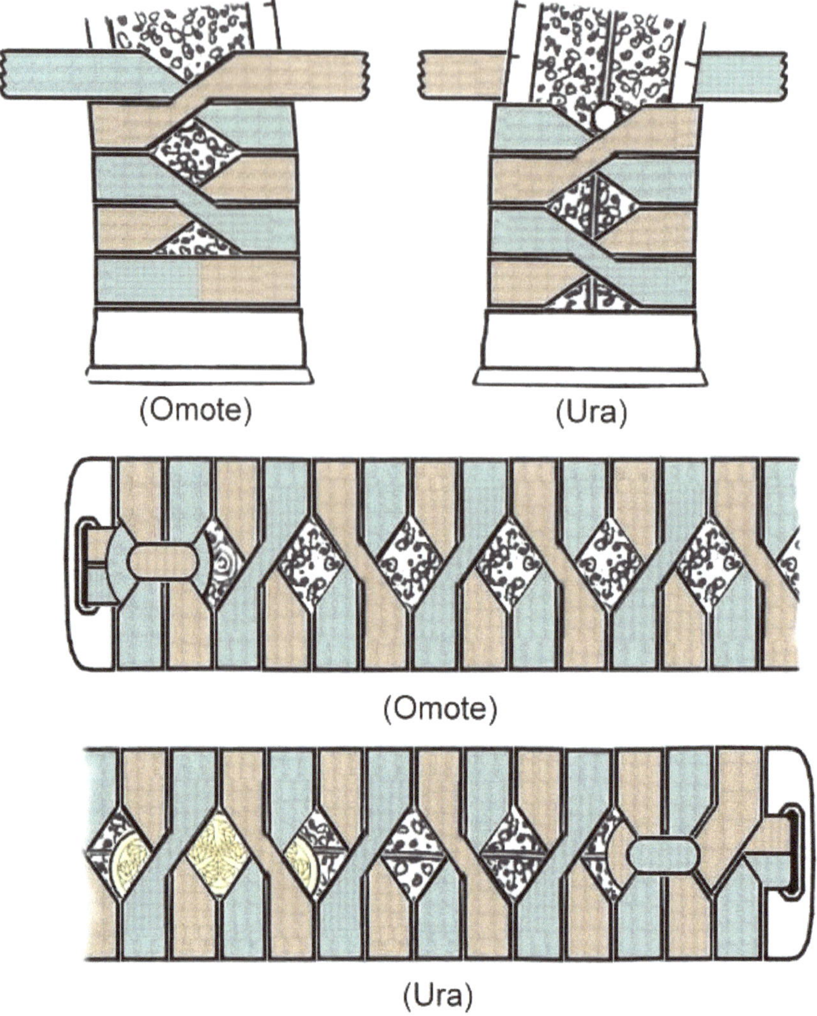

Figure 3.96 The crossover technique, menuki placement and end knots.

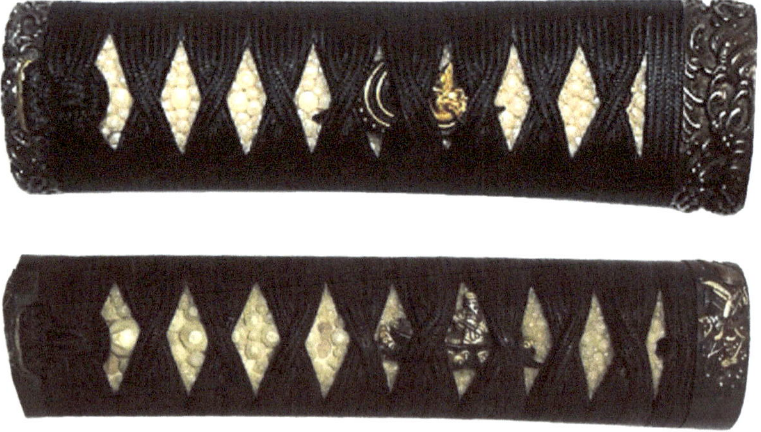

Figure 3.97 Two Edo Period tsuka wrapped in the tsumami maki style.

3.25 Yagyu Ryu Hiramaki

This version of *tsukamaki* specifically uses lacquered leather, or sealed leather, and is one of the hallmarks of *Yagyu Ryu*, a *kenjutsu* style founded by Kamiizumi Ise no Kami Nobutsuna and passed through the Yagyu family.

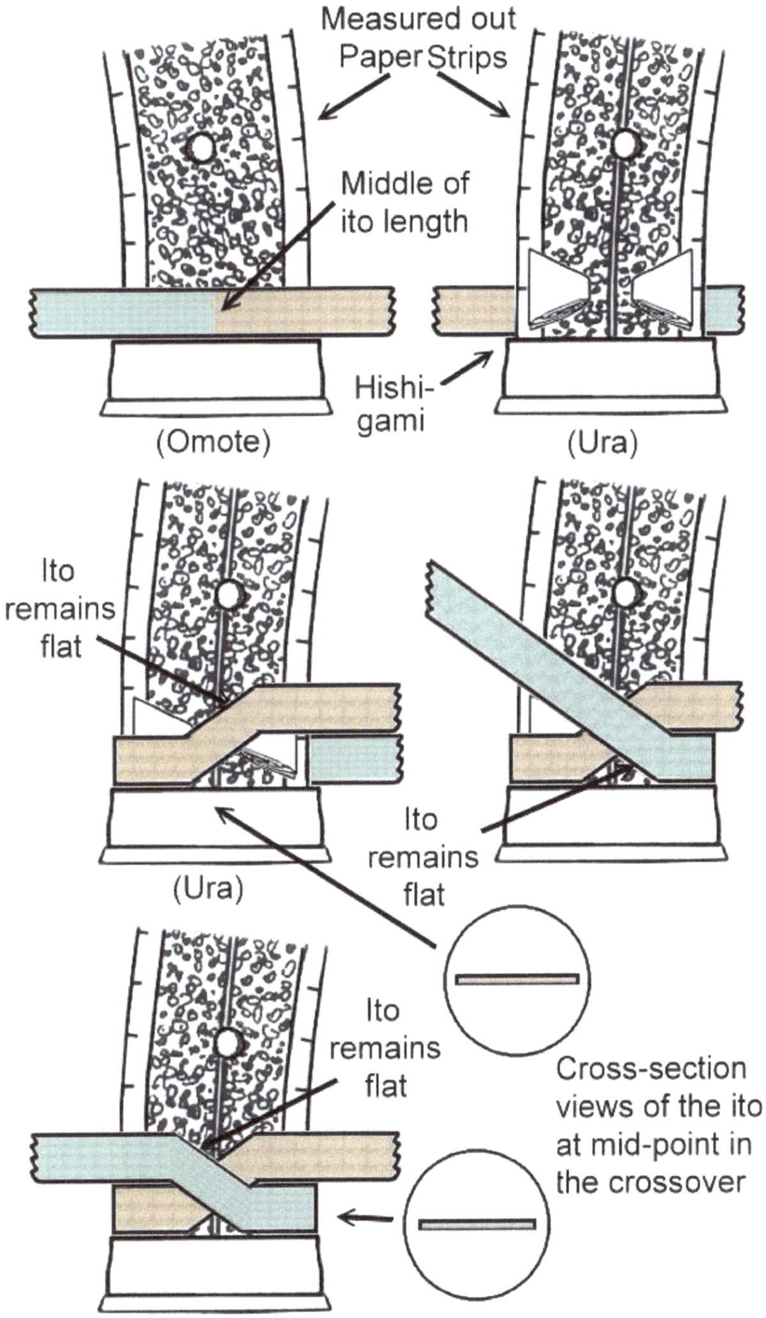

Measured out Paper Strips

Middle of ito length

Hishi-gami

(Omote)

(Ura)

Ito remains flat

(Ura)

Ito remains flat

Ito remains flat

Cross-section views of the ito at mid-point in the crossover

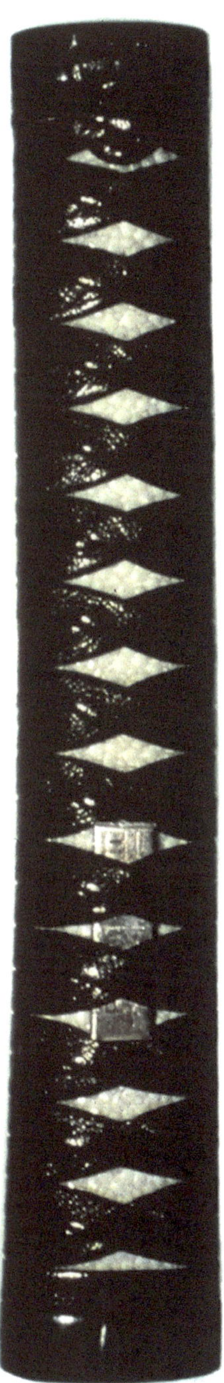

Figure 3.98 Above, a tsuka wrapped in the yagyu ryu hira-maki style.

Figure 3.99a (Left) The beginning steps and crossover technique.

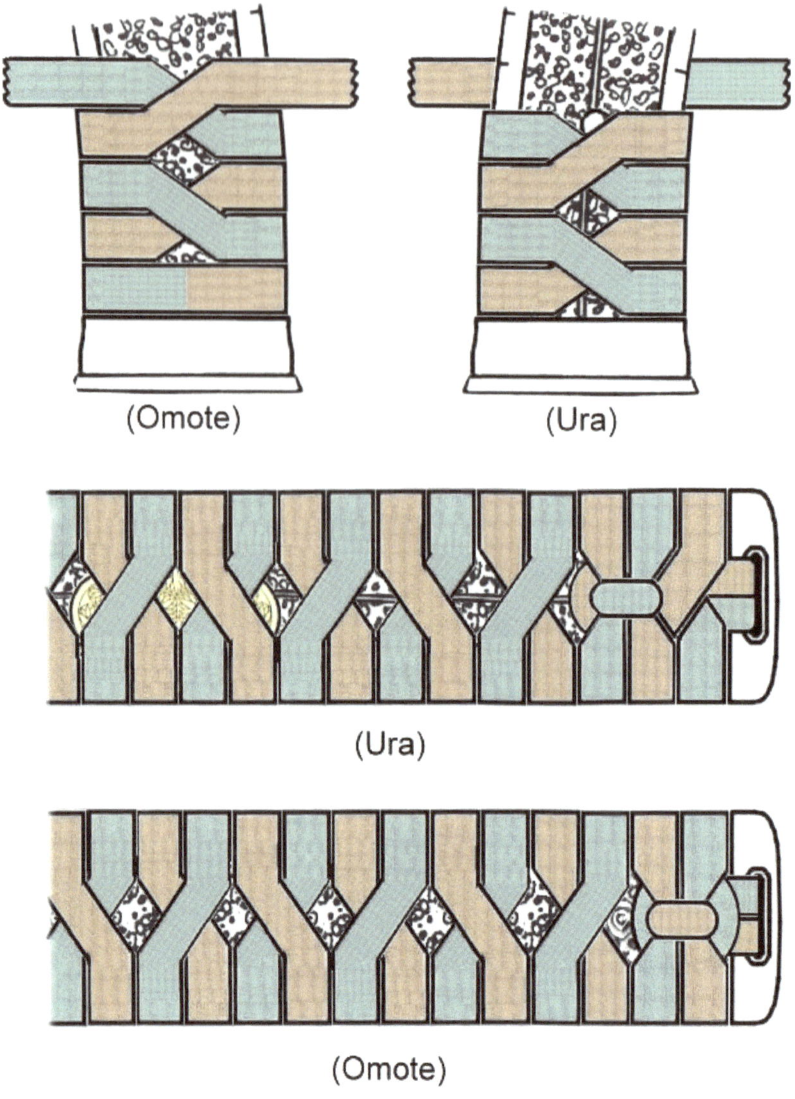

Figure 3.99b The crossover technique continued and the ending knots.

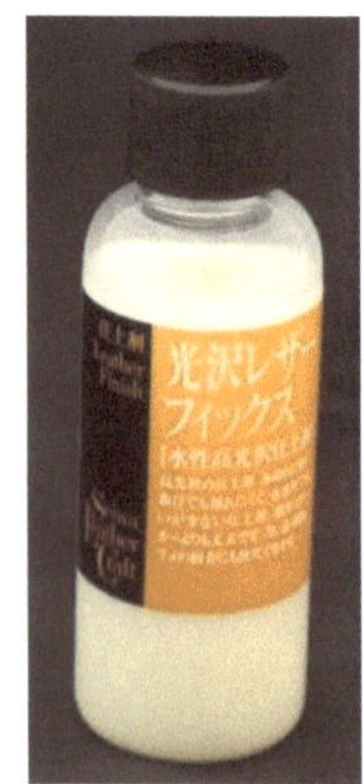

Figure 3.99c A 100 ml (4 fluid ounces) bottle of Seiwa lacquer sealant.

The high gloss leather finish on the *yagyu ryu hiramaki* style is unique in that it uses a water-based leather lacquer, instead of oil, that both seals the leatherwork from the elements and protects it from bumps, scrapes and heavy use. Unlike oil based lacquered leather finishes, it is more flexible and tends not to crack or peel. Seiwa (Fig. 3.99c) is a modern version of this traditional sealant.

4 A Visual Dictionary

Introduction

In studying the art of tsukamaki, or Japanese swords in general, an understanding of specific terms, components, and characteristics is a must. The goal of this section isn't to give an in depth comprehensive of sword concept and vocabulary, instead it is to provide easy-to-understand definitions and illustrations for quick reference, and a guide to further research. The main sections of this chapter are as follows:

COMPONENTS: SWORD MOUNTINGS

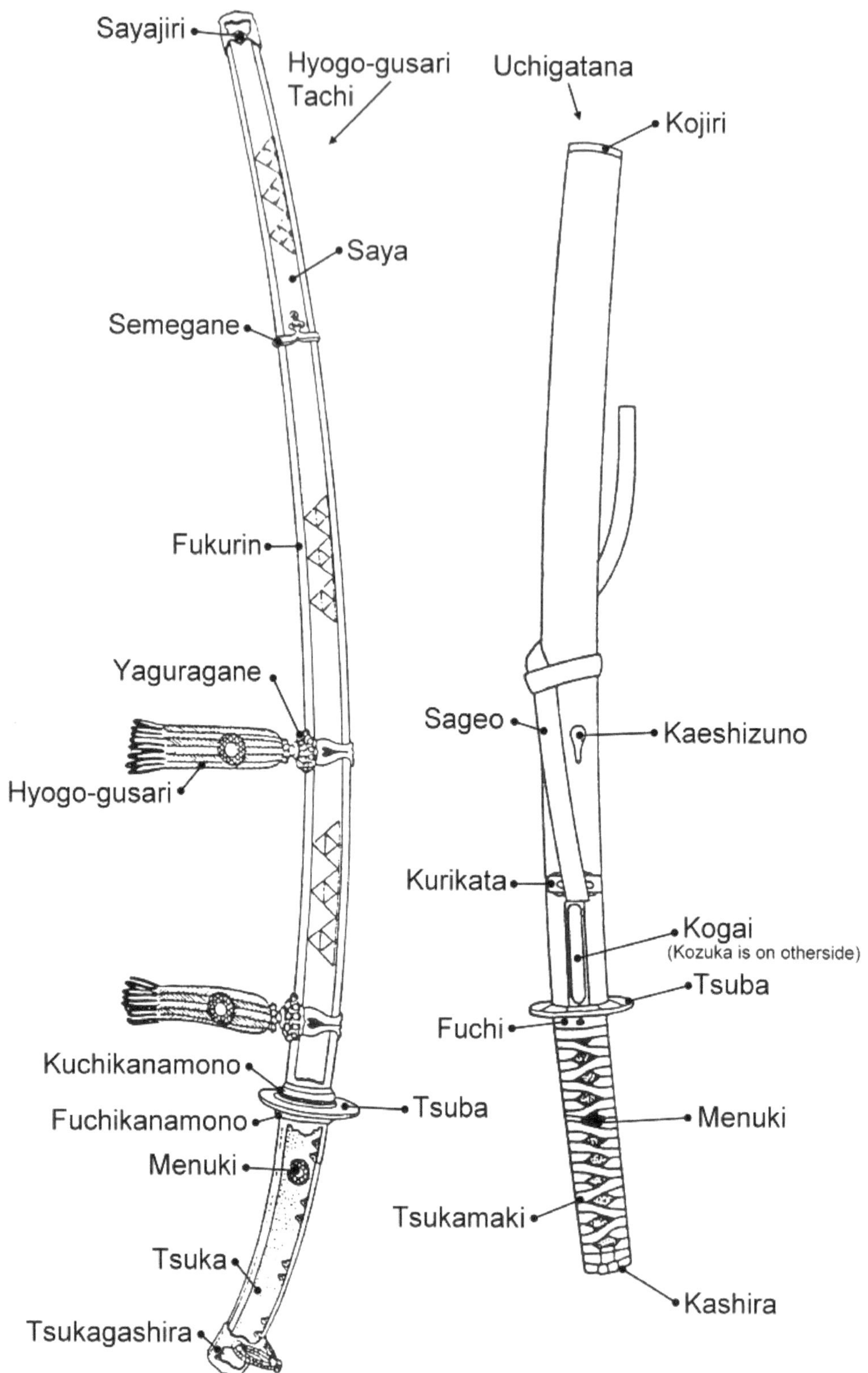

COMPONENTS: SWORD BLADE

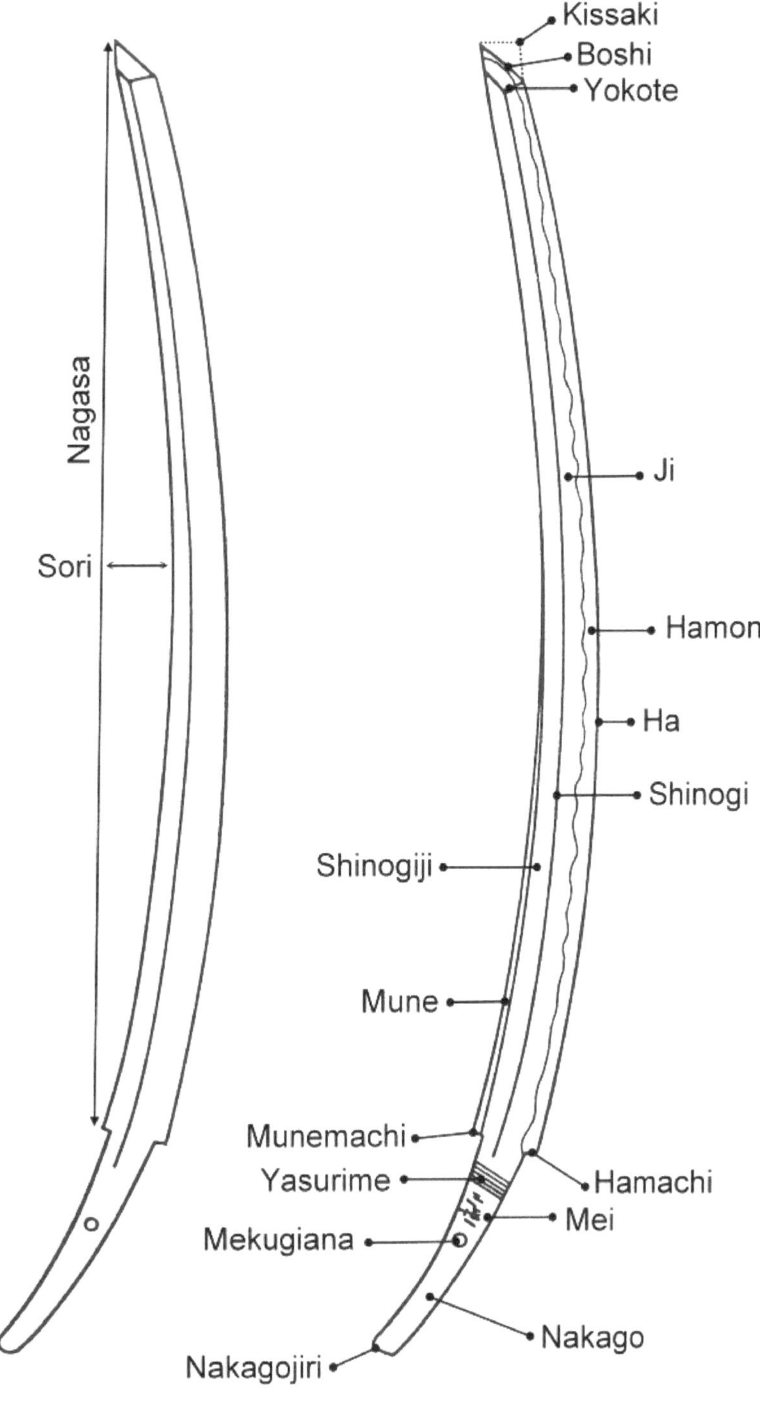

The Nakago: Shapes

In *tsukamaki*, a working knowledge of the specific *nakago*, or tang, characteristics (shape, markings, etc.) is essential.

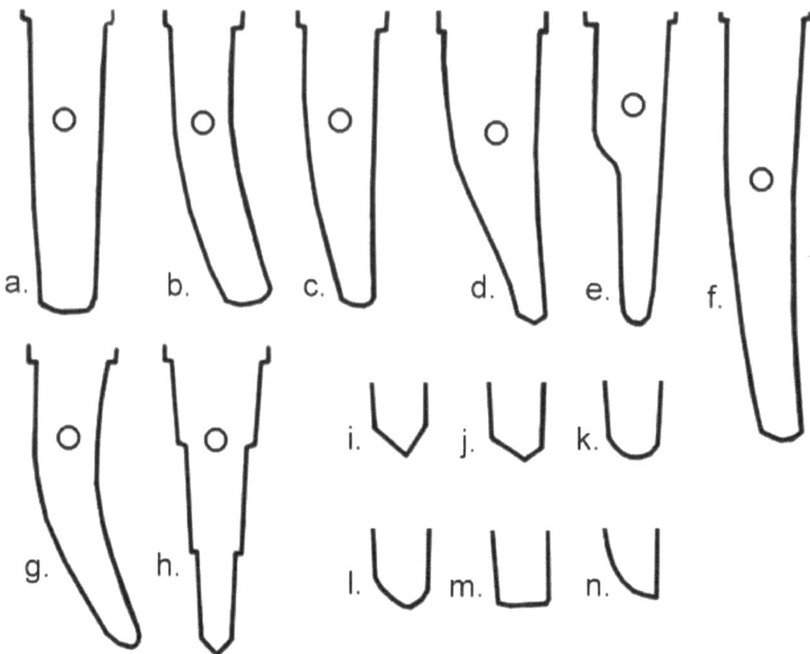

a. Shirihari (尻張り) – Tang with wide base flaring outward.
b. Furisode (振袖) – Tang tip curves back like kimono sleeve.
c. Tangobara (鱮腹) – Tang bulges like a fish's belly.
d. Tangobara (鱮腹) – Extreme fish belly.
e. Kijimata (雉子股) – Narrow tang flares slightly like pheasant tail.
f. Futsu (普通) – Standard, straight, gently tapered tang shape.
g. Funasoko (舟底) – Rounded tang end, like a boat bottom.
h. Goheigata (御幣形) – Stylized tang shaped like Shinto paper streamer.
i. Kengyo (剣形) – Pointed tang end with fan-like shape.
j. Katayama-kengyo (片山剣形) – Off-center pointed tang.
k. Kurijiri (栗尻) – Chestnut-shaped rounded end, common on tachi.
l. Haagari (刃上がり) – Tang slopes upward toward the cutting edge.
m. Kiri (切) – Flat, square-cut tang end; very common.
n. Katasogi (片削ぎ) – One-sided cut tang; asymmetrical tang end.

THE NAKAGO: FILE PATERNS

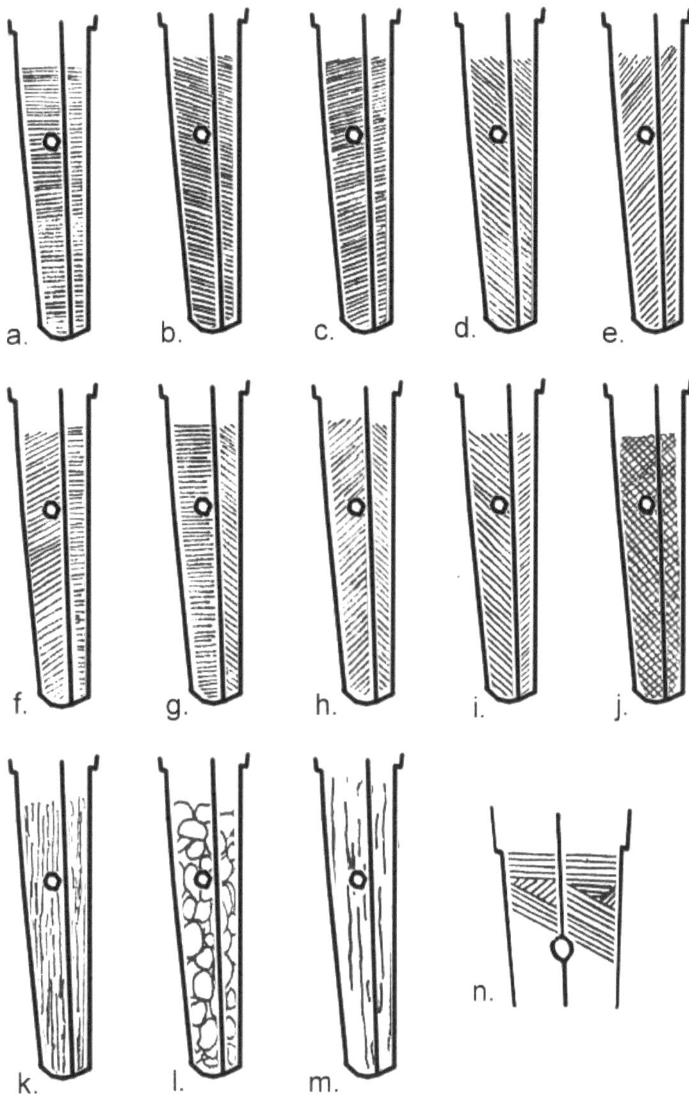

a. Yokoyasuri (横鑢) – Horizontal file marks across the nakago surface.
b. Katesagari (勝手下がり) – Diagonal marks slanting down to the left.
c. Kateagari (勝手上がり) – Diagonal marks slanting up to the right.
d. Sujikai (筋違い) – Regular oblique file marks across the tang.
e. Hidari-sujikai (左筋違い) – Reverse oblique file marks slanting.
f. Hirasujikai (平筋違い) – Oblique marks on the flat (hira) surface.
g. Hira-kiri shinogi sujikai (平切鎬筋違い) – Horizontal and oblique.
h. Takanoha (鷹の羽) – V-shaped file marks resembling hawk feathers.

i. Gyaku-takanoha (逆鷹の羽) – Reverse hawk feather pattern.
j. Higaki (檜垣鑢) – Criss-cross pattern like a cypress-lattice fence.
k. Midare (乱れ鑢) – Irregular or uneven file marks on tang.
l. Tsuchime (槌目) – Hammered texture; not a file mark pattern.
m. Sensuki (銑すき) – Draw-shaving marks left by shaping tools.
n. Kesho-yasuri (化粧鑢) – Decorative file patterns.

BLADE CROSS SECTIONS: COMPOSITION

Tsukamaki not only requires an understanding of the outside shape of the nakago, but also its cross-section shape and general composition. As illustrated below, to help obtain strength and sharpness, various methods of lamination were used of different levels of complexity, ranging from two to as many as seven pieces of soft to hard steel.

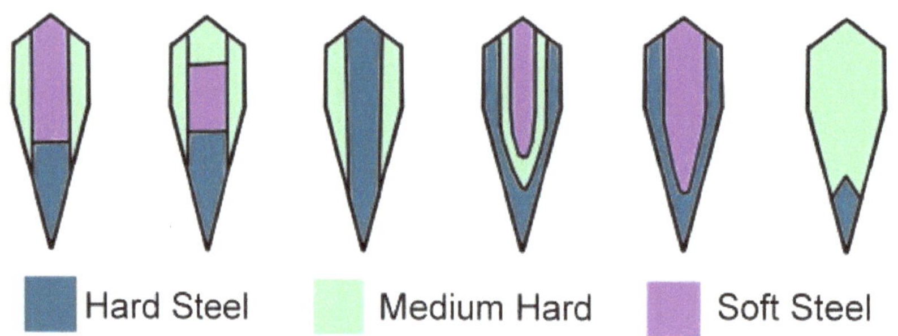

BLADE CROSS SECTIONS: SHAPE

In general, cross-section shapes can be broken down into three sections 1) the back, or mune; 2) the upper surfaces, or shinogi; and, 3) the cutting edge surfaces, or ji. The mune were everything from rounded to square; the shinogi were parallel or slanted; and, the ji was flat (no meat) or rounded (having meat). See illustration below.

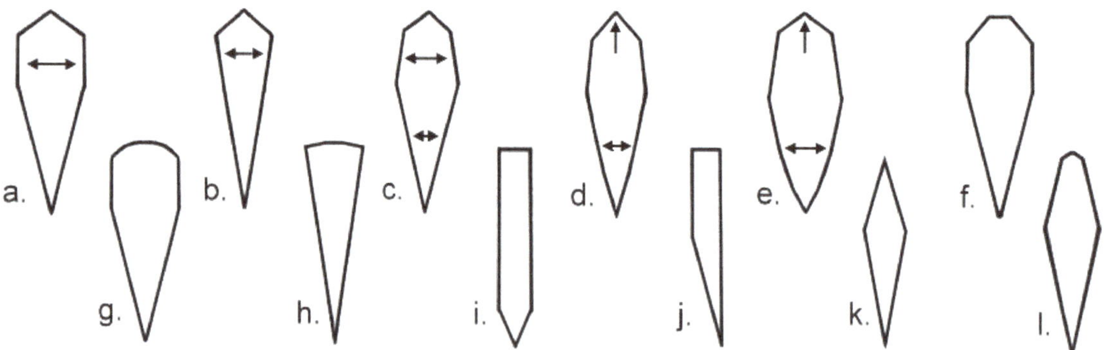

BLADE CROSS SECTIONS: SHAPE (cont.)

a. Parallel shinogi.
b. Low shinogi.
c. High shinogi; shishi-nashi (no meat).
d. High ihori-mune; sukunashi (little meat).
e. Normal ihori-mune; shishiari (much meat).
f. Shin-no-mune (three surface back).
g. Maru mune (round).
h. Hira mune (flat).
i. Kiriha-zukuri (ancient shape).
j. Katakiri edge (ancient shape).
k. Moroha tsukuri (diamond shaped).
l. Normal shape.

GENERAL TEMPER PATTERNS IN CHRONOLOGICAL ORDER

Late Heian to Early Kamakura Periods

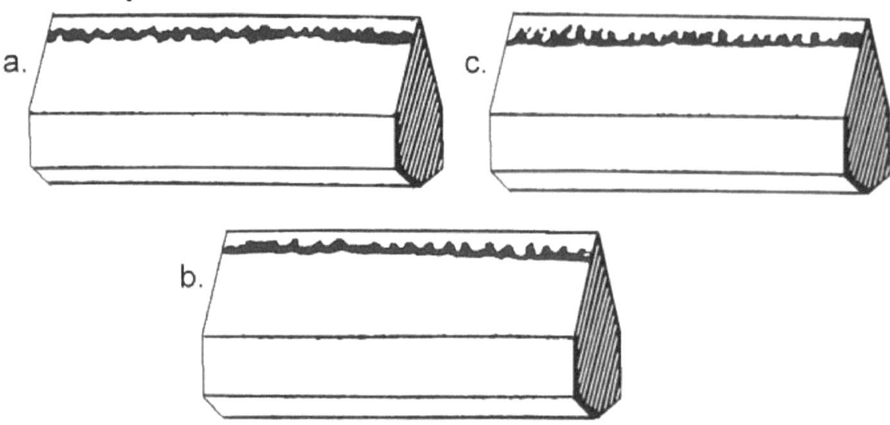

Mid Kamakura Period

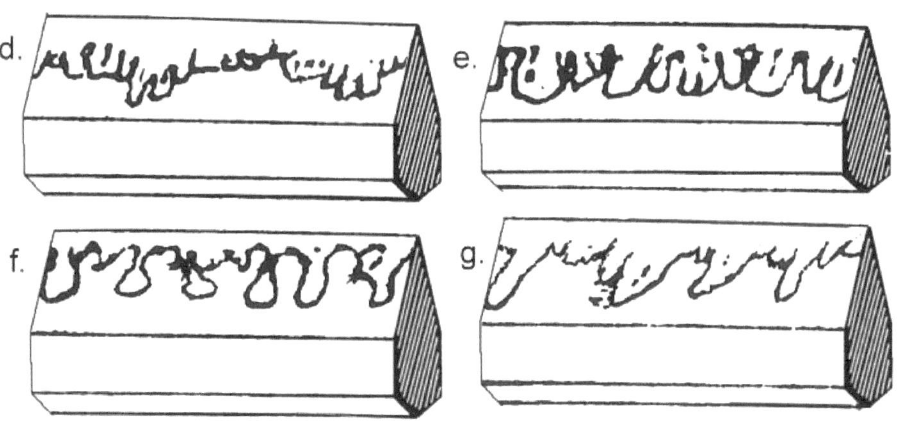

Late Kamakura Period

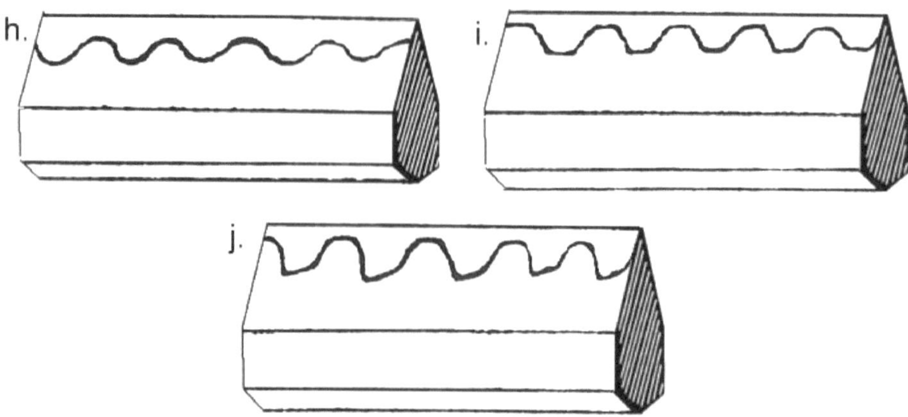

Nanbokucho Period

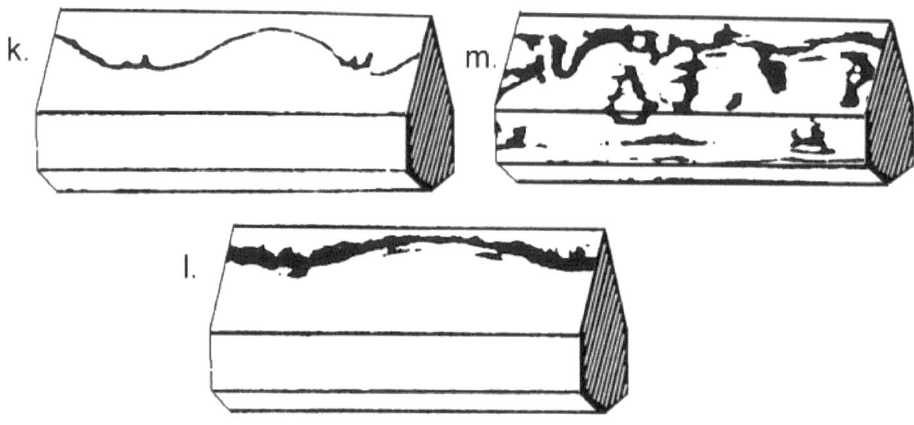

Early Muromachi Period

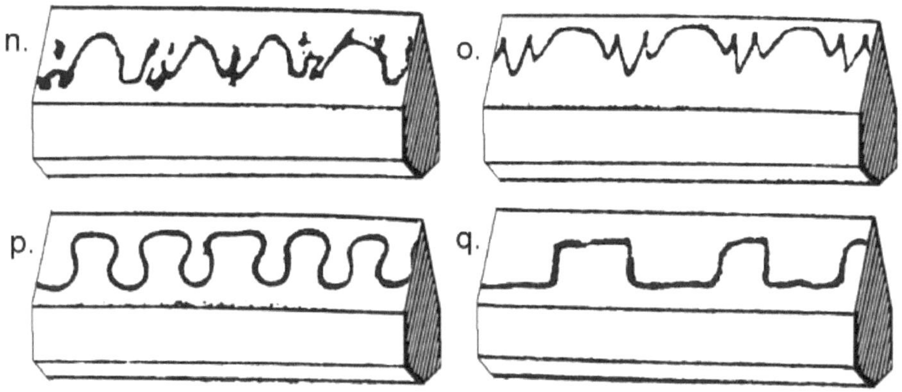

Late Muromachi Period

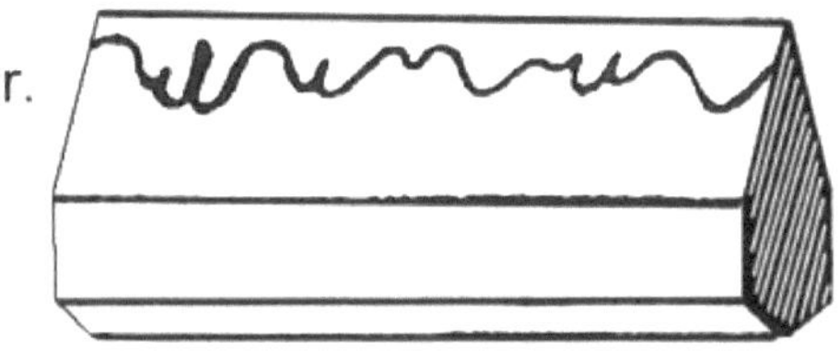

Momoyama to Mid Edo Period

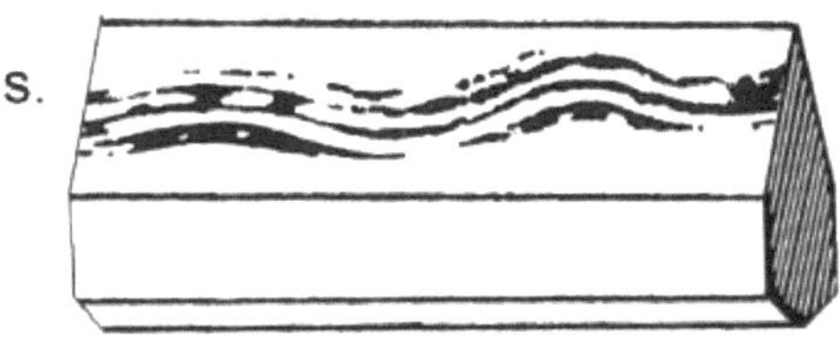

Mid Edo Period

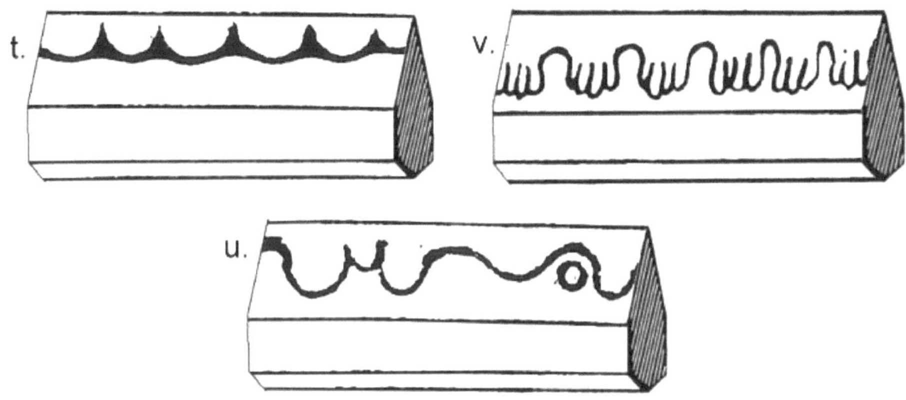

Common to All Times

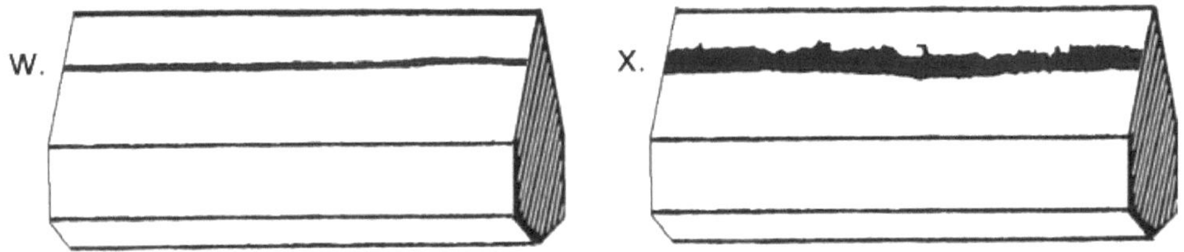

a. Ko midare in suguha
b. Ko choji in suguha
c. Ko gunome in suguha
d. Fuka-choji
e. Obusa-choji
f. Kawazuka-choji
g. Saka-choji
h. Gunome
i. Kakubari gunome
j. Kataochi gunome
k. Notare
l. Nie dominant notare
m. Hitatsura
n. Widely spaced complex gunome

o. Sanbonsugi
p. Kanehusa midare
q. hukoba.
r. widely spaced gunome mixed with choji
s. sudareba
t. sujuba
u. toranba
v. kengata-choji
w. nioi – tight suguha
x. nioi – deep suguha

SPECIFIC TEMPER PATTERNS CHARACTERISTICS

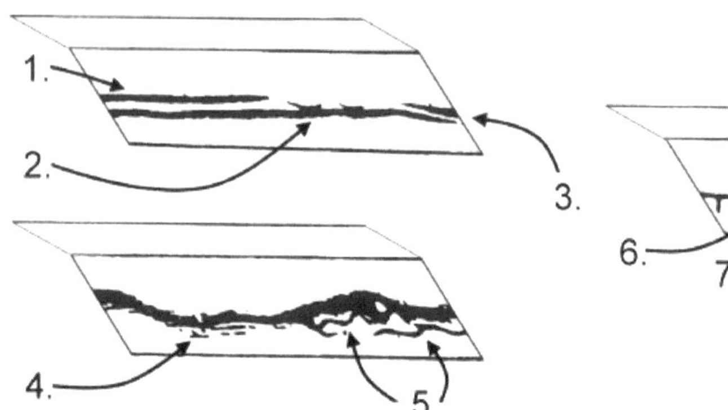

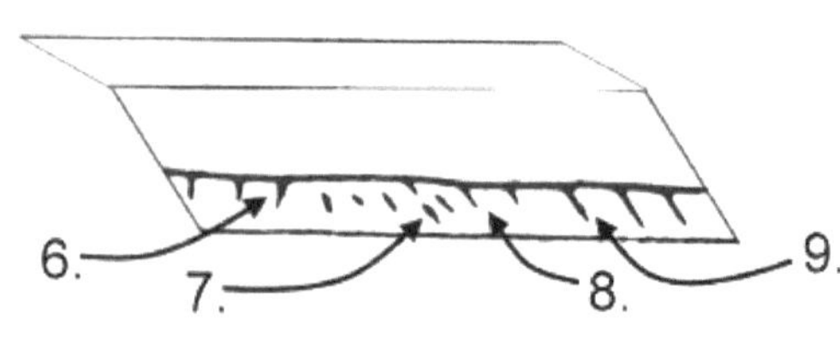

1. *Nijuba* – a second line of *hamon*, or temper, that appears parallel to the main *hamon* line.
2. *Uchinoke* – small 'new moon' shaped *nie* lines on blades of master smiths.
3. *Kuichigaiba* – lines of hamon which are not completely aligned, allowing for a gap between the tempered lines.
4. Long *ashi* – lines of *nioi* projecting into the ha at right angles.
5. *Ko-ashi* – a larger version of long *ashi*.
6. *Yo* – spots of *nioi* suspended in the *hamon*.
7. *Saka-ashi* – lines of *nioi* projecting into the *hamon* at slanted angles.
8. *Kinsuji* – literally 'Golden Line'; activity in the *hamon* resembling lightening.
9. *Sunagashi* – activity in the *hamon* that resembles brushed sand.

Common Signature Characters

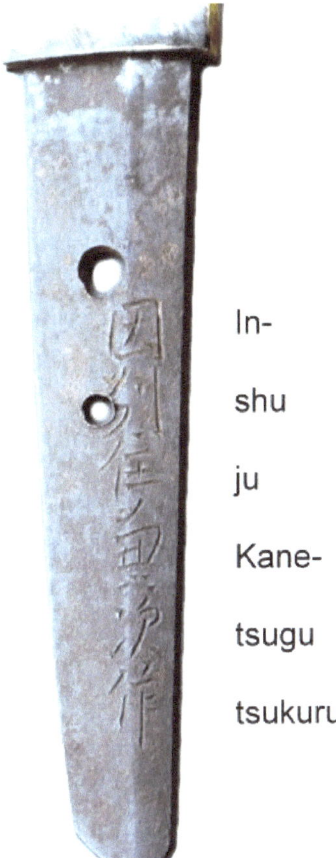

One of the difficulties in translating an artisan's *mei*, or signature, is in actually indentifying the signature's characters. Based on B. W. Robinson's work (Robinson, 1961), the following pages of this section include over 270 examples of the most common characters, or *kanji,* used in sword related signatures.

Reading Mei

In the signature to the left, the *mei* reads as "Inshu ju Kanetsugu tsukuru" or "this was made by Kanetsugu of Inshu." When reading signatures, it is important to remember that the name is at the end followed by the character "tsukuru," which means "made," and, in general, the first two characters list the town, province or tradition that he worked in. It should also be mentioned that in general the two character name is not the name given by parents at birth, but one selected by the artisan when he started signing works. It is a trade name that could be changed at will. Many artisans selected a name they used until they became experts. Ashamed of some of their early works, they later would change their name. Sometimes, when a pupil showed great ability, his instructor gave him a character from his own name as an honor. Regardless, an artisan adopted a new name when he considered himself proficient. To give a better idea of the difficulty in reading mei, below are *kanji* examples modeled after ones originally done by John Yumoto (Yumoto, 1958) illustrating various ways just these two signature characters could possibly appear.

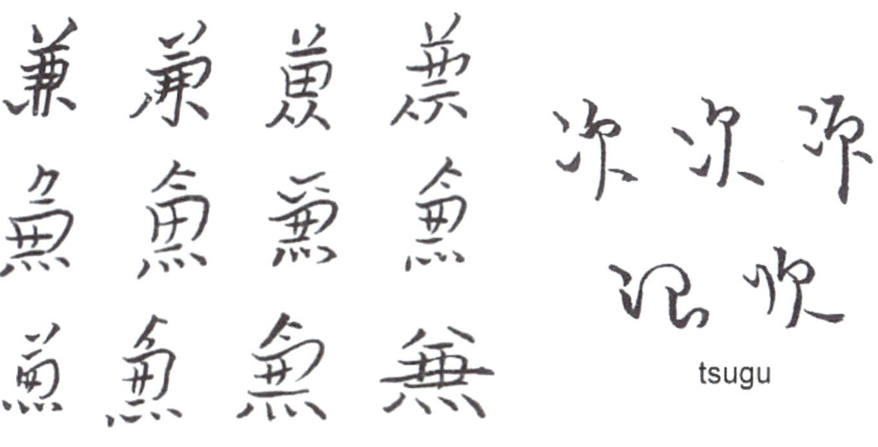

一 1	了 2	入 3	力 4	卜 5	三 6	下 7	千 8	久 9
上 10	大 11	丸 12	山 13	水 14	元 15	王 16	天 17	手 18
戸 19	氏 20	介 21	方 22	友 23	月 24	永 25	代 26	加 27
功 28	弘 29	外 30	正 31	平 32	生 33	冬 34	本 35	末 36
左 37	世 38	包 39	用 40	任 41	次 42	行 43	汎 44	西 45
舟 46	先 47	充 48	守 49	安 50	吉 51	在 52	有 53	旨 54
光 55	辻 56	作 57	阪 58	改 59	村 60	邦 61	利 62	助 63
里 64	秀 65	谷 66	良 67	完 68	克 69	孝 70	辰 71	延 72
成 73	戒 74	国 75	治 76	法 77	阿 78	政 79	明 80	門 81
刻 82	長 83	昌 84	命 85	京 86	宗 87	定 88	幸 89	奇 90
道 91	忠 92	房 93	虎 94	武 95	近 96	周 97	胤 98	信 99
保 100	俊 101	恒 102	持 103	秋 104	紀 105	則 106	軍 107	盈 108
是 109	重 110	泉 111	宣 112	春 113	貞 114	美 115	若 116	英 117

茂 118	屋 119	風 120	倫 121	城 122	峰 123	院 124	格 125	時 126
神 127	祐 128	師 129	能 130	兼 131	乘 132	島 133	鬼 134	息 135
胃 136	高 137	家 138	泰 139	真 140	峯 141	座 142	御 143	清 144
陳 145	祥 146	教 147	野 148	章 149	常 150	基 151	康 152	通 153
國 154	順 155	隆 156	植 157	勝 158	雄 159	統 160	朝 161	雲 162
尊 163	景 164	奥 165	爲 166	森 167	堯 168	貴 169	盛 170	菊 171
賀 172	進 173	傳 174	經 175	路 176	歳 177	業 178	義 179	資 180
照 181	遊 182	道 183	圓 184	綱 185	實 186	壽 187	榮 188	遠 189
徹 190	德 191	隣 192	輝 193	寛 194	蓮 195	髪 196	慶 197	廣 198
儔 199	諶 200	賴 201	興 202	憲 203	繁 204	鎮 205	藏 206	麿 207
藤 208	繼 209	寶 210	續 211	鶴 212	顯 213	鷹 214	金 215	惠 216
子 217	仁 218	内 219	之 220	文 221	太 222	丹 223	四 224	仲 225
如 226	庄 227	兵 228	孚 229	赤 230	甫 231	序 232	味 233	知 234

雨 235	昆 236	易 237	宜 238	東 239	奈 240	典 241	芝 242	尚 243
珉 244	珍 245	彦 246	喜 247	哉 248	幽 249	悦 250	矩 251	郎 252
夏 253	節 254	勘 255	貫 256	就 257	善 258	琴 259	登 260	幹 261
意 262	與 263	墨 264	樂 265	隨 266	龍 265	親 266	霍 267	篤 268
盧 271	齋 272	竹 273	克 274	受 275	俗 276	理 277	尋 278	董 279

1. ichi; kazu
2. rio
3. niu
4. riki
5. boku
6. san; mitsu
7. shita; shimo
8. sen; chi
9. hisa
10. ko; ozuke
11. dai; o
12. maru
13. san; yama
14. sui; midzu
15. gen; moto
16. o
17. ten; ama
18. te;ju
19. to
20. uji
21. suke
22. kata
23. tomo
24. gwatsu
25. yei; naga
26. yo
27. ka
28. koto
29. hiro
30. to
31. masa
32. hei; hira
33. sho
34. fuyu
35. hon; moto
36. suye
37. sa
38. yo
39. kane
40. yu; mochi
41. tomo
42. tsugi; tsugu
43. gio; yuki
44. hiro
45. sai
46. fune
47. -zaki
48. mitsu
49. mori
50. yasu
51. yoshi
52. ari
53. ari
54. mune
55. mitsu
56. tsuji
57. saku
58. saka
59. kai
60. mura
61. kuni
62. toshi
63. suke
64. zato
65. hide
66. tani
67. rio; yoshi
68. kwan; sada
69. yoshi
70. taka
71. tatsu
72. yen; nobu
73. nari
74. kai
75. kuni
76. ji; haru
77. nori
78. a
79. masa
80. mei; mio; aki
81. mon; kado

82. toki
83. cho; naga
84. masa
85. mio
86. kei
87. so; mune
88. sada
89. yuki; yoshi
90. ki
91. kao
92. tada
93. bo; fusa
94. ko; tora
95. take
96. chika
97. chika
98. tane
99. shin; nobu
100. yasu
101. toshi
102. tsune
103. mochi
104. aki
105. ki
106. nori
107. gun
108. mitsu
109. kore
110. shige
111. sen
112. nobu
113. haru
114. sada
115. yoshi
116. waka
117. fusa
118. shige
119. ya; iye
120. kaze; fu
121. tomo
122. ki; jo; shiro
123. ho
124. in
125. kaku; nori
126. toki
127. shin
128. suke; yu
129. moro; shi
130. yoshi
131. kane
132. ju; nori
133. shima
134. ki; oni
135. soku
136. mune
137. taka
138. iye
139. yasu
140. shin; sane
141. ho
142. za
143. go
144. kiyo
145. chin; nobu
146. yoshi
147. nori
148. no
149. aki
150. tsune
151. moto
152. yasu
153. michi
154. kuni
155. jun
156. taka
157. uye
158. katsu
159. o
160. mune
161. tomo
162. un
163. son
164. kage
165. oku
166. tame
167. mori
168. taka
169. taka
170. mori
171. kiku
172. yoshi
173. shin
174. ten; den
175. tsune
176. michi
177. toshi
178. nari
179. yoshi
180. suke
181. teru
182. yu
183. michi
184. yen
185. tsuna
186. sane
187. ju; toshi
188. yei
189. to
190. tetsu
191. toku; nori
192. rin; chika
193. teru
194. kwan; hiro
195. ren
196. kami
197. kei; yoshi
198. hiro
199. tomo
200. shin
201. yori
202. oki
203. nori
204. han
205. shige
206. kura
207. maro
208. fuji; to
209. tsugi; tsugu
210. ho
211. tsugi; tsugu
212. tsuru
213. aki
214. taka
215. kin; kana
216. kei
217. ko
218. nin
219. nai
220. yuki

221. fumi
222. ta
223. tan
224. shi
225. naka
226. jo
227. sho
228. hei
229. sane
230. aka
231. ho
232. tsune
233. mi
234. tomo
235. u
236. kon
237. yasu
238. yoshi
239. to
240. na
241. ten
242. shi
243. nao
244. min
245. shin
246. hiko
247. yoshi
248. sai
249. yu
250. yetsu
251. nori
252. ro
253. natsu
254. chu
255. kan
256. tsura
257. nari
258. yoshi
259. kin
260. nari
261. moto
262. i
263. yo
264. boku
265. raku
266. yuki; zui
267. tatsu
268. chika
269. kwaku
270. toku
271. yoshi
272. sai
273. chiku
274. katsu
275. tsugu
276. yo
277. masa
278. jin
279. tada

Glossary of Sword Terms

A

Aikuchi – tanto up to 30 cm long (1 foot) mounted without tsuba.

Ara-nie (荒沸) – coarse or large nie (large nie crystals)

Arashiage (荒仕上げ) – the rough finishing on a sword.

Asai-notare (浅いのたれ) – a shallow undulating hamon.

Ashi (足) – leg or foot. Short lines extending from patterns of nie or nioi.

Ashi kanamono (足金物) – a metal suspension fitting or band attached to a tachi's saya (scabbard), through which cords are threaded to suspend the sword edge-down from the obi.

Ashi sadamaru (足定まる) – a steady hamon pattern either straight or wavy.

Ashi-naga (足長) – long ashi.

Azuki midare (小豆乱れ) – temper line like a row of small beans.

B

Bakufu (幕府) – military government of the shogun

Bizen (備前) – archaic province of Japan, modern day Okayama prefecture

Bizen-to (備前刀) – swords produced in Bizen

Bizen-zori (備前反り) – deep curvature close to the tang area of the sword; also known as koshi-zori

Bohi (棒樋) – wide groove almost fitting shinogi surface.

Bohi soyebi (棒樋添樋) – wide groove beside a narrow groove.

Boshi (帽子) – shape of temper line at the kissaki (point).

Boshisaki (帽子先) – the very tip of the boshi temper line.

Bugei (武芸) – military arts – use of sword, etc.

C

Chigau midare (違う乱れ) – oblique hamon of Bitchu blades.

Chiisa gatana (小さ刀) – a general term for swords shorter than a standard katana, often referring to blades between wakizashi and katana lengths.

Chiji komasame (縮小小杢目) – undulating fine straight grain of suwo nio smiths.

Chiji midare (縮み乱れ) – wrinkled irregular hamon by miike & kongobyoe groups.

Choji (丁子) – clove seed shape folds in hamon. Many varieties.

Choji-midare (丁子乱れ) – clove shapes mixed with irregular patterns in hamon.

Chu-kissaki (中切先) – medium sized point (kissaki).

Chu-suguba (中直刃) – medium width straight hamon (follows curve of sword).

D

Daimyo (大名) – feudal lord.

Daisho (大小) – (large-small) a matched pair of swords or fittings for same.

Daito (大刀) – long sword (over 60.6 cm or 24 inches)

Dambira (ダンビラ / 段平) – very wide blade.

Doran or *toran* (濤欄 / 波濤乱れ) – high wave patterns of hamon.

F

Fuchi (縁) – collar on hilt.

Fuchi-kanamono (縁金物) – the ornamental ring around the end of a tachi tsuka next to the tsuba.

Fuchi-kashira (縁頭) – set of hilt collar (fuchi) and butt cap (kashira)

Funagata (舟形) – ship bottom shaped nakago (tang).

Furisode (振袖) – a tang shape with the end deeply curved toward the back side which resembles a kimono sleeve.

G

Gassan hada (月山肌) – grain made by gouging with round chisel then flatten.

Gendaito (現代刀) – traditionally forged sword blades by modern , particularly before and during World War II. These are not mass-produced and follow traditional methods.

Gimei (偽銘) – a false signature on a blade. Usually a copy of a famous smith to increase the sword's value.

Gunome (互の目) – undulating or semi-circular hamon pattern.

Gunto (軍刀) – army or military sword mountings.

H

Ha (刃) – cutting edge of a sword.

Hada (肌) – grain in steel, pattern of folding the steel.

Hamachi (刃区) – the notch at the end of the edge that the habaki rests against.

Hamidashi (はみ出し) – tanto with small guard.

Hamon (刃文) – temper pattern along blade edge

Handachi (半太刀) – tachi mountings used on a katana or wakizashi

Hi (樋) – grooves cut in a sword.

Hiki hada (引き肌) – leather scabbard cover.

Horimono (彫物) – carvings on blades.

Hyogo-gusari (兵庫鎖) – the chain link or leather attachment that the tachi is suspended by.

J

Ji (地) – sword surface between the shinogi and the hamon.

Ji-hada (地肌)– surface texture – course or fine of various patterns of hada.

Jin wakizashi (陣脇差) – medium length sword worn with a tachi.

K

Kabuto-gane (兜金) – tachi style pommel cap.

Kaeshizuno (返し角) – a hook on the side of the saya designed to catch on the obi, or sash, of the wearer.

Kai gunto (海軍刀) – naval sword produced during WWII.

Kantei (鑑定) – study and appraisal of swords.

Kashira (頭) – cap on the end of handle – pommel.

Kasumi no oshie (霞の教え) – a misty nioi in blades of hizen yoshikage.

Katana (刀) – long sword worn edge up in sash by samurai.

Katana mei (刀銘) – signature side that faces out when worn edge up.

Katana kake (刀掛け) – sword stand for horizontal display.

Katana hira (刀平) – flat of the blade.

Ken (剣) – straight double edged sword.

Kinko (金工) – soft metal sword fittings (not iron).

Kiri-ha (切刃造り) – flat sword with both sides beveled to the edge.

Kiri nakago (切り茎) – tang cut off square, usually in shortened blades.

Kiri suji-chigai (切筋違い) – file marks.

Kissaki (切先) – the point of a blade. Many shapes.

Kodomo daisho (子供大小) – a child's pair of swords.

Kogai (笄) – hair arranger fitted in pocket opposite kozuka, on some swords.

Kogatana (小刀) – a small utility knife with a kozuka handle, sometimes said to have been used for marking or carrying trophy heads (though this use is debated).

Koiguchi (鯉口) – the mouth of the scabbard or its fitting.

Kojiri or sayajiri (鐺 / 鞘尻) – bottom end fitting on scabbard.

Koshirae (拵え) – sword mountings including scabbard, handle and fittings.

Koto (古刀) – old sword period (prior to 1596).

Ko-uchi katana (小打刀) – short fighting sword before wakizashi came in style.

Ko-wakizashi (小脇差) – short wakizashi of 1 foot to 1 foot 4 inches (about 30–42 cm) long.

Kozuka (小柄) – a small utility knife fitted into a pocket on the side of a saya. It is part of the koshirae and paired with a kogatana blade.

Kuchikanamono (口金物) – the ornamental ring around the mouth of a tachi scabbard.

Kuni (国) – province, town or city.

Kuri-jiri (栗尻) – chestnut shape tang end.

Kurikata (栗形) – scabbard (saya) fitting for attaching the sageo.

M

Maki ito (巻糸) – braid for handle wrapping.

Mei (銘) – signature chiseled on a blade, mostly on the tang. Signature is away from body when worn - katana - edge up, tachi - edge down. A few exceptions.

Mekugi (目釘) – bamboo peg used to secure the tsuka (handle) to the nakago (tang).

Mekugi-ana (目釘穴) – the hole in the nakago through which the mekugi is inserted..

Menuki (目貫) – ornaments under handle wrapping to improve grip.

Mi (身) – the main body of the sword blade, excluding the nakago (tang). Includes the edge, surface, ridge, and point.

Midare choji (乱れ丁子) – irregular clove seed shapes in hamon.

Mon (紋) – family crest.

Mumei (無銘) – no signature (unsigned blade).

Mune (棟) – back ridge of sword blade.

Munemachi (棟区) – the notch at the end of the mune that the habaki rests against.

N

Nagasa (長さ) – blade length (from tip of kissaki to munemachi).

Naginata (薙刀) – A polearm featuring a curved blade mounted on a long shaft..

Nakago (茎) – tang of a blade.

Nakago-jiri (茎尻)– the end of the tang.

Nakago mune – back of a tang. Several shapes; flat or rounded.

Nanako (魚子地) – a fine, raised dimpled texture on soft metal surfaces of sword fittings (e.g., fuchi, kashira), resembling fish roe. Indicates refined workmanship.

Naoshi (直し) – a repaired or remounted sword blade.

Nie (沸) – fine white crystals formed in the hamon or ji.

Nioi (匂) – crystals like nie but much finer and darker. Hamon patterns may be made of nioi or a thread-like line of nioi may parallel or be mixed in with nie hamon (cloud like hamon). Presence of both is considered good.

O

O (大) – large or great. Used as a prefix to indicate size.

Obi (帯) – belt or sash.

O-choji (大丁子) – hamon of large choji (clove seed) patterns.

O-dachi (大太刀) – very long sword (over 30 inches).

O-kissaki (大切先) – large kissaki.

O-midare (大乱れ) – large irregular hamon pattern.

Omote (表) – the outer side of the sword as worn. On a katana (worn edge-up), omote faces outward. On a tachi (worn edge-down), the opposite side is the omote. Often bears the mei (signature); the reverse is called ura.

O-seppa (大切羽) – large seppa (usually on tachi).

Oshigata (押形) – rubbing of tang with inscription.

O-suriage (大磨上げ) – a blade that has been greatly shortened, typically with the mei (signature) removed. Common in older swords.

O-tachi (大太刀) – very long tachi, some are 5 or 6 feet long.

O-wakizashi (大脇差) – a longer wakizashi, typically approaching 2 shaku (~60 cm), close in length to a short katana.

S

Sageo (下緒)– cord or braid attached to kurikata on side of scabbard.

Saka-choji (逆丁子) – choji shapes slanting down toward base of blade.

Saka-gonome (逆互の目) – slanted gonome hamon pattern.

Saki (先) – tang end of a sword blade.

Saku (作) – kanji on tang meaning "made".

Saku kore (作是) – "made this".

Sanbonsugi (三本杉) – three cedar trees pattern hamon; Mino School.

Saya (鞘) – the scabbard of the sword, often made of wood and lacquered.

Sayajiri (鞘尻) – the end of the tachi scabbard.

Sayashi (鞘師) – scabbard maker.

Semegane (責金) – the bands on the scabbard of a tachi.

Seppa (切羽) – washers to fill out space provided for tsuba on blade.

Shakudo (赤銅) – copper and gold alloy used for sword fittings

Shinogi (鎬) – ridges on each side of a blade.

Shinogi ji (鎬地) – sword flat between the mune and shinogi.

Shinogi zukuri (鎬造り) – a blade shape with a well-defined shinogi ridge and kissaki, typical of most katana.

Shin no kurikara (真の倶利伽羅) – horimono of dragon twined around sword.

Shinto (新刀) – new sword period (1596 to 1781).

Shin-shinto (新新刀) – new-new sword period (1781 to 1868).

Shira-saya (白鞘) – plain wood storage scabbard.

Shitodome (鵐目) – small collars in the kurikata and/or kashira.

Shoto (小刀) – short sword (between 12 and 24 inches).

Showa-to (昭和刀) – traditionally hand-forged sword in Showa Period – 1926 on. Not gunto.

Sori (反り) – the curvature of the blade.

Suguha (直刃) – straight temper line.

Suguba hotsure (直刃ほつれ) – straight hamon somewhat frayed in places.

Suriage (磨上げ) – shortened blade. All or part of tang cut off.

T

Tachi (太刀) – long sword worn with cutting-edge down.

Tachi mei (太刀銘) – signature facing away from body when worn edge down

Tameshi mei (試し銘) – gold inscription on tang describing test and by whom.

Tanto (短刀) – dagger or knife less than one foot long.

Togari (尖り) – pointed hamon patterns; saw teeth.

Togi mei (研ぎ銘) – polisher's signature inscribed with needle at base of blade.

Tsuba (鍔) – sword guard.

Tsuka (柄) – handle of a Japanese sword, covering the nakago (tang), traditionally wrapped in samegawa (rayskin) and ito (cord).

U

Uchigatana (打刀) – long fighting sword with tsuba, worn edge up.

Uchiko (打粉) – fine powder for cleaning swords.

Uki-menuki (浮目貫) – menuki outside the wrappings.

Ura-mei (裏銘) – signed on the ura (usually the date).

W

Wakizashi (脇差)– medium length sword from 1 shaku to 2 shaku (30.3 to 60.6 cm, or 12 to 24 inches)

Ware (割れ) – a flaw or opening in the steel of the blade. Can affect both appearance and structural integrity.

Y

Yamazakura (山桜) – small clove pattern resembling wild cherry blossoms.

Yari (槍) – straight spear; variants: futamoto-yari (二本槍) – 2 prongs; mitsumoto-yari (三本槍) – 3 prongs.

Yokote (横手線) – line between ji (blade) and kissaki (tip).

APPENDIX 1
TACHI SAYAMAKI

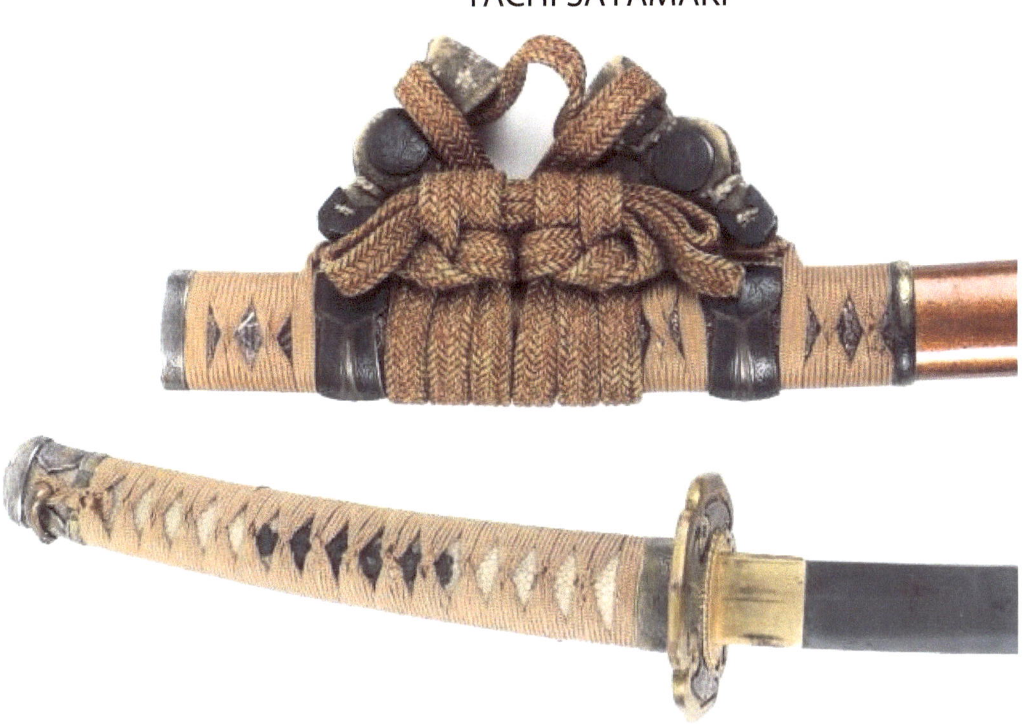

(An example of a mid-Edo period Tachi with Sayamaki)

Wrapping a tachi saya (scabbard) with ito is both a decorative and functional technique often seen on Kamakura period thru Edo period tachi that were worn with armor. This process, known as sayamaki (鞘巻き), is less common than tsukamaki, but follows similar principles. Here's a step-by-step overview of the process.

Step 1: Perform the same basic starting crossover style and techinques as you would when wrapping the tachi's tsuka, as displayed in the following diagrams.

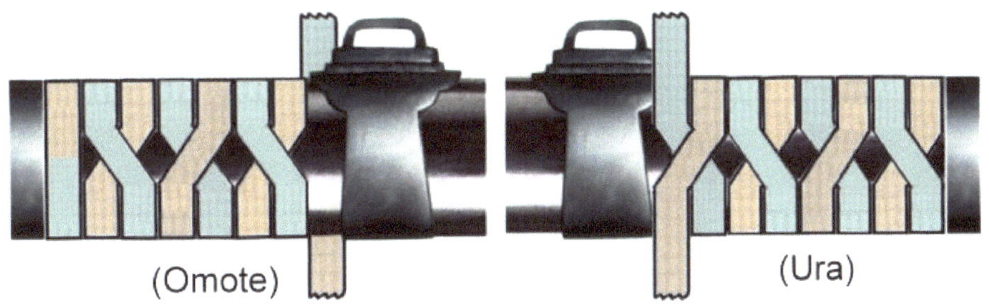

Appendix Figure 1.1 The opening steps and crossover techniques.

Step 2: Once the maki has reach the *Yaguragane* (suspension band), starting on the Omote side of the saya, loop the ito around the top of the *Yaguragane* as shown in figure 1.2 below. This helps to secure the suspension band in its desired position.

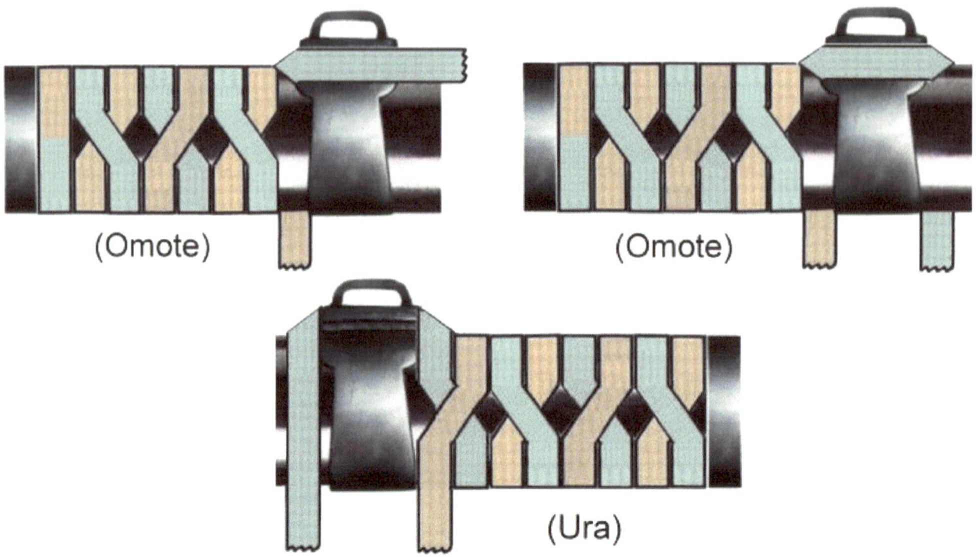

Appendix Figure 1.2 Looping the ito around the Omote side of the Yaguragane.

Step 3: Next, repeat the process of looping the second end of the ito over the top of the *Yaguragane*, but on the opposite Ura side of the suspension band, as shown in figure 1.3 below.

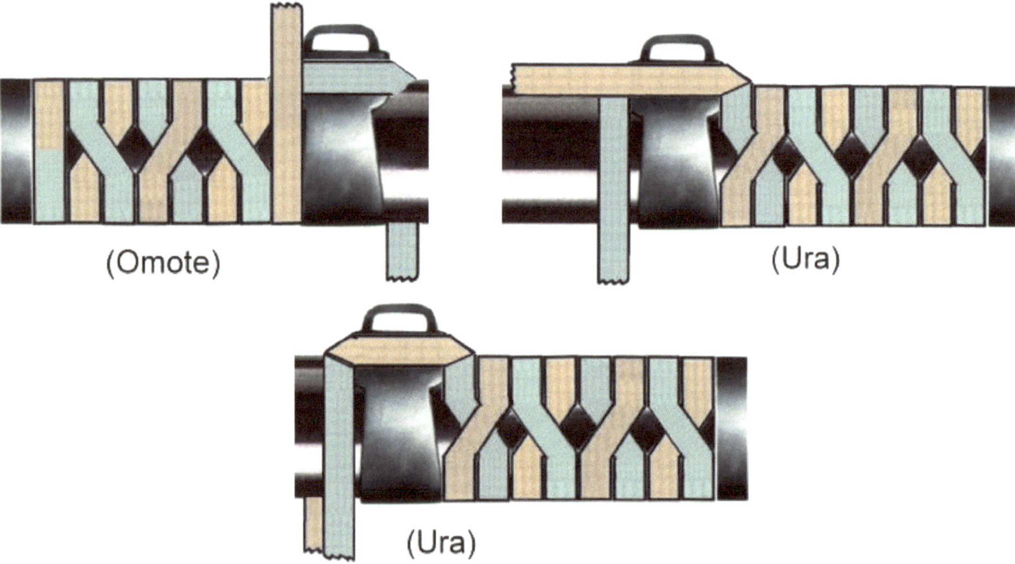

Appendix Figure 1.3 Looping the ito around the Ura side of the Yaguragane.

Step 4: Once the first Yaguragane is secured by the ito loops, as displayed in figure 1.3, starting on the Ura side resume wrapping in the crossover patern as before until you reach the position of the second Yaguragane, then repeat the looping process as shown in figure 1.3. This is followed by a continaution of the given crossover patern as shown below in figure 1.4.

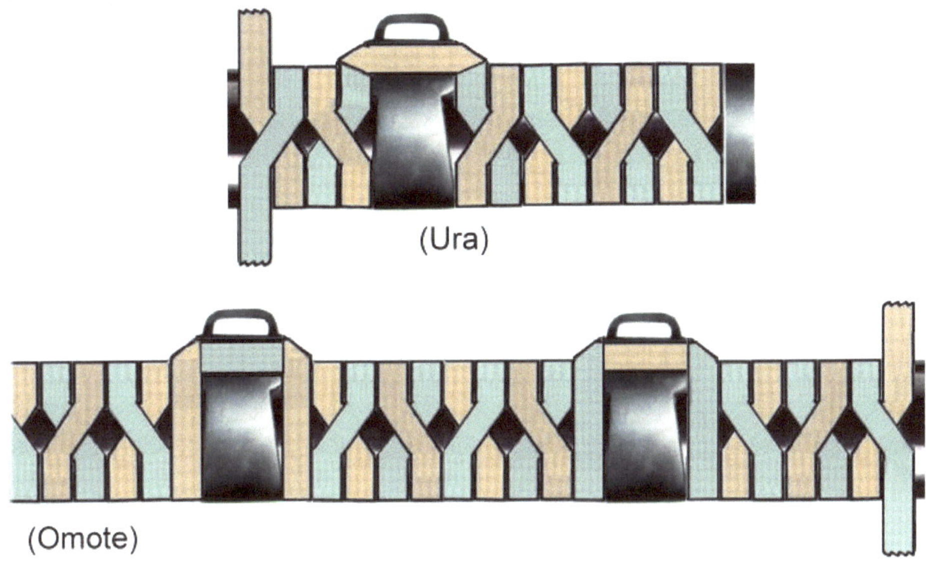

Appendix Figure 1.4 Continuing the crossover.

Step 5: On the Omote side, once you've complete the same number of crossovers after the second Yaguragane as you have before the first Yaguragane side, it's time to begin the final knots. Depending on whether or not you want a final knot on the Omote side, the last crossover may differ from the crossover style on the tsuka and rest of the saya.

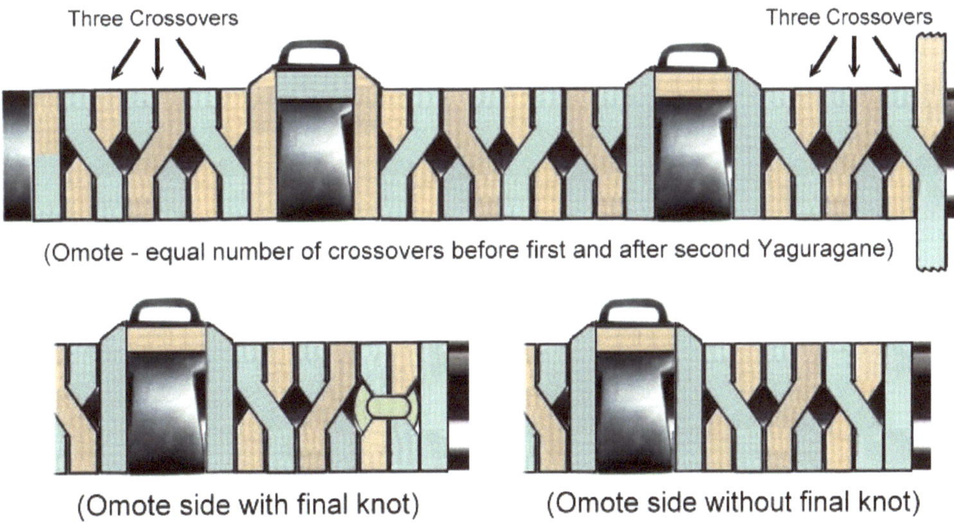

Appendix Figure 1.5 Final crossovers with Omote knot (left), and without knot **(right).**

Assuming you are going to complete both the Omote and Ura knots, prepare the last two crossovers by having them in menpumaki moyo iri, as shown below.

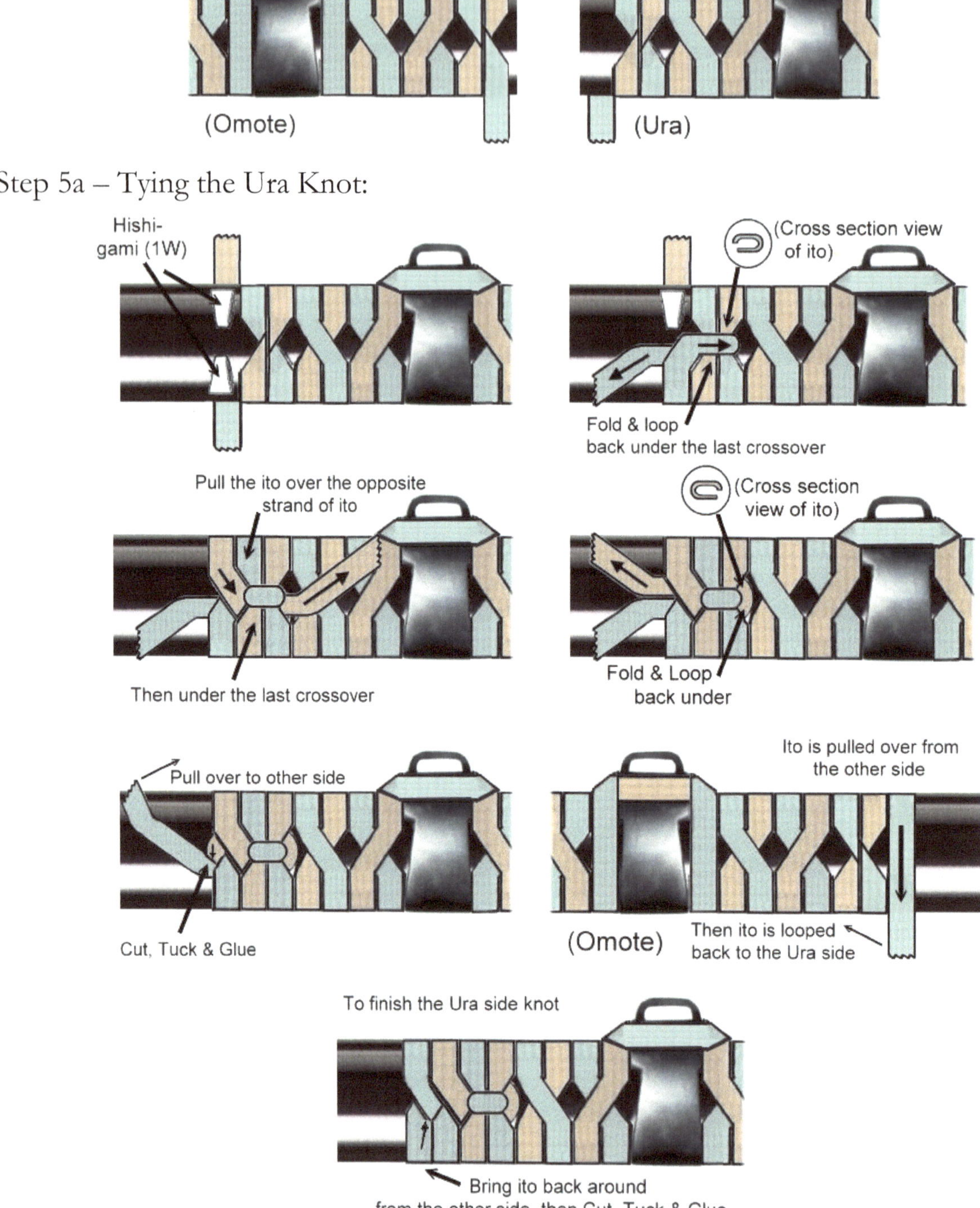

Step 5a – Tying the Ura Knot:

Step 5b – Tying the Omote Knot:

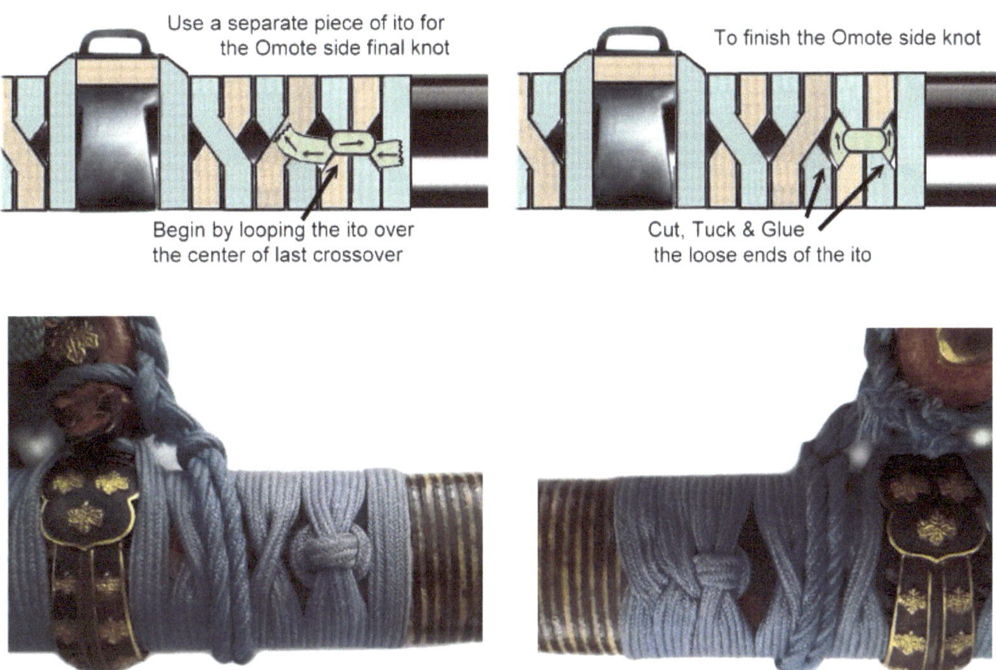

Appendix Figure 1.6 Examples of the Final Omote and Ura knots on a Mid-Edo tachi saya.

APPENDIX 2
COMMERCIALLY PRODUCED HANDLE WRAPPING STAND AND CLAMP SCHEMATICS

Wrapping Stand Schematic

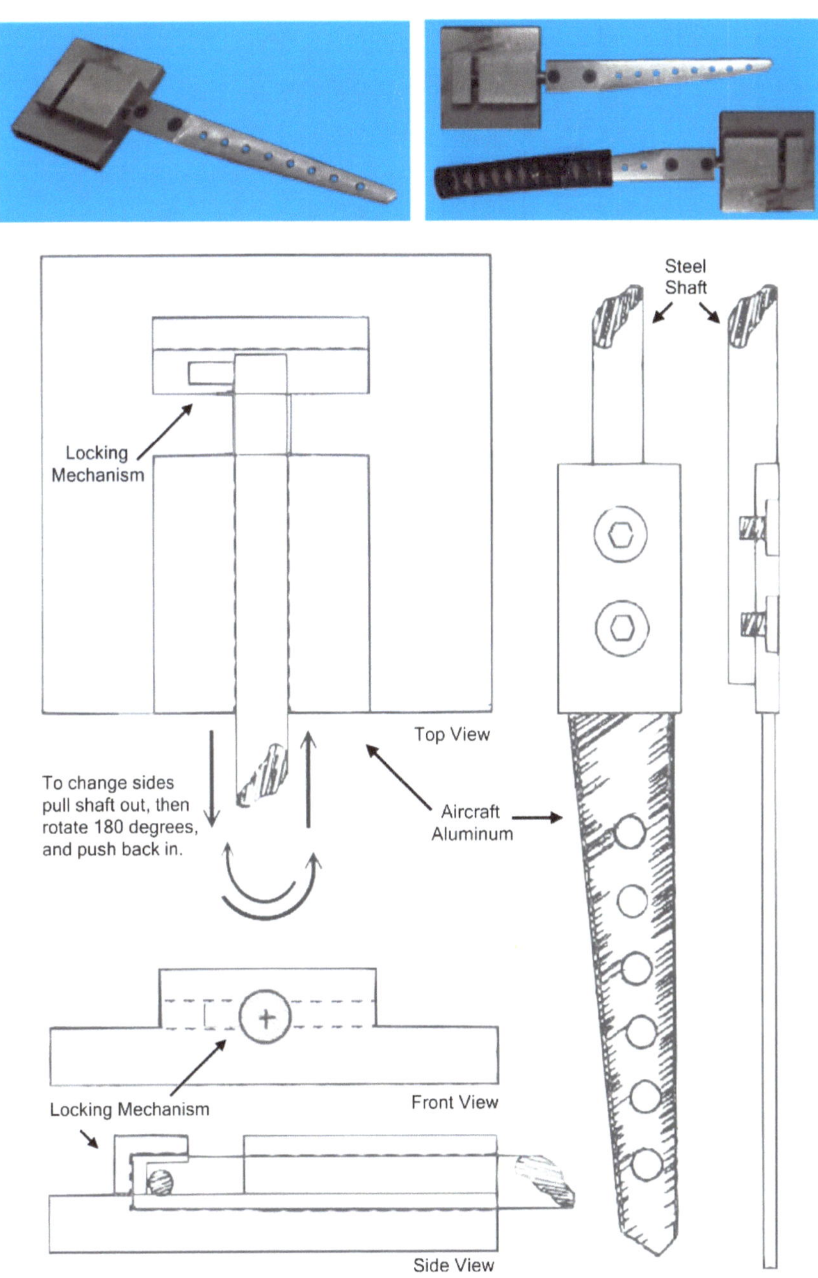

Wrapping Clamp Schematic

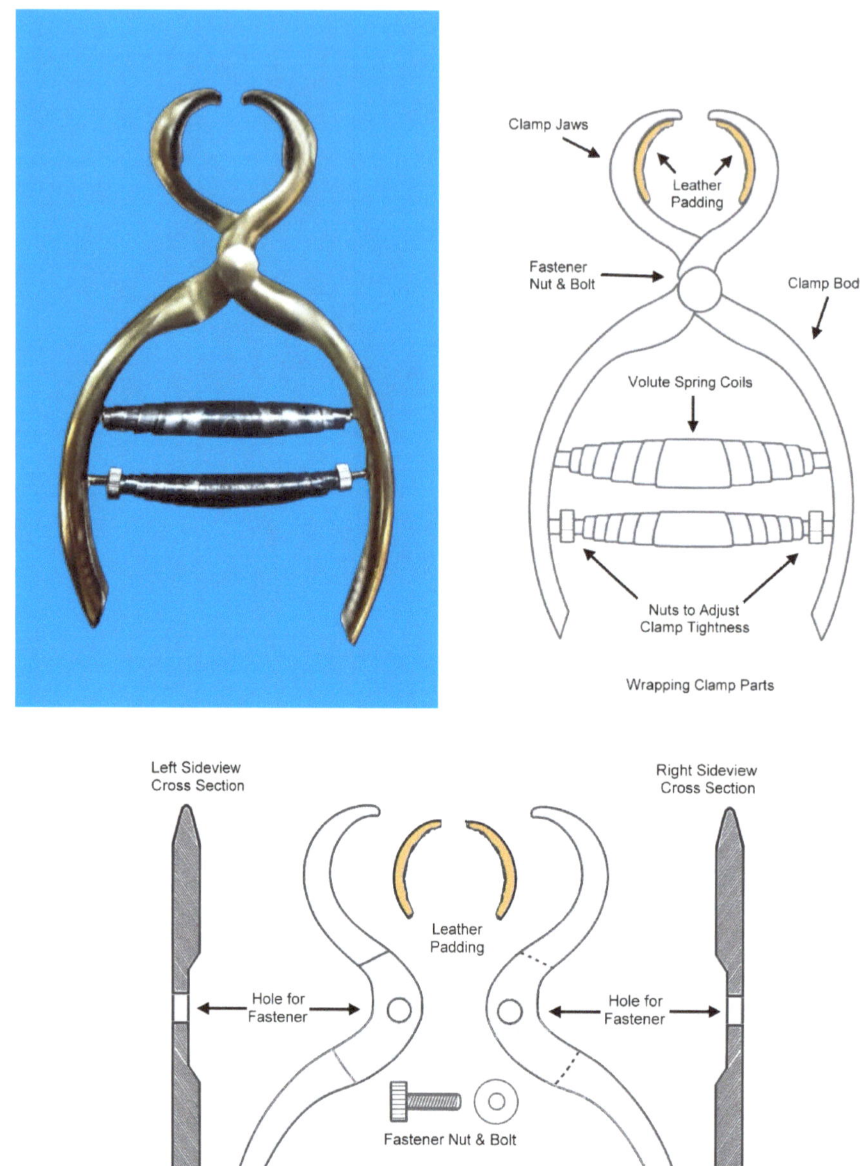

Appendix Figure 2.2 A commercially produced wrapping clamp with leather padding and volute springs.

BIBLIOGRAPHY

Fuller, Richard, & Gregory, Ron (1987). *Military Swords of Japnan: 1868-1945.* New York, NY: Arms and Armour Press.

Hawley, W. M. (1981). *Japanese Swordsmiths Revised.* Hollywood, CA: Hawley Publications.

Irvine, Gregory (2000). *The Japanese Sword – The Soul of the Samurai.* London, England: Victoria and Albert Museum.

Kapp, L., Kapp, H. & Yoshihara, Y. (1987). *The Craft of the Japanese Sword.* New York, NY: Kodansha International.

Kapp, L., Kapp, H. & Yoshihara, Y. (2002). *Modern Japanese Swords and Swordsmith: From 1868 to the Present.* New York, NY: Kodansha International.

Kokubo, Kenichi. (1993). The complete illustrated book of the Japanese sword furnishings. Tokyo, Japan: Kogei Shuppan.

Nagayama, Kokan (1998). *The Connoisseur's Guide to Japanese Swords.* New York, NY: Kodansha International.

Nakao, Seigo (1997). The Random House Japanese-English English-Japanese Dictionary. New York, NY: Random House, Inc.

Ogasawara, Nobuo. (1994). The art of Japan 1, No. 332: The mountings of Japanese swords. Tokyo, Japan: Shibun Do.

Ogawa, Morihiro (2009). Art of the Samurai: Japanese Arms and Armor, 1156-1868 (Metropolitan Museum of Art). New York, NY: Metropolitan Museum of Art.

Roach, Colin (2010). *Japanese Swords: Cultural Icons of a Nation.* North Claendon, VT: Tuttle Publishing.

Robinson, B. W. (1961). *The Arts of the Japanese Sword.* London, England: Faber & Faber, Ltd.

Sato, Kanzan, & Earl, Joe (1983). *The Japanese Sword.* New York, NY: Kodansha International.

Sinclaire, Clive (2001). *Samurai: The Weapons and Spirit of the Japanese Warrior.* Guilford, CT: Salamander Books Ltd.

Stone, G. C. (1961). A Glossary of the Construction, Decoration and Use of Arms and Armor, in all countries and in all times. New York, NY: Jack Brussel.

Takeuchi, S. Alexander. (2003). "Typology of *katate-maki* (i.e., battle wrap) and its relevance to historically accurate menuki placement." In *Dr. T's Nihon-to Random Thoughts Page*. Florence, Ala: University of North Alabama, , USA.

Tsuji, Kyojiro. (1973). Tsuka maki. In Tadashi Oono (Ed.), *Nihon-to shokunin shokudan.* (1st Ed.). Pp. 169-179. Tokyo, Japan: Kogei Shuppan.

Turnbull, Stephen (2004). *Samurai: The Story of Japan's Great Warriors.* London: PRC Publishing, Ltd.

Yumoto, J. M. (1958). *The Samurai Sword – A Handbook.* North Claendon, VT: Tuttle Publishing.

Zusho, Ichiro. (2003). *Satsuma Koshirae.* Tokyo, Japan: Ribun Shuppan.

INDEX

PHOTO CREDITS

Tsuka by Takao Ichinose
Courtesy of Robert Benson, photos by Dr. R. M. Lewert
p. 44, p. 47, p. 50, p. 52, p. 54, p. 56, p. 58, p. 60, p. 62, p. 64, p. 66, p. 67, p. 69, p. 71, p. 73, p. 75, p. 77, p. 78, p. 80, p. 82, p. 84, p. 85, p. 87, p. 88, p. 90.

Tsuka and Saya by
Kazuki Takayama & Yasuo Toyama
Courtesy of Kenji Mishina
p. 12.

Christie's
p. 5, p. 50.

Japanese Imperial Collection
Courtesy of Nobuo Ogasawara
p. 3, p. 4, p. 8, p. 9, p. 10.

Denver Art Museum
p. 13, p. 16, p. 17.

Japanese Sword Museum
p. 10, p. 11, p. 13, p. 14, p. 16.

Tokugawa Art (Sanmei Trading Co., Ltd)
p. 19.

All other Pictures and Diagrams
Created and/or Sourced by Author

LIST OF FIGURES

ABOUT THE AUTHOR

Dr. Thomas Buck has been collecting and studying the Japanese Art Sword for over fifty years, acquiring his first Samurai Sword in October, 1975. In 1987, with the guidance of Dr. W. Y. Takahashi, Sensei, he began a three year intensive study/apprenticeship of the restoration and preservation techniques of John Grimmitt and Takahiro Ichinose, concentrating his research on Tsukamaki and Japanese Lacquer-ware. Since 1988, he has been performing restoration and research work on tsuka for various institutions, private collectors, and dealers.

Dr. Buck's educational background is wide ranging and complex. He completed his BA's in Eastern History and Philosophy (double major) in 1985 with minors in Mandarin Chinese and Mathematics, followed by an MA in Elementary Education (1990), an MS in Curriculum and Instruction (1996), and PhD's in Educational Psychology and Applied Information Systems (1998 & 2004 respectively), as well as an MBA (2017) in Rural Healthcare and an MS (2021) in Health Informatics.

ALSO BY THOMAS BUCK

Functional Sculpture: A Photo Essay – Denver Art Museum Conservancy Works by Thomas Buck. ISBN: 978-09843779-9-2.

Historic Japanese Swords and Fittings: A Collection of Digitally Restored and Translated 19th Century Manuscripts. ISBN: 978-09843779-4-7.

Across the spectrum: Historical trends in Japanese lacquer-ware. ISBN: 0-9843779-1-3

Ancient Japanese Swords and Fittings: A Collection of Restored and Translated Nineteenth Century Woodblock Manuscripts. ISBN: 0-9843779-0-5

www.ingramcontent.com/pod-product-compliance
Lightning Source LLC
LaVergne TN
LVHW070124110826
845147LV00002B/184
9780984377954